Approaches to the Study of Intercultural Transfer

Approaches to the Study of Intercultural Transfer

Thomas Adam

Anthem Press
An imprint of Wimbledon Publishing Company
www.anthempress.com

This edition first published in UK and USA 2020
by ANTHEM PRESS
75–76 Blackfriars Road, London SE1 8HA, UK
or PO Box 9779, London SW19 7ZG, UK
and
244 Madison Ave #116, New York, NY 10016, USA

First published in the UK and USA by Anthem Press 2019

Copyright © Thomas Adam 2020

The author asserts the moral right to be identified as the author of this work.

All rights reserved. Without limiting the rights under copyright reserved above,
no part of this publication may be reproduced, stored or introduced into
a retrieval system, or transmitted, in any form or by any means
(electronic, mechanical, photocopying, recording or otherwise),
without the prior written permission of both the copyright
owner and the above publisher of this book.

British Library Cataloguing-in-Publication Data
A catalogue record for this book is available from the British Library.

ISBN-13: 978-1-78527-579-1 (Pbk)
ISBN-10: 1-78527-579-8 (Pbk)

This title is also available as an e-book.

CONTENTS

	Introduction	1
1.	New Ways to Write the History of Western Europe and the United States: The Concept of Intercultural Transfer	9
2.	Social Housing Reform and Intercultural Transfer in the Transatlantic World before World War I	29
3.	Cultural Excursions: The Transnational Transfer of Museums in the Transatlantic World	57
4.	The Intercultural Transfer of Football: The Contexts of Germany and Argentina	75
5.	Interreligious and Intercultural Transfers of the Tradition of Philanthropy	101
6.	Change through Non-Violence: The Rationalization of Conflict Solution	127
7.	From *Weihnachten* to Christmas: The Invention of a Modern Holiday Ritual and Its Transfer from Germany to England and the United States	155
	Index	179

INTRODUCTION

With this volume we start our new series in intercultural transfer studies, which aims to present innovative scholarship that reveals the interconnected nature of human cultures and societies. The concept of intercultural transfer studies is based on the recognition that humans have always lived in an interconnected world. They moved around and, in the process, transferred ideas and objects across continents and oceans. Such transfers shaped all human societies and cultures across the globe. And even though limitations on transportation and information exchange in the premodern world could cause one to believe that such transfers of ideas and objects were more characteristic of the modern world, intercultural transfers are nothing new.[1] Historians of the modern era have, however, one decisive advantage over historians of the premodern area when it comes to the exploration of intercultural transfers. Intercultural transfers in the nineteenth and twentieth centuries were much better documented than intercultural transfers in the twelfth and thirteenth centuries.

Our series focuses on the circulation of notions, images, things, living beings, capital, and practices across cultures and societies around the globe and the creation or disruption of relations and spaces that shaped the perception and reality of individuals. These circulations created spaces of their own that overlapped and competed with spaces created by states, empires, and nations. This series provides a home for scholars who explore and analyze historical phenomena in their entirety rather than segments of such phenomena within specific and isolated regional or national settings. Such an approach provides for a comprehensive understanding of specific phenomena that could never be reached within a state- or nation-centered approach.

Nation-centered accounts of history seem to have exhausted themselves. Phenomena such as football have, for instance, received much attention by scholars in the context of nation-building and the creation of national identity. And while there is no doubt that football has become intertwined with nationalism, historians have largely failed to explore how this sport came into existence and how it spread across the globe.[2] Football was born at English public schools (Rugby and Eaton) and was transferred from there to high schools across Europe and South America as part of school reform efforts. Neglecting this dimension of transfer isolated football from the context in which it emerged: the context of school reform. Football was not accepted into societies and cultures as a sport but as a teaching tool that gave high school students a way of self-determination and self-disciplining. Football was, furthermore, not introduced into emerging national cultures but rather into subcultures that were defined by socioeconomic status and social class. In many places, competing football cultures emerged that were only later nationalized. Football, further, found acceptance first among students from entrepreneurial families since this game provided opportunities of learning teamwork and experiencing (capitalist) competition that other physical exercises of the time did not. Applying the intercultural transfer studies approach to the history of football reveals its long-lost connections with school reform and the creation of market economies.

Telling the story of past phenomena from this perspective is not merely about getting the story right, but more importantly about providing students and readers with a narrative that matters in a globalized world. The increasingly globalized and interconnected world requires academics to engage in research and to produce publications that provide answers to questions about the nature of the modern world. Globalization and the information revolution changed the context for research fundamentally. Existing historical approaches that remain focused on narrow fields and contexts seem to be out of touch with an audience that lives in this globalized world and needs guidance for tackling challenges that are global in nature. This series will provide readers with a fresh look at topics and themes that are familiar and locate these topics within their global context. It will highlight the interconnected nature of the modern world by exploring the processes that resulted in the global spread and expansion of specific phenomena.

This first volume presents essays that have, with the exception of the essay on the history of Christmas, previously been published in specialized journals and volumes across the historical discipline. Bringing them together in this inaugural volume was motivated by the desire to show the wide range of possible topics. Each chapter, further, provides the application of the intercultural transfer studies paradigm to a specific and distinct historical phenomenon, including football, social housing reform, museums, philanthropy, nonviolent resistance, and holiday rituals. Each chapter, thereby, reveals specific aspects of the intercultural transfer of phenomena, the role of agents of intercultural transfer and the transformations of ideas transferred between cultures. These chapters, thereby, contribute to our understanding of the mechanisms of intercultural transfers.

The approach of intercultural transfer studies differs significantly from traditional and vertical ways of doing history. Traditionally, historians have explored a specific phenomenon within a narrowly defined (national, regional, or local) space over time. The study of intercultural transfers does not limit itself to such a vertical and spatially limited approach. Instead it combines a horizontal approach with a vertical approach as it explores the separation of a specific idea or object from a giving society, the transformation of that idea or object by an agent of intercultural transfer, the transportation of that idea or object from a giving society to a receiving society and the integration of the idea or object into a receiving society. The integration of ideas into receiving societies often took years and decades and required extensive lobbying for the introduction and integration of a new idea by agents of intercultural transfer. It took Harvard professor George Ticknor more than two decades to realize his dream of introducing a public lending library in Boston that was based on libraries he had encountered in Göttingen and Dresden.

The approach of intercultural transfer studies also goes beyond the horizontal approach of comparative studies.[3] Intercultural transfer studies are not merely concerned with comparing and, thereby, solidifying the notion of different cultures and societies. Instead, they seek to undermine the perception that there were distinct cultures that could be treated as disconnected entities. The intercultural transfer approach seeks to study the objects moving between ever-changing cultures and the contribution of these transfers to the making and transformation of these cultures. Objects and ideas transferred, changed, and transformed the places and spaces into which they moved. They, further, created cultural spaces of their own that provided bridges between cultures. The transfer of models for philanthropic activities between Islam, Christianity, and Judaism linked these three religions and provided for the formation of modern concepts of civil society with foundations, endowments, and associations as the core of civic engagement.

The approach of intercultural transfer studies builds on cultural transfer concepts that were developed in the context of transfers between French and German society in the era of Enlightenment and the French Revolution.[4] The concept introduced here goes beyond this approach, which was still centered on states and nation-building, and abandons the framework of the state and instead focuses on spaces created by the circulation of ideas and objects between smaller units, such as cities and institutions, and larger units, such as ethnolinguistic groups and religious communities. Transfers, thus, occurred between cities such as Dresden and Boston; institutions such as the Rugby Public School and the Gymnasium Martino-Katharineum at Braunschweig; and religions such as Islam and Christianity. The study of intercultural transfer, as it is introduced here, further combines structuralist with individualized interpretations of history. Transfers depended on the activities of agents of intercultural transfer. This approach is, thus, centered on human agency.

Agents of intercultural transfer were essential for the transfer process. These agents almost always belonged to the receiving society. For transfers to succeed it was highly beneficial if the agents of transfer came from the receiving society. Agents such as the high school teacher Konrad Koch, who championed the introduction of football as it was played at the Marlborough Public School into the curriculum of his Braunschweig High School, and George Ticknor, who introduced the Christmas ritual that he had encountered in Dresden into Boston society, were successful in their advocacy for transferring football and the Christmas ritual, respectively, because they belonged to the receiving society.

These agents acted on their own volition and were not agents of states or governments. Intercultural transfers occurred outside the activities of political bodies and were the field of nonstate actors. Social reformers such as Henry I. Bowditch concerned themselves with the problem of housing for working-class families and sought to find ways for improvement. Often these agents belonged to the upper class and had the financial means to encounter other cultures. Travel presented an opportunity to explore other cultures and to identify ideas and objects that could be appealing to society back home.

The experience of travel and study brought agents of intercultural transfer into direct contact with other societies and new ideas. George Ticknor learned about the Christmas ritual during his stay in Göttingen and Dresden, and American disciples of Mahatma Gandhi's nonviolent resistance movement such as Benjamin Mays and Howard Thurman traveled to India to meet with Gandhi. Such contacts provided the basis for intercultural transfer and allowed agents of intercultural transfer to claim authority. Even after Gandhi was long dead, traveling to India and visiting the site of Gandhi's activities still provided an aura of knowledge and expertise that was essential in appropriating the idea of Satyagraha by African American civil rights leaders such as Martin Luther King Jr. However, modern media increasingly provided opportunities to learn about ideas that emerged beyond one's own culture without encountering it firsthand. The American labor leader César Chávez and the Philippine opposition leader Cory Aquino learned, for instance, about Gandhi not from direct contact and travel but from watching news reels and fictional movies.

Agents of intercultural transfer selected ideas and objects in the giving society for transfer. The giving society had little to no control over the transfer process. Members of the giving society provided some guidance in introducing agents of intercultural transfer to a specific idea or institution. George Ticknor was invited to a Christmas party in Dresden. This invitation and the acceptance of the invitation provided the basis for the intercultural transfer of the Christmas ritual. However, the giving society played no role in the transfer process beyond the presentation of the idea or object. Intercultural transfer processes such as the transfer of the Christmas tree and gift giving succeeded only because the receiving society had full control over the transformation, translation, and integration of these phenomena into its culture. Interference into the transfer process by members of the giving society would have doomed such transfers.

The interest in the transfer of objects has always been motivated by feelings of inferiority within the receiving society as it becomes clear in the formation of museum associations in New York. The poet William Cullen Bryant reminded his audience in his speech at the meeting that finalized the transfer of such associations from Leipzig to New York of the rich museums in Dresden as a sign of cultural superiority of that city over New York. Bryant skillfully played with the feeling of cultural inferiority to motivate his audience to support the formation of the museum association. Whether such claims were true is not important. Such claims were always made with a strategic goal and motivation. The individual making such claims wanted to convince their audience of the necessity to introduce a new idea or object that was always portrayed as enhancing the quality of culture. Acknowledging or accepting that something was missing in one's own culture or that one's own culture could be improved was a necessary precondition for intercultural transfers to succeed.

Agents of intercultural transfer selected, redefined, modified, transferred, and integrated ideas and objects into the receiving society. In the process, ideas and objects were transformed in many ways. These transformations resulted from the interpretation of the ideas or objects by the agents of intercultural transfer and from the agent's desire to fit an idea or object into the receiving society. Limited foreign language skills and lack of cultural knowledge regularly lead to misinterpretations and misappropriations. Analyzing these transformations provides historians with an opportunity to study both the giving and the receiving societies.

The transfer of an idea from one place to another always creates a circulatory system that connects two or more places. When nineteenth-century social reformers sought ways and means to improve the housing of working-class families, a global network emerged from the transfer of the limited dividend housing company model that was born in London in the 1840s. From London it was first transferred to Berlin and Frankfurt am Main from the 1840s to the 1860s, and then in the 1870s to Boston and New York. Furthermore, the modified social housing companies in places such as Leipzig that had applied ideas and concepts of social housing invented first in London became the object of observation for American social reformers who were able to study the integration of these social housing models into a foreign culture. In the process, primary transfers of ideas from the place of their origin to another place (in this specific case from London to Berlin and from London to Boston) were later joined by secondary transfers of ideas (here from Leipzig to New York). Such secondary transfers resulted from the observation of an idea that was integrated into a place in which it did not originate. Such secondary transfers were of great interest to observers since they had already proven the possibility of transferring the object from one culture to another and of successfully integrating the idea into this second culture. What worked once could also work a second time.

Secondary transfers could also result in the return of an idea in modified form to its place of origin. When at the beginning of the twentieth century the advisor to the Royal Art Museum in Dresden, Woldemar von Seidlitz, suggested that the American museum associations could provide a model for the funding of German museums, he overlooked or ignored the genesis of these American models. The formation of museum associations such as the one for the Metropolitan Museum of Art in New York City was in the 1860s inspired by museum associations in Leipzig. Intercultural transfers were, thus, rarely monodirectional, but they often led to exchanges between cultures in both directions.

These transfers did not, however, result in a unified and homogenous world, but rather in a highly diversified world. The museum associations of New York differed in their hierarchical structure significantly from the ones in Leipzig. This transformation reflected the different historical contexts. While such associations in Leipzig were part of the bourgeois desires for an egalitarian society that challenged the monarchical society, which gave the nobility social dominance, museum associations in American society served to create hierarchies in a society that otherwise lacked social hierarchies. Such transformations have always been typical for intercultural transfers. Sometimes they simply reflected the inability of individuals from the receiving society to grasp the complexity of an object or idea selected for transfer. In the context of Gandhi's Satyagraha, Western scholars who were interested and fascinated by Satyagraha showed a remarkable inability to find a proper translation. Too many intellectuals suggested to mistranslate Satyagraha with passive resistance. Such intentional and unintentional modifications, misunderstandings, and reinterpretations were characteristic of intercultural transfers and were even unavoidable.[5] Every idea and object that was moved from one place to another was multiply transformed. These transformations were the very reason that these transfers did not create homogeneity but strengthened diversity. Intercultural transfers, thereby, contributed to the conundrum of the modern world, which appeared to become more similar and more dissimilar at the same time.

Notes

1. Wolfram Drews and Christian Scholl, "Transkulturelle Verflechtungsprozesse in der Vormoderne. Zur Einleitung," in: Wolfram Drews and Christian Scholl (eds.), *Transkulturelle Verflechtungsprozesse in der Vormoderne*, Berlin and Boston: Walter De Gruyter, 2016, VII–XXIII; Georg Christ, Saskia Dönitz, Daniel G. König, Şevket Küçükhüseyin, Margit Mersch, Britta Müller-Schauenburg, Elrike Ritzerfeld, Christian Vogel and Julia Zimmermann, *Transkulturelle Verflechtungen: Mediävistische Perspektiven*, Göttingen: Universitätsverlag Göttingen, 2016; Thomas Adam, *Intercultural Transfers and the Making of the Modern World, 1800–2000*, New York: Palgrave Macmillan, 2012.
2. Todd Cleveland, *Following the Ball: The Migration of African Soccer Players across the Portuguese Colonial Empire*, Athens: Ohio University Press, 2017.
3. Heinz-Gerhard Haupt and Jürgen Kocka, "Comparative History: Methods, Aims, Problems," in: Deborah Cohen and Maura O'Connor (eds.), *Comparison and History: Europe in Cross-National Perspective*, New York and London: Routledge, 2004, 23–39; Heinz-Gerhard Haupt and Jürgen Kocka (eds.), *Comparative and Transnational History. Central European Approaches and New Perspectives*, New York and Oxford: Berghahn Books, 2009; Jürgen Osterhammel, "Transferanalyse und Vergleich im Fernverhältnis," in: Hartmut Kaelble and Jürgen Schriewer (eds.), *Vergleich und Transfer. Komparatistik in den Sozial-, Geschichts-, und Kulturwissenschaften*, Frankfurt am Main and New York: Campus-Verlag, 2003, 439–66.
4. Michel Espagne and Michael Werner, "Deutsch-französischer Kulturtransfer als Forschungsgegenstand. Eine Problemskizze," in: *Transferts Les Relations Interculturelles dans L'Espace Franco-Allemand (XVIIIe et XIXe Siècle). Textes réunis et présentés par Michel Espagne et Michael Werner*, Paris: Editions Recerce sur les Civilisations, 1988, 11–34; Johannes Paulmann, "Internationaler Vergleich und interkultureller Transfer. Zwei Forschungsansätze zur europäischen Geschichte des 18. bis 20. Jahrhunderts," in: *Historische Zeitschrift* 267, 3 (1998): 649–85.
5. Daniel T. Rodgers, *Atlantic Crossings: Social Politics in a Progressive Age*, Cambridge and London: Belknap Press of Harvard University Press, 1998, 31.

Bibliography

Adam, Thomas. *Intercultural Transfers and the Making of the Modern World, 1800–2000*, New York: Palgrave Macmillan, 2012.

Christ, Georg, Saskia Dönitz, Daniel G. König, Şevket Küçükhüseyin, Margit Mersch, Britta Müller-Schauenburg, Elrike Ritzerfeld, Christian Vogel, and Julia Zimmermann. *Transkulturelle Verflechtungen: Mediävistische Perspektiven*, Göttingen: Universitätsverlag Göttingen, 2016.

Drews, Wolfram, and Christian Scholl. "Transkulturelle Verflechtungsprozesse in der Vormoderne. Zur Einleitung." In: *Transkulturelle Verflechtungsprozesse in der Vormoderne*, edited by Wolfram Drews and Christian Scholl. Berlin and Boston: Walter De Gruyter, 2016, VII–XXIII.

Espagne, Michel, and Michael Werner. "Deutsch-französischer Kulturtransfer als Forschungsgegenstand. Eine Problemskizze." In: *Transferts Les Relations Interculturelles dans L'Espace Franco-Allemand (XVIIIe et XIXe Siècle). Textes réunis et présentés par Michel Espagne et Michael Werner*. Paris: Editions Recerce sur les Civilisations, 1988, 11–34.

Haupt, Heinz-Gerhard, and Jürgen Kocka, eds. *Comparative and Transnational History. Central European Approaches and New Perspectives*. New York and Oxford: Berghahn Books, 2009.

Haupt, Heinz-Gerhard, and Jürgen Kocka. "Comparative History: Methods, Aims, Problems." In: *Comparison and History: Europe in Cross-National Perspective*, edited by Deborah Cohen and Maura O'Connor. New York and London: Routledge, 2004, 23–39.

Osterhammel, Jürgen. "Transferanalyse und Vergleich im Fernverhältnis." In: *Vergleich und Transfer. Komparatistik in den Sozial-, Geschichts-, und Kulturwissenschaften*, edited by Hartmut Kaelble and Jürgen Schriewer. Frankfurt am Main and New York: Campus-Verlag, 2003, 439–66.

Paulmann, Johannes. "Internationaler Vergleich und interkultureller Transfer. Zwei Forschungsansätze zur europäischen Geschichte des 18. bis 20. Jahrhunderts." *Historische Zeitschrift* 267, 3 (1998): 649–85.

Rodgers, Daniel T. *Atlantic Crossings: Social Politics in a Progressive Age*. Cambridge and London: Belknap Press of Harvard University Press, 1998.

Chapter 1

NEW WAYS TO WRITE THE HISTORY OF WESTERN EUROPE AND THE UNITED STATES: THE CONCEPT OF INTERCULTURAL TRANSFER

Abstract

The concept of intercultural transfer was originally developed in the 1980s for the study of exchange processes between France and Germany in the time of the Enlightenment and the French Revolution. More recently, various scholars have applied it to the exchange processes across the Atlantic (and between Germany and the United States in particular) and across the British Chanel (and between Germany and Great Britain in particular). Its focus is cultural transformation, since the transferred elements reflect the influence of the agents of intercultural transfer as well as both the giving and the receiving society. This chapter seeks to provide an alternative to traditional accounts of German and American history by highlighting transfers that occurred in the realm of culture, education, and customs in the nineteenth century. Such transfers included concepts for the organization of the urban infrastructure of American cities (from museums and schools to city parks) as well as models for education (from kindergarten to university). Both cultures and societies were deeply connected by these intercultural transfers even though they occurred outside the realm of state action and apart from the increasing control of both nation states over the movement of its citizens within civil society. Intercultural transfers were organized and carried out by agents of intercultural transfer. These agents were private citizens who acted on their own initiative as agents of civil society but not as agents of nation states. The development of German and American society and culture in the nineteenth century was, thus, intrinsically linked and resulted in a multitude of cross-cultural interconnections that contributed to the diversification of both societies. The Atlantic represented in this narrative a "connective lifeline" rather than a separating gulf.

This chapter was first published in *History Compass* 11, 10 (2013): 880–92.

Introduction

While the end of the Cold War was certainly not the end of history,[1] it was, one might argue, the beginning of the decline of national history as a dominating paradigm in research and instruction. Even though we are far from removing the nation as an organizing principle from the historical profession, more and more dissertations and books are written outside traditional national frameworks and instead embrace topical and global approaches.[2] The perceived increase in geographic mobility as well as the globalized effects of the recent economic crisis seem to contribute to a sense in which national governments are no longer in control of economic and political forces. National sovereignty seems to have been replaced by the transnational powers of international markets (both for commodities and jobs) and rating agencies which appear to be far more powerful than individual national governments and elected parliaments.

Yet, at the same time, nation states continue to reassert their relevance in class rooms through curricula and textbooks which highlight the values of nations and celebrate the heroic deeds of national heroes. Conservative historians such as Larry Schweikart and Michael Allen do not hide their belief that history's most important task is to produce admiration for national heroes and undivided patriotism. In response to the perceived "leftist destruction of American identity" Schweikart and Allen write in their introduction to their college-level textbook *A Patriot's History of the United States*: "we remain convinced that if the story of America's past is told fairly, the result cannot be anything but a deepened patriotism, a sense of awe at the obstacles overcome, the passion invested, the blood and tears spilled, and the nation that was built."[3]

Since history was part of the "national project" from its inception and provided legitimacy to the nation states created in the course of the nineteenth century, a mutually beneficial relationship emerged between the historical profession and the nation states they helped create. This is not to say that the historical profession should be reduced to a tool of state governments in their pursuit of national projects. Historians simply absorbed and reflected the culture in which they grew up, in which they were trained, and which they perceived as the framework for their research and writing.[4] This symbiotic relationship lasted as long as historians accepted the nation as the natural body for the object of their study. When historians began to question the legitimacy of national history and began to see the nation, to use Daniel T. Rodgers famous phrase, as an "analytical cage" rather than a logical and self-explanatory container for history, conflicts began to emerge.[5]

In the last two decades, federal and state governments in Europe and the United States interfered with school curricula to a degree that, according to Maria Grever, bordered on "moral panic." For Grever, this struggle over school curricula was due to the states' realization that they were "losing control over who and what constitutes the 'common' past."[6] The power to define a "correct" history of their nation seemed to slip away leaving governments to feel threatened by revisionist historians who wanted to give a voice to various groups excluded from the traditional canon. This is best illustrated by the various attempts in a number of Texas cities from San Antonio to Dallas to honor labor activist César Chávez by naming a street after him. When in May 2011 the city council of San Antonio voted in favor of naming a main thoroughfare after Chávez, the San Antonio Conservation Society sued to prevent the street renaming arguing that "it is important that we protect the integrity of our history" and a district judge ruled that this renaming of the road would interfere with "maintain[ing] the integrity of our history."[7] As this example highlights, the stakes are in the case of the United States particularly high since the country's perceived historical identity as being of English origin serves as the background for current policies about immigration, identity, and citizenship.

The Need for a Transnational History

Since the publication of the La Pietra Report[8] by Thomas Bender in 2000, transatlantic and transnational approaches to American history gained some ground in academic culture. However, history teaching in high schools and community colleges still embraces a traditional interpretation of American history. Even though Daniel T. Rodgers' *Atlantic Crossings* and Ian Tyrrell's *Transnational Nation* received much praise within the academic world, the impact of both books on the structure of our academic culture remains rather limited.[9] Yet, a transnationalization of the historical canon seems to be the next logical phase of the grand narrative; after all, more and more people live their lives no longer within the confines of nation states but in the borderless digital world of Facebook. Already in the early 1990, Yasemin Soysal suggested, "that national citizenship has lost its importance in the postmodern era, since most of the basic rights, namely social and civil rights linked to the institution of citizenship, are now given automatically by postnational membership, to those who are not even citizens of a specific nation-state."[10] And Thomas Bender believed that the traditional nation-centered approach to history "has exhausted itself."[11] If history does not want to lose relevance in the modern globalized world, it needs to shed the skin of the nation state and embrace a new transnational paradigm. No longer can we assume that the nation is the natural vantage point of history; instead, we might focus on the broad spectrum of influences on humans' lives which originated inside and outside of the communities in which people lived.

Transnational forces from economic crisis to terrorism, increased mobility and migration, and the prolific growth of non-state and non-nation actors in form of multinational enterprises and non-governmental organizations in the course of the last century contributed to a sense of an interconnected world which had been largely neglected by traditional political historians who sought to force history into the straitjacket of national history. But neither the development of railways nor the introduction of sewage and water lines into cities, to take just two examples of historical changes which fundamentally transformed our lives, can be sufficiently explained if one limits history to the space created by the political borders of any one nation. Modern societies emerged from extensive cultural contacts which facilitated extensive exchanges of ideas, concepts, and models which shaped the structures of all societies and cultures involved. Since the 1970s and 1980s, European and American historians have increasingly turned toward cultural and social history approaches in which social and cultural contacts between people in distant regions have taken center stage. In this context, the nation state has largely lost its interpretative value and has been replaced with transnational frameworks. This cultural and transnational turn has even impacted diplomatic and international relations studies. Nation states are no longer just perceived of as political communities but also as cultural communities and relations between them, in the words of Akira Iriye, as "intercultural relations."[12]

Cultural contacts and intercultural transfers are not, however, a novel phenomenon of modern times. People, cultures, and civilizations have always encountered other people, cultures, and civilizations through migration, trade, conflict, and conquest. Ideas moved often freely between different cultures and found as much acceptance as they found resistance. Such cultural contacts have contributed to the shaping of all societies, religions, and cultures in history.[13] The establishment of history as an academic discipline in the nineteenth century and the adoption of the nation state as its sole framework and key concept forced professional historians to stress national distinctions and differences at the cost of mutual exchanges and influences. Historians strove to write the history of one nation by highlighting its particularities and not the characteristics it shared with other nations. In the process, cultural contacts and intercultural transfers were written out of history and have, thus, become invisible.

The study of intercultural transfers, as it will be introduced in this chapter, could, therefore, be compared to an archaeological excavation since the task of the scholar is to unearth connections and influences which have been buried deep under many layers of interpretation and modification. Terminology and naming often obscure relatedness between objects in two different cultures. Inquiry into intercultural transfers is as much uncovering lost and hidden connections as it is an endeavor into rearranging available knowledge by reassessing perceived differences between societies and cultures. In the process, scholars (re)construct transnational connections and, thus, challenge entrenched interpretations of separate development and uniqueness. This type of research produces a transnational counter-narrative to traditional national narratives, and, thus, opens up new ways for understanding our modern world.[14]

Nation states still matter in this new approach to history, but they are no longer accepted as the "natural skin of history." Since both national spaces and transnational spaces are constructed through human interaction and human imagination, historians need to make a case for using either one as the framework for their research. It remains also possible to assign the nation state a prominent role in transnational history as Patricia Clavin and Sebastian Conrad have done.[15] Clavin and Conrad's interpretation of transnational history seems to accept the existence and power of national (state) borders and focuses on the crossing of these borders.[16] Another way to define transnational history is to consider it a history "below and beyond the nation state." Such an approach emphasizes the connections and exchanges that occurred outside the purview and control of nation states. The focus here is not on the crossing of borders but rather on the creation of transnational spaces that transcend national spaces.[17] For transnational historians, it appears necessary to historicize both the nation as an invented community of traditions and values and the state as one actor among others in the production of the social, economic, and cultural fabric of modern societies. Both Ian Tyrell and Daniel T. Rodgers agreed that nation states did neither emerge nor exist in isolation, but where Tyrrell and Rodgers limit this transnational production of nations to phenomena such as migration and demographic change, economic competition, the formulation of national policies (and social policies in particular), and the creation and maintenance of national identities, transatlantic historians need to go further and investigate the entire fabric that constitutes society and culture. All societies and cultures within the Atlantic world have been created through extensive intercultural transfers that have affected every aspect of modern life from food and religion to education and culture. These transfers might have increased in intensity through modern means of technology such as television and internet, but they are not a new phenomenon. While ships and carriages certainly slowed down contacts between places within the Atlantic world, nineteenth-century societies depended on intercultural transfer as much as twentieth- and twenty-first-century societies.[18]

The Intercultural Transfer Approach

Developed in the 1980s by Michel Espagne and Michael Werner to conceptualize the cross-cultural contacts and influences of French and German societies, the concept of intercultural transfer does—in contrast to traditional ways of doing history—not serve to legitimize national cultures. In fact, it undermines established notions of separateness, uniqueness, and superiority/inferiority. The goal of this approach is to recover the interconnectedness of cultures and societies throughout history.[19]

Although intercultural transfer depends upon the comparative method, it is designed specifically to go beyond comparison and into the realm of connectivity. Comparing two societies is only the first step, for the goal of transfer studies is to circumvent the heuristic problems of the comparative method. The fundamental problem of comparative studies rests with the selection and, thus, creation, of the objects of comparison. Looking at the same space, distinct observers will choose different aspects and different objects for their comparison. By selecting a particular aspect or object of two societies for comparison, the observer artificially, but necessarily, creates these two objects through the process of selection and, thus, isolation from their context, naming, and, finally, describing and characterizing. These aspects were an undivided portion of the societal continuum until selected as an object and isolated for comparison. The observer freezes the objects of his study in time and by doing so negates changes and cross-cultural influences in order to compare them. Further, since the observer is in most cases part of one of the two societies, he intends to compare, he cannot claim a third point external to the two objects or spaces of comparison. He is, therefore, closer to and more familiar with one of his two objects/spaces of comparison, which often results in distortions to the comparison.[20]

The selection of objects is in many cases informed by research interests and questions which derived from the culture and time of the observer but not from the culture and time of the object of comparison. While this is of course legitimate, it takes the objects of comparison out of their historical context and brings them closer to the present time. Further, the observer is challenged to find a language and terminology external to the two societies under study in order to avoid a linguistic trap. Different signifiers in the two languages of the societies which are compared suggest semantic differences when the signified objects might actually be more similar, and the major difference only lays in the naming.

In contrast to the comparative approach in which the objects of study are immobilized and interactions between the objects of comparison are suspended, the study of intercultural transfer focuses on the interactions between the objects studied and the transformations that result from these interactions. While comparative scholars limit their study to a synchronic level and static objects, scholars interested in intercultural transfer studies chase ever changing and mutating objects through time and space. The study of intercultural transfer is part of what Michael Werner and Bénédicte Zimmermann called "relational approaches" but transfers themselves were hardly limited, as Rodgers claims, to societies characterized by a "common economic and social experience but also a recognition of underlying kinship."[21] Perceived inferiority to another society and contact with that society were the only necessary preconditions for intercultural transfer to occur.

Because of the transformations and mutations ideas and objects undergo in the process of intercultural transfer scholars such as Gabriele Lingelbach have doubted that such transfers actually occurred. For Lingelbach who studied the introduction of the "German university model" into American higher education, public claims of American reformers such as Herbert Baxter Adams to having brought the superior model of German graduate education to American universities appear simply as public relations trick rather than a successful implementation of a perceived German model. The systems of education seemed to be too far apart, the understanding of German ways of instruction among American observers too superfluous, and the result of the publicly claimed transfer too different from graduate education at German universities.[22] As Rodgers reminds us, however, no idea "came through the transnational networks of debate and connection unaltered" and "every imported idea and scheme was, by necessity, multiply transformed."[23] In many cases, the transferred idea appeared to be so different from its origin that it quickly became unrecognizable as an alien idea by members of the receiving society: a fact which was used from time to time by those involved in the transfer and who recognized that this actually might be an advantage for the success of the transfer. Few Americans, for instance, might know that one of the iconic pictures of the American Revolution, *Washington Crossing the Delaware*, was painted in Germany by the German-American painter Emanuel Leutze and intended for a German audience. *Washington Crossing the Delaware* was Leutze's artistic response to the failure of the democratic revolution of 1848/49. Painted in the Romantic tradition, Leutze's picture was to remind the badly beaten German liberals that "the demoralized, nearly paralyzed men of 1848, caught in the tight web of the reaction, could yet rally and overcome their defeat" in the same way that "Washington had led the Americans from despair to victory."[24] When the painting was partially destroyed by fire, Leutze produced a copy of the original painting, which became the property of the Metropolitan Museum of Art in New York. The original and restored painting was bought by the Bremer Kunsthalle where it was shown until its destruction in an aerial bomb raid during World War II. The American audience embraced Leutze's painting not as a Romantic painting about a failed revolution but as an artistic and realistic (as opposed to Romanticized) documentation of an important event in the American War of Independence.[25]

Therefore, the task of the historian who studies intercultural transfer is, as Rodgers reminds us, not to focus on "identities but processes, not essences but geneses."[26] We are interested in the transfer of an object, the mutations it underwent, and its integration into the receiving society. It should not be enough to just identify ideas and objects that were transferred; it is also necessary to show how these ideas and objects were integrated into the receiving culture and how they transformed the receiving culture.

Agents of Intercultural Transfer

The study of intercultural transfers offers a unique opportunity to combine structuralist with individualist approaches to the study of history since transfers depend on human agency. In the process of transfer, the object is remodeled and reinvented by the individuals involved in the transfer. The agents of intercultural transfer therefore became the authors of the object they sought to introduce into their society, for the modifications they applied to the transferrable object were intentionally designed to adapt the object to the conditions of the receiving society, thereby turning the objects of transfer into new models of implementation.[27]

Acting as an agent of intercultural transfer was not a profession but happened by chance. Wealth, leisure time, and the ability to and experience of travel were necessary preconditions for this calling, but they did not always lead to intercultural transfer. Agents of intercultural transfer almost always belonged to the receiving culture. In rare cases such as the transfer of the Pilates exercise movement from Germany to the United States, a member of the giving society could function as agent of intercultural transfer. However, great flexibility was expected of such individuals. In the case of Joseph Pilates, his exercise technique offered a solution to a societal need: the treatment of injured dancers in New York. But only after he abandoned his plan to name his exercise technique "contrology," and after his technique was embraced by famous American artists such as dance icons George Balanchine, Martha Graham, and Jerome Robbins, and only with the help of the Pilates Elders who came from mainstream American society, did Pilates slowly succeed in establishing his invention in the United States.[28]

Contacts through travel and migration proved essential for intercultural transfer in the nineteenth century. Even though the concept of intercultural transfer shares some similarities with Mary Louise Pratt's concept of transculturation, it refers to a very different form of cultural contact and cultural contact zones. While Pratt's contact zones were often characterized by "highly asymmetrical relations of domination and subordination,"[29] intercultural transfer brings together individuals on a level playing field. This did not exclude, however, the existence of feelings of cultural inferiority on the side of the observers. In fact, such feelings were a precondition for intercultural transfer to occur.

As the modification process demonstrates, successful intercultural transfers depended on the acceptance of the idea transferred among the members of the receiving society. Travel by members of the receiving society to regions and places beyond the borders of their nation proved to be, as the example of the kindergarten idea shows, advantageous for intercultural transfer. Friedrich Froebel's concept of early childhood education was brought to the United States first by Margarethe Schurz who opened the very first kindergarten in Watertown (Wisconsin) in 1856. Schurz had been involved in the training of kindergarten teachers in Hamburg before she moved together with her husband Carl Schurz to the United States in 1852. After her arrival in Wisconsin, Schurz set up a kindergarten for the German-American community. From here, the kindergarten spread across the United States but remained largely confined to the cities with large German populations such as Chicago, New York, Milwaukee, Philadelphia, and St. Louis. Anglo-American parents were concerned about the "German character" of these kindergartens and complained about Froebelian rigidity as well as the emphasis on German songs, games, and folk stories. Only after Elizabeth Peabody became interested in the kindergarten concept and "translated" it for an English-speaking audience, did the kindergarten concept have a chance of being accepted into mainstream American education. Peabody relied on Schurz' inspiration and knowledge but also traveled to Germany in 1867 in order to learn first-hand about the kindergarten in its land of origin. The Americanized kindergarten focused on the experience of immigrant children's life in American cities and replaced playful learning with academic instruction and preparation for school.[30]

As this case reveals, it seems as though intercultural transfer works best when the initiative originated from a member of the receiving society. Travel by wealthy Anglo-Americans proved to be essential for the transfers from Europe to the United States in the course of the nineteenth century. After the end of the Napoleonic Wars an increasing flow of American travelers made their way across the Atlantic to drink at the fountains of European culture. Even in the 1860s, European societies were perceived as superior to the American nation when it came to education and culture. Among the many American visitors was George Ticknor who studied at the University of Göttingen and later became the first Harvard Professor of Romance Languages.

When Ticknor, during his first stay in Germany, was enrolled as a student at the University of Göttingen, he extensively used its university library. In his travel journals he repeatedly compared the library in Göttingen with the library in Dresden, which he also visited during his German stay. He concluded: "Each has its advantages—This has a great number of old books—the Göttingen a greater number of recent ones—This is better arranged on the shelves and more elegant—the Göttingen has a catalog which is beyond any work of the kind extant and is a more practical library."[31]

Both libraries allowed users to take out books: a practice which left a great impression on Ticknor and which stayed in his mind for the rest of his life. When American travelers identified something of interest—a museum, a library, a particular high school, a park, or a social housing charity—they produced extensive texts in which they described in detail the particular characteristics of these institutions or they simply talked up the idea among their fellow citizens back home. Ticknor wrote about his experiences in his travel journals, which were circulated among Boston's rich families as we know from a letter written by Elizabeth Peabody, and thus informed public discourse in Boston's High Society after Ticknor's return.[32]

After George Ticknor returned home, he never grew tired of talking about the advantages of the libraries in Göttingen and Dresden, which with time and distance became apparently more and more idealized. But even highly motivated agents of intercultural transfer needed an audience and financial support to realize their dreams. As a result, Ticknor had to wait for nearly 20 years before the Boston Public Library—which was conceived of as a free lending library—became a reality.[33] The libraries in Dresden and Göttingen served for Ticknor as reference points in his lobbying for a public library. And even though there were public lending libraries created in the United States before, it was the cultural significance and perceived superiority of the German libraries that helped Ticknor convince his fellow Bostonians of the necessity of such an institution. In many ways, Dresden was, according to the mental maps of individuals such as Ticknor, closer to Boston than New York or Philadelphia.

As is the case with all transfers, the Boston Public Library was of course not an identical copy of the libraries in Dresden and Göttingen. Intercultural transfer always includes modification and transformation of ideas found in a specific society, which also results in the creation of new models in the minds of the agents through the process of transfer. To stay with the example of the library, Ticknor encountered two libraries—the one in Göttingen and the one in Dresden—both had certain advantages.[34] One had more books, the other had very rare books, yet both offered readers the opportunity to take out books, albeit in a limited fashion in the case of Göttingen. Ticknor compared both libraries and when he returned to Boston, he seemed to have merged these two libraries into a single model of a free lending library, to which he added new ideas about libraries as educational institutions for the betterment of a readership from lower-class and immigrant (Irish) background. The model of a free lending library resulted from Ticknor's contact with the libraries in Göttingen and Dresden, but the Boston Public Library was by no means a mere copy of these two libraries. The function, organization, and the targeted audience had undergone significant modifications in the process of intercultural transfer: the Boston Public Library acquired multiple copies of books that were deemed beneficial for the moral improvement of its readers; it was not intended to house a collection of rare or academic books; and the opening hours were more extensive than those at the Dresden and Göttingen libraries. These modifications were not just a response to the conditions of the receiving society, but rather a result of Ticknor's visions for the function of a library in the receiving society.[35]

Intercultural transfer should, therefore, not be confused with the mere replication of a model in the receiving society. Ideas and institutions became models for social and cultural organization in the receiving society only through the activities of the agent of intercultural transfer. The agent did not find a model for an institution in another culture; he rather found elements and inspiration for the creation of a model, which was a product of his creativity and imagination. Agents of intercultural transfer were always the authors of the model they proclaimed to be an import from another society, which they portrayed as superior. The process of intercultural transfer was, thereby, also a process of changing authorship of the "model." Created in a particular society, the object of transfer was reinvented in the process of transfer and most likely underwent further transformations after its integration and establishment in the receiving society. This process was driven entirely by members of the receiving society who had admiration for the giving society and no direct connection to the society of origination. In fact, such a background would, as the example of the kindergarten shows, have severely limited the success of intercultural transfer and diminished the chances for acceptance of such models in mainstream (Anglo-) American society.

The intercultural transfer of the German custom of Christmas and the Christmas tree to American homes seems to be another example for the necessity of the involvement of Anglo-Americans in the process of transfer in order to secure its success. The trimming of Christmas evergreens emerged as part of the modern form of Christmas celebration among wealthy families in Germany during the Romantic period.[36] From here it quickly spread across Europe and even to the New England states in the 1830s and 1840s. German migrants to North America brought the tradition of Christmas trees with them when they moved to Pennsylvania and New York. For other migrants, the German Christmas trees quickly "became a point of fascination."[37] However, only after Anglo-Americans such as George Ticknor embraced this new custom, did the decorated Christmas tree as well as gift giving become a staple of the American Christmas celebration. This acceptance might also have been helped by the transfer of this custom to England and its quick acceptance into English society around the same time. Ticknor's first encounter with a Christmas tree happened, however, not in New England but during his stay in Göttingen in 1815/16. During his second journey to Saxony in the winter of 1835, he and his daughter encountered a particularly memorable Christmas celebration with a trimmed tree and the giving of presents in the home of Freiherr von Ungern-Sternberg. He wrote in his travel journal about a secret room separated by a folding door from the rest of the house in which the parents had prepared a tree with wax lights under which the presents for each child were presented on round tables.[38] After their return to Boston, the Ticknors introduced this custom to Boston society when they celebrated a Christmas Party with their friends in 1843. The wife of Henry Longfellow wrote about the "beautiful Christmas tree decorated with presents" and the excitement of the children "when the folding doors opened and the pyramid of lights sparkled from the dark boughs of a lofty pine."[39]

The advocacy for the German-style Christmas celebration of Charles Loring Brace might also have contributed to the Anglo-American acceptance of this custom. In his book *Home-Life in Germany*, Brace contrasted "our hollow home-life in many parts of America—the selfishness and coldness in families—the little hold HOME has on any one" with the warmth, meaningfulness, and happiness of German life. "There is something about this German Festival," Brace wrote, "which one would seldom see in our home enjoyments. People do not seem to be enjoying them selves, because it is a 'duty to be cheerful;' and because a family-gathering is a very beautiful and desirable thing. They are cheerful, because they cannot help it, and because they all love one another."[40] Candies, toys, and candles proved to be significant reasons for Americans of all backgrounds to embrace Christmas trees and gift giving.

From the beginning, the giving society did not have any significant role in the process of intercultural transfer other than simply presenting an idea to the interested and selective eye of the observer. Interest and selection through an agent of intercultural transfer were the first steps in the process of transfer. This selection might be guided and determined by introductions of the agent of intercultural transfer to the idea through members of the giving society. The ultimate choice, however, was still left with the member of the receiving society. Location and access determined the selection of the idea as much as human factors. The giving society, thus, lost control over its product fairly early in the process of intercultural transfer. With the movement of the agent of intercultural transfer beyond the borders of the giving society, it forwent in most cases all influence and control over its product.

If a member of the giving society attempted to control the object of intercultural transfer after it had been introduced into the receiving society, such transfers regularly resulted in failure. The best documented example of such a failure is the first introduction of Maria Montessori's teaching method to American schools. After Maria Montessori successfully introduced her teaching philosophy in Italian schools and achieved astonishing success with her new child-centered approach, American school reformers were drawn to her ideas and began traveling to Italy to study with her. Montessori's book *The Montessori Method* was published in the United States in 1912, and the popular women's magazine *The Delineator* ran a series of articles on Montessori's teaching methods in 1914. Across the country, Montessori schools were founded by teachers who had studied with Montessori in Rome.

However, she considered any attempts by American educators to modify her teaching philosophy such that it would fit better into the American school system as detrimental to the success of her approach. Moreover, she was afraid of losing control over her teaching philosophy. Therefore, she intervened and attacked those Americans who "translated" her ideas into English. In newspaper articles, she voiced her disapproval of unauthorized guidance books about the Montessori Method and even suggested that she could not be held responsible for any damages to the development of the children that might result from these unauthorized and presumably dangerous translations. These attempts at controlling the transfer process and maintaining the purity of the Montessori Method quickly backfired and prevented the widespread acceptance of her teaching method. While initially being embraced by more than 2000 schools across the country and even being adopted for the entire school system of Rhode Island, Montessori's teaching philosophy disappeared from American schools almost completely by 1920. Only after Montessori died in 1952 and the Cold War caused Americans to fear lagging behind the Soviet Union (Sputnik Shock) did a second wave of interest in her teaching philosophy surface and lead to a successful introduction of her concept into American education.[41]

The Paradox of Intercultural Transfer

The models that emerged in the process of intercultural transfer differed significantly from the objects that inspired their creation. The integration of these models into the socio-economic and cultural context of the receiving society contributed to the changes and mutations these models underwent before they were fully integrated into their new environment. The layers of these changes often obscured the origin of these institutions and made them alien even for members of the giving society. When in 1893 Constantin Nörrenberg, the chief librarian of the university library at Kiel, came to the United States and encountered the free lending library movement started in Boston, he did not realize that the Boston library was connected by intercultural transfer to the libraries in Göttingen and Dresden. Calling the free lending library a truly American phenomenon, he championed the introduction of this superior model to Germany.[42] And this was no exception. The modern concept of museum associations, which originated with art museums across German cities in the middle of the nineteenth century, became the blueprint for American museum associations before they were reintroduced to Germany at the end of the nineteenth century as truly American inventions.[43] Intercultural transfer, thus, often occurs in both directions over long periods of time and leads to the reintroduction of concepts and ideas into the giving society, which no longer recognizes these ideas as their own since the other society modified and transformed the idea in the process of transfer.

These changes also reveal the paradox of intercultural transfer: societies connected by intercultural transfer became more similar and at the same time more different. In contrast to older concepts such as Americanization, which suggested that the acceptance of American ideas and products by other cultures made non-American cultures essentially identical with the American culture, the notion of intercultural transfer does not suggest that one unified and uniform global culture emerged. The twentieth century was certainly the century of the United States and American products from jeans to chewing gums enticed people across Europe.[44] However, as Rob Kroes so succinctly observed "American icons may have become the staple of a visual lingua franca" but it would be foolish to assume that its idioms carry the same meaning everywhere in Europe.[45] Instead, American icons have been appropriated in very distinct ways and often been ascribed new meanings and interpretations which were still somehow connected to its original meaning but it would be wrong to assume that Americans and Germans ascribed the same meaning to the wearing of jeans.

While the concept of Americanization cannot provide an explanation for these shifts in meaning and interpretation, the concept of intercultural transfer thrives on analyzing the modifications that occurred in every instance of transfer. Since the process of intercultural transfer is not one of simple replication and the exercising of control by the giving society through the movement of concepts and ideas across its borders, it makes sense of the two processes of modern life: the increasing interconnectedness of societies and cultures over the last two centuries and the continuing differentiation and fragmentation of societies and cultures around the world. While Americanization suggests the existence of one center, the concept of intercultural transfer refers to a multi-polar and fragmented world in which control is exercised by the receiving rather than the giving end. Agents of intercultural transfer almost always belonged to the receiving society. Intercultural transfer refers not to missionary work executed by members of the giving society. The selection of the object or idea, the transfer of it, and its integration into the receiving society is completely in the hands of the agents of intercultural transfer and, thus, under the control of the receiving society. The example of Maria Montessori and her attempts to prevent modifications of her teaching method when introduced to American schools led to the failure of this intercultural transfer from Italy to the United States and highlights the dependence of successful intercultural transfers on the willingness of the giving society to let go of an idea and to stay out of its transfer.

Notes

1 Francis Fukuyama, "The End of History," in: *National Interest* No. 16, 1989: 3–18.
2 Akira Iriye, *Global and Transnational History: The Past, Present, and Future*, New York: Palgrave Macmillan, 2013; Akira Iriye and Pierre-Yves Saunier (eds.), *The Palgrave Dictionary of Transnational History*, New York: Palgrave Macmillan, 2009.
3 Larry Schweikart and Michael Allen, *A Patriot's History of the United States: From Columbus's Great Discovery to the War on Terror*, New York: Penguin Book, 2004, XXI.
4 John Breuilly, "Historians and the Nation," in: Peter Burke (ed.), *History and Historians in the Twentieth Century*, New York: Oxford University Press, 2002, 55–87; Stefan Berger, "The German Tradition of Historiography, 1800–1995," in: Mary Fulbrook (ed.), *German History since 1800*, London: Arnold, 1997, 477–92.
5 Daniel T. Rodgers, *Atlantic Crossings: Social Politics in a Progressive Age*, Cambridge and London: The Belknap Press of Harvard University Press, 1998, 2.
6 Maria Grever, "Plurality, Narrative and the Historical Canon," in: Maria Grever and Siep Stuurman (eds.), *Beyond the Canon: History for the Twenty-First Century*, New York: Palgrave Macmillan, 2007, 32.
7 http://thinkprogress.org/politics/2011/05/24/169016/texas-cesar-chavez-street/?mobile=nc (accessed December 1, 2012).
8 The LaPietra Report can be found at: http://www.oah.org/activities/lapietra/. See also: Thomas Bender (ed.), *Rethinking American History in a Global Age*, Berkeley, Los Angeles, London: University of California Press, 2002.
9 Rodgers, *Atlantic Crossings*; Ian Tyrrell, *Transnational Nation: United States History in Global Perspective since 1789*, New York: Palgrave Macmillan, 2007.
10 Ayhan Kaya and Ayşegül Kayaoğlu, "Is National Citizenship Withering Away? Social Affiliations and Labor Market Integration of Turkish-Origin Immigrants in Germany and France," in: *German Studies Review* 35, 1 (2012): 114; Yasemin Soysal, *Limits of Citizenship: Migrants and Postnational Membership in Europe*, Chicago and London: University of Chicago Press, 1994.
11 Bender, *A Nation Among Nations*, 3.
12 Iriye, *Global and Transnational History*, 8.
13 Lisa Bailey, Lindsay Diggelmann, and Kim M. Phillips (eds.), *Old Worlds, New Worlds: European Cultural Encounters, c. 1000–1750*, Turnhout: BREPOLS, 2009; Erdmut Jost and Holder Zaunstöck (eds.), *Goldenes Zeitalter und Jahrhundert der*

Aufklärung: Kulturtransfer zwischen den Niederlanden und dem mitteldeutschen Raum im 17. und 18. Jahrhundert, Halle: Mitteldeutscher Verlag, 2012; Jerry H. Bentley, *Old World Encounters: Cross-Cultural Contacts and Exchanges in Pre-Modern Times*, New York and Oxford: Oxford University Press, 1993.

14 Thomas Adam, *Intercultural Transfers and the Making of the Modern World, 1800–2000*, New York: Palgrave Macmillan, 2012.

15 Patricia Clavin, "Defining Transnationalism," in: *Contemporary European History* 14, 4 (2005): 421–39; Sebastian Conrad and Jürgen Osterhammel (eds.), *Das Kaiserreich Transnational: Deutschland in der Welt 1871–1914*, Göttingen: Vandenhoeck & Ruprecht, 2006.

16 Deborah Cohen and Maura O'Connor (eds.), *Comparison and History: Europe in Cross-National Perspective*, New York and London: Routlegde, 2004.

17 Thomas Adam and Uwe Luebken (eds.) *Beyond the Nation: United States History in Transnational Perspective*, Washington DC: Bulletin of the German Historical Institute Supplement no. 5 (2008).

18 Mark Rennella, *The Boston Cosmopolitans: International Travel and American Arts and Letters*, New York: Palgrave Macmillan, 2008, 17–21; Tyrrell, *Transnational Nation*, 95–96.

19 Michel Espagne and Michael Werner, "Deutsch-französischer Kulturtransfer als Forschungsgegenstand. Eine Problemskizze," in: *Transferts Les Relations Interculturelles dans L'Espace Franco-Allemand (XVIIIe et XIXe Siècle)*. *Textes réunis et présentés par Michel Espagne et Michael Werner*, Paris: Editions Recherce sur les Civilisations, 1988, 11–34; Gabriele Lingelbach, "Comparative History, Intercultural Transfer Studies, and Global History: Three Modes of Conceptualizing History beyond the Nation State," in: *Yearbook of Transnational History* 2 (2019): XX–XX; Johannes Paulmann, "Internationaler Vergleich und interkultureller Transfer. Zwei Forschungsansätze zur europäischen Geschichte des 18. bis 20. Jahrhunderts," in: *Historische Zeitschrift* 267, 3 (1998): 649–85.

20 Michael Werner and Bénédicte Zimmermann, "Beyond Comparison: Histoire Croisée and the Challenge of Reflexivity," *History and Theory* 45, 1 (2006): 30–50.

21 Werner/Zimmermann, "Beyond Comparisons," 31; Rodgers, *Atlantic Crossings*, 33.

22 Gabriele Lingelbach, "Cultural Borrowing or Autonomous Development: American and German Universities in the Late Nineteenth Century," in: Thomas Adam and Ruth Gross (eds.), *Traveling Between Worlds: German-American Encounters*, College Station: Texas A&M University Press, 2006, 100–123.

23 Rodgers, *Atlantic Crossings*, 31.

24 Barbara S. Groseclose, *Emanuel Leutze, 1816–1868: Freedom Is the Only King*, Washington DC: Smithsonian Institution Press, 1975, 37.

25 Groseclose, *Emanuel Leutze*, 37–38; Barbara Gaehtgens, "Fictions of Nationhood: Leutze's Pursuit of an American History Painting in Düsseldorf," in: Thomas W. Gaehtgens and Heinz Ickstadt (eds.), *American Icons: Transatlantic Perspectives on Eighteenth- and Nineteenth-Century American Art*, Santa Monica: Getty Center for the History of Art and Humanities, 1992, 147–82.

26 Rodgers, *Atlantic Crossings*, 31.

27 Thomas Adam, *Buying Respectability: Philanthropy and Urban Society in Transnational Perspective, 1840s to 1930s*, Bloomington and Indianapolis: Indiana University Press, 2009, 5–6.

28 I am very grateful for this information, which was provided by Jacqueline Zeledon, a former doctoral student of mine in the history department at the University of Texas

at Arlington, who was working on a dissertation about Joseph Pilates and the transfer of his exercise technique from Germany to the United States.
29 Mary Louise Pratt, *Imperial Eyes: Travel Writing and Transculturation*, London and New York: Routledge, 2008, 7–8.
30 Ann Taylor Allen, "Children Between Public and Private Worlds: The Kindergarten and Public Policy in Germany, 1840–Present," in: Robert Wollons (ed.), *Kindergarten and Cultures: The Global Diffusion of an Idea*, New Haven and London: Yale University Press, 2000, 16–41; Barbara Beatty, "'The Letter Killeth': Americanization and Multicultural Education in Kindergartens in the United States, 1856–1920," in: Wollons (ed.), *Kindergarten and Cultures*, 42–58.
31 Thomas Adam and Gisela Mettele (eds.), *Two Boston Brahmins in Goethe's Germany: The Travel Journals of Anna and George Ticknor*, Lanham, Boulder, New York, Toronto, Oxford: Lexington Books, 2009, 38.
32 Letter of Elizabeth Peabody to Mary (Peabody), dated June 12, 1822, Peabody Family Papers, Sophia Smith Collection, Smith College, Northampton, Massachusetts.
33 Adam, *Buying Respectability*, 31–38.
34 Adam/Mettele, *Two Boston Brahmins in Goethe's Germany*, 23–24, 36–38, 141–42, 208–9.
35 *Report of the Trustees of the Public Library of the City of Boston*, July 1852, 17.
36 Joe Perry, *Christmas in Germany: A Cultural History*, Chapel Hill: The University of North Carolina Press, 2010.
37 Penne L. Restad, *Christmas in America: A History*, New York and Oxford: Oxford University Press, 1995, 59.
38 Adam/Mettele, *Two Boston Brahmins in Goethe's Germany*, 110–11.
39 Cited after Restad, *Christmas in America*, 60–61.
40 Charles Loring Brace, *Home-Life in Germany*, New York: Charles Scribner, 1853, 224–25.
41 Adam, *Intercultural Transfers*, 77–110.
42 Adam, *Buying Respectability*, 38.
43 Adam, *Buying Respectability*, 15–31; Karsten Borgmann, "'The Glue of Civil Society': A Comparative Approach to Art Museum Philanthropy at the Turn of the Twentieth Century," in: Thomas Adam (ed.), *Philanthropy, Patronage, and Civil Society: Experiences from Germany, Great Britain, and North America*, Bloomington: Indiana University Press, 2004, 34–54; Judith Huggins Balfe (ed.), *Paying the Piper: Causes and Consequences of Art Patronage*, Urbana and Chicago: University of Illinois Press, 1993.
44 Victoria de Grazia, *Irresistible Empire: America's Advance Through Twentieth-Century Europe*, Cambridge and London: The Belknap Press of Harvard University Press, 2005.
45 Rob Kroes, "American Empire and Cultural Imperialism: A View from the Receiving End," in: Bender (ed.), *Rethinking American History*, 310–12.

Bibliography

Primary Sources

Brace, Charles Loring. *Home-Life in Germany*. New York: Charles Scribner, 1853.
Letter of Elizabeth Peabody to Mary (Peabody), dated June 12, 1822, Peabody Family Papers, Sophia Smith Collection, Smith College, Northampton, Massachusetts.
Report of the Trustees of the Public Library of the City of Boston, July 1852.

Secondary Sources

Adam, Thomas. *Intercultural Transfers and the Making of the Modern World, 1800–2000*. New York: Palgrave Macmillan, 2011.

Adam, Thomas. *Buying Respectability: Philanthropy and Urban Society in Transnational Perspective, 1840s to 1930s*. Bloomington and Indianapolis: Indiana University Press, 2009.

Adam, Thomas and Gisela Mettele, eds. *Two Boston Brahmins in Goethe's Germany: The Travel Journals of Anna and George Ticknor*. Lanham, Boulder, New York, Toronto, Oxford: Lexington Books, 2009.

Adam, Thomas and Uwe Luebken, eds. *Beyond the Nation: United States History in Transnational Perspective*. Washington DC: Bulletin of the German Historical Institute Supplement no. 5. (2008).

Allen, Ann Taylor. "Children Between Public and Private Worlds: The Kindergarten and Public Policy in Germany, 1840–Present." In: *Kindergarten and Cultures: The Global Diffusion of an Idea*, edited by Robert Wollons. New Haven and London: Yale University Press, 2000, 16–41.

Bailey, Lisa, Lindsay Diggelmann, and Kim M. Phillips, eds. *Old Worlds, New Worlds: European Cultural Encounters, c. 1000–1750*. Turnhout: BREPOLS, 2009.

Balfe, Judith Huggins, ed. *Paying the Piper: Causes and Consequences of Art Patronage*. Urbana and Chicago: University of Illinois Press, 1993.

Beatty, Barbara. "'The Letter Killeth': Americanization and Multicultural Education in Kindergartens in the United States, 1856–1920." In: *Kindergarten and Cultures: The Global Diffusion of an Idea*, edited by Robert Wollons. New Haven and London: Yale University Press, 2000, 42–58.

Bender, Thomas, ed. *Rethinking American History in a Global Age*. Berkeley, Los Angeles, London: University of California Press, 2002.

Bender, Thomas. *A Nation Among Nations: America's Place in World History*. New York: Hill and Wang, 2006.

Bentley, Jerry H. *Old World Encounters: Cross-Cultural Contacts and Exchanges in Pre-Modern Times*. New York and Oxford: Oxford University Press, 1993.

Berger, Stefan. "The German Tradition of Historiography, 1800–1995." In: *German History since 1800*, edited by Mary Fulbrook. London: Arnold, 1997, 477–92.

Borgmann, Karsten. "'The Glue of Civil Society': A Comparative Approach to Art Museum Philanthropy at the Turn of the Twentieth Century." In: *Philanthropy, Patronage, and Civil Society: Experiences from Germany, Great Britain, and North America*, edited by Thomas Adam. Bloomington: Indiana University Press, 2004, 34–54.

Breuilly, John. "Historians and the Nation." In: *History and Historians in the Twentieth Century*, edited by Peter Burke. New York: Oxford University Press, 2002, 55–87.

Clavin, Patricia. "Defining Transnationalism." *Contemporary European History* 14, 4 (2005): 421–39.

Cohen, Deborah and Maura O'Connor, eds. *Comparison and History: Europe in Cross-National Perspective*. New York and London: Routledge, 2004.

Conrad, Sebastian and Jürgen Osterhammel, eds. *Das Kaiserreich Transnational: Deutschland in der Welt 1871–1914*. Göttingen: Vandenhoeck & Ruprecht, 2006.

Espagne, Michel and Michael Werner. "Deutsch-französischer Kulturtransfer als Forschungsgegenstand. Eine Problemskizze." In: *Transferts Les Relations Interculturelles dans L'Espace Franco-Allemand (XVIIIe et XIXe Siècle). Textes réunis et présentés par Michel Espagne et Michael Werner*. Paris: Editions Recherce sur les Civilisations, 1988, 11–34.

Fukuyama, Francis. "The End of History." *National Interest* No. 16 (1989): 3–18.
Gaehtgens, Barbara. "Fictions of Nationhood: Leutze's Pursuit of an American History Painting in Düsseldorf." In: *American Icons: Transatlantic Perspectives on Eighteenth- and Nineteenth-Century American Art*, edited by Thomas W. Gaehtgens and Heinz Ickstadt. Santa Monica: Getty Center for the History of Art and Humanities, 1992, 147–82.
Grazia, Victoria de. *Irresistible Empire: America's Advance Through Twentieth-Century Europe*. Cambridge and London: The Belknap Press of Harvard University Press, 2005.
Grever, Maria. "Plurality, Narrative and the Historical Canon." In: *Beyond the Canon: History for the Twenty-First Century*, edited by Maria Grever and Siep Stuurman. New York: Palgrave Macmillan, 2007, 31–47.
Groseclose, Barbara S. *Emanuel Leutze, 1816–1868: Freedom Is the Only King*. Washington DC: Smithsonian Institution Press, 1975.
Iriye, Akira. *Global and Transnational History: The Past, Present, and Future*. New York: Palgrave Macmillan, 2013.
Iriye, Akira and Pierre-Yves Saunier, eds. *The Palgrave Dictionary of Transnational History*. New York: Palgrave Macmillan, 2009.
Jost, Erdmut and Holder Zaunstöck, eds. *Goldenes Zeitalter und Jahrhundert der Aufklärung: Kulturtransfer zwischen den Niederlanden und dem mitteldeutschen Raum im 17. und 18. Jahrhundert*. Halle: Mitteldeutscher Verlag, 2012.
Kaya, Ayhan and Ayşegül Kayaoğlu. "Is National Citizenship Withering Away?: Social Affiliations and Labor Market Integration of Turkish-Origin Immigrants in Germany and France." *German Studies Review* 35, 1 (2012): 113–34.
Kroes, Rob. "American Empire and Cultural Imperialism: A View from the Receiving End." In: *Rethinking American History in a Global Age*, edited by Thomas Bender. Berkeley/Los Angeles/London: University of California Press, 2002, 295–313.
Lingelbach, Gabriele. "Comparative History, Intercultural Transfer Studies, and Global History: Three Modes of Conceptualizing History beyond the Nation State." *Yearbook of Transnational History* 2 (2019): XX–XX.
Lingelbach, Gabriele. "Cultural Borrowing or Autonomous Development: American and German Universities in the Late Nineteenth Century." In: *Traveling Between Worlds: German-American Encounters*, edited by Thomas Adam and Ruth Gross. College Station: Texas A&M University Press, 2006, 100–123.
Paulmann, Johannes. "Internationaler Vergleich und interkultureller Transfer. Zwei Forschungsansätze zur europäischen Geschichte des 18. bis 20. Jahrhunderts." *Historische Zeitschrift* 267, 3 (1998): 649–85.
Perry, Joe. *Christmas in Germany: A Cultural History*. Chapel Hill: The University of North Carolina Press, 2010.
Pratt, Mary Louise. *Imperial Eyes: Travel Writing and Transculturation*. London and New York: Routledge, 2008.
Rennella, Mark. *The Boston Cosmopolitans: International Travel and American Arts and Letters*. New York: Palgrave Macmillan, 2008.
Restad, Penne L. *Christmas in America: A History*. New York and Oxford: Oxford University Press, 1995.
Rodgers, Daniel T. *Atlantic Crossings: Social Politics in a Progressive Age*. Cambridge and London: The Belknap Press of Harvard University Press, 1998.
Schweikart, Larry and Micael Allen. *A Patriot's History of the United States: From Columbus's Great Discovery to the War on Terror*. New York: Penguin Book, 2004.

Soysal, Yasemin. *Limits of Citizenship: Migrants and Postnational Membership in Europe.* Chicago and London: University of Chicago Press, 1994.

Tyrrell, Ian. *Transnational Nation: United States History in Global Perspective since 1789.* New York: Palgrave Macmillan, 2007.

Werner, Michael and Bénédicte Zimmermann. "Beyond Comparison: Histoire Croisée and the Challenge of Reflexivity." *History and Theory* 45, 1 (2006): 30–50.

Chapter 2

SOCIAL HOUSING REFORM AND INTERCULTURAL TRANSFER IN THE TRANSATLANTIC WORLD BEFORE WORLD WAR I

Abstract: Previous scholarship has pointed to the transatlantic transfers that occurred in the realms of social welfare policies and state involvement in the solution of the "social question." Both, Daniel T. Rodgers and Axel Schäfer, reminded historians that social policy was created nowhere in the North Atlantic world in national isolation. American and European reformers developed a transatlantic network that furthered exchange and learning processes. And although Rodgers already reminded his audience that this exchange was characterized by an "asymmetry of the exchange"—meaning that the United States received many more ideas and concepts in the field of social policy during the nineteenth century than it exported during the twentieth century—he still neglected to take into account the extensive exchange of ideas within the field of private social welfare. An investigation of the European roots of American private social housing projects in Boston and New York will show the extent of this transfer and its impact on social reform debates in the United States. From the 1840s to the turn of the nineteenth century, American housing reformers such as Henry I. Bowditch, Alfred T. White, and Elgin R. L. Gould traveled repeatedly to Europe in search of models for the solution of the pressing housing problems back home. In this process, British and German organizational and architectural models for social housing companies were imported by social reformers and philanthropists who did not have a government mandate but acted on their own or in company with like-minded individuals. London and Leipzig became the favorite destinations of these reformers who observed social housing models in various economic, social, and cultural settings to find the best fit for solving the housing crisis at home.

This chapter was first published online as a working paper of the International Society for Third Sector Research Conference in 2008. Parts of it were later included in my book *Buying Respectability: Philanthropy and Urban Society in Transnational Perspective, 1840s to 1930s*, Bloomington and Indianapolis: Indiana University Press 2009, 39–79.

Introduction

Previous scholarship has pointed to the transatlantic transfers that occurred in the realms of social welfare policies and state involvement in the solution of the "social question." Both, Daniel T. Rodgers and Axel Schäfer, reminded historians that social policy was created nowhere in the North Atlantic world in national isolation.[1] American and European reformers developed a transatlantic network that furthered exchange and learning processes. And although Rodgers already reminded the readers of his book *Atlantic Crossings* that this exchange was characterized by an "asymmetry of the exchange," meaning that the United States received many more ideas and concepts in the field of social policy during the nineteenth century than it exported during the twentieth century,[2] he still neglected to take into account the extensive exchange of ideas within the field of private social welfare. Long before American reformers such as Carroll Davidson Wright (1840–1909),[3] U.S. commissioner of labor from 1884 to 1905, became interested in European social policies,[4] private individual such as Henry I. Bowditch (1808–1892) and Alfred T. White (1846–1921) traveled to Europe during the 1870s for the purpose of finding models for private social housing companies that would elevate the dreadful living condition of the poor in the big American cities that were swamped with European immigrants.[5]

Bowditch and White's decision to travel to London rather than to Paris or Berlin for finding models for social housing is less confirmation of a perceived established "colonial habit,"[6] than the recognition that London was the only place with social housing enterprises, which could build upon a thirty-year experience.[7] Bowditch and White were not the only housing reformers who visited London and who followed the progress of social housing enterprises in the British metropolis. Since the 1840s, German social reformers such as Victor Aimé Huber (1800–1869), Johann Georg Varrentrapp (1809–1866), and Gustav de Liagre (1842–1904) either visited London to learn about its various social housing enterprises or followed the widespread publication and propagation of its social housing concepts in newspapers and travel reports. From the 1840s to World War I, an intensive transfer of social hosing models occurred between London and various German and American cities. From the 1840s to the 1880s, London social housing models informed the creation of similar enterprises in German (Berlin, Frankfurt am Main, and Leipzig), and American cities (Boston, New York, and Philadelphia). At the end of the nineteenth century, American reformers cast their net wider and considered social housing enterprises in German cities such as Leipzig as models that could be emulated back home.

This chapter will analyze the complexity of transfers in the realm of private social housing enterprises between London, Berlin, Leipzig, Boston, and

New York focusing on the concept of "Philanthropy and Five Percent." This nineteenth-century concept refers to a type of philanthropy that combined market mechanisms with the provision of social welfare. Its proponents argued that philanthropy would be most effective when both sides—giver and receiver—benefitted from the act of philanthropy. Receiving a limited return (a maximum of five percent compared to much higher profits on investments in other industrial ventures) was considered "truly philanthropic." It was assumed that this "true philanthropy" would provide the people who depended on philanthropy with a certain degree of independence and self-respect. "Philanthropy and Five Percent," thus, was seen as more helpful than "pure philanthropy." Proponents of "Philanthropy and Five Percent" such as Lord Stanley considered it as a "fair and equal bargain between man and man" for "there was no sacrifice of independence on either side. They [the investors] got a fair return for their capital, and the workman got a better quality of lodging."[8] Furthermore, the main function of such profitable (although limited) social housing enterprises was to provide a model that would attract attention from wealthy citizens who did not have a direct interest in social housing and philanthropy. The essential element of nineteenth-century philanthropy was the creation of a model that was to spark widespread imitation. This understanding of philanthropy recognized the large-scale character of providing affordable and healthy housing for lower-class families. Nineteenth-century philanthropy was certainly, as Kathleen Woodroofe pointed out, an individualized answer to a perceived individual failure and not a failure of society. The expectation that social housing projects should not only provide space for a certain number of poor families in need but rather serve as models for larger changes reflects, however, the recognition of the extent of the social question. It already points toward a transformation of philanthropy from an individualized solution toward a general conceptualization of the social question in terms of social and environmental causes.[9]

This discussion of the transfer of social housing models between different cities in different countries reflects the renewed interest in a history researched and written beyond the nation state.[10] However, while newer approaches such as transnational[11] and transfer history[12] still take the overarching importance of the nation state for granted and, therefore, focus on exchanges that occurred between nation states, my investigation of transfer processes shows that the state and the nation played no role in the location of social housing models, the transfer of these models, and their replication in the receiving urban society. Intercultural transfer across the British Channel and across the Atlantic occurred not between nation states but between smaller social communities (cities and towns). The actors involved in the transfer (agents of intercultural transfer) were not ambassadors or political functionaries of nation states. In most cases, they were private individuals concerned with the improvement of their hometown or scholars on research and study trips. To become an agent of intercultural transfer was not a choice or a profession. It happened by chance and was always related to travel and social privilege. It was the wealthy upper-class citizen who traveled for education and enjoyment who encountered models for the creation of an urban infrastructure. Knowledge about such concepts and the direct experience during travel, however, were not sufficient preconditions for a successful transfer. Sometimes it took decades before the model could be replicated in the receiving culture.[13] The desire for the establishment of such institutions by the receiving society is as important as the knowledge about the models that could be implemented. For intercultural transfer to happen, both the giving and the receiving culture had to be fairly open.[14] Feelings of inferiority and superiority played an important role as motivating factors for intercultural transfer. For Americans traveling to Europe in search for social housing models, London and later Leipzig were considered superior with regards to how it dealt with social problems.

The following discussion is divided into three parts. First, this chapter will investigate the transfer of social housing models between London, Berlin, and Frankfurt am Main in the 1840s and 1860s, then we will turn our attention to the transfer of the limited dividend company model from London to Boston in the 1870s, before we finally will discuss the transfer triangle of social housing models between British, German, and American cities at the end of the nineteenth century.

From Limited Dividend Companies to Housing Cooperatives

Since England had a head start in industrialization, it faced its social repercussions much earlier than the United States or Germany. In response to the emerging housing problem for the lower classes, a number of limited dividend housing companies were founded in London. The first such company, the *Metropolitan Association for Improving the Dwellings of the Industrious Classes*, was created in 1841. These companies differed from other housing enterprises in that they limited the dividend paid to investors to five percent (Philanthropy and Five Percent). Common to these companies was the desire to combine making a modest profit with providing healthy and affordable housing for working-class families.[15]

While making a profit with the construction of urban tenement buildings was not a novelty and certainly not philanthropic, the idea to provide affordable and hygienic tenements that satisfied basic standards for human housing was both new and philanthropic. London landlords had been accustomed to providing housing to working-class families that German observers such as Victor Aimé Huber likened to the housing of animals in barns. Huber was even more enraged by the very fact that London's landlords, ignoring the social and cultural repercussions of these living conditions, earned enormous profits by renting out these tenements.[16]

During his many visits to London, Huber witnessed the emergence of philanthropic housing companies and came into contact with its chief founders. In early 1847 he was introduced to Lord Ashley, the later Lord Shaftesbury (1801–1885), who had founded the *Society for Improving the Condition of the Labouring Classes* in 1844. Full of new ideas with regards to cooperation and shared responsibility Huber approached Ashley with a text he had just written in which he argued that renters should be included in the financing schemes and administration of social housing associations. Although Ashley fundamentally disagreed with the young and idealistic Huber on that point, he still arranged for Huber to visit the new tenement buildings of his limited dividend housing company.[17] And although Huber's nineteenth-century biographer, Rudolf Elvers, consistently denies any English influence on Huber's ideas, it seems clear that his English experience had an impact on his concept of "innere Colonisation" (internal colonization).[18] It would be wrong to assume, however, that Huber simply adopted English ideas in their original form. As it always happens, ideas traveling between places mutate in the process of transfer. In the case of Huber, two concepts merged and provided a new approach for the solution of the housing problem in cities such as Berlin. Huber, who saw the necessity for reform, advocated the combination of two modes of social action that he had found and observed in England: philanthropic assistance by well-off citizens and noblemen combined with the self-help of the working people in the form of cooperatives. For Huber, the improvement of the social conditions of the working classes had to begin with the improvement of their living conditions. However, the provision of healthy and affordable housing was just the beginning of the reform Huber envisioned. It had to be followed by a moral and intellectual transformation of the workers and their emancipation by the formation of associations (cooperatives).

In 1846, Huber published "Über innere Colonisation" ("About Internal Colonization"), in which he attacked earlier attempts at social reform and cooperation (Robert Owen) and advocated reform within the existing capitalist system in order to avoid class conflict. Based on his deep religious beliefs, Huber believed in the solidarity between men of all social classes and the possibility of cooperation between nobility, factory owners, and workers. However, the central point of his reform was to enable workers to gain a position of self-determination and self-reliance. Since he did not see a possibility for workers to achieve such a position on their own, Huber believed that the concept of self-help (association) was flawed. Therefore, Huber propagated the combination of social assistance with the concept of self-help. In order to raise the living conditions of working-class families, he further suggested the creation of factory villages outside big cities, which he identified with material and moral decay. These factory villages were to be built in close proximity to the workplace and connected to industrial areas as well as the city by trains. They were to provide healthy and affordable housing and gardens for each family. Since workers could not finance the construction of these complexes, Huber believed that factory owners, the nobility, and the government should provide the necessary funding. From the beginning, Huber envisioned these settlements as profitable enterprises, which were to accrue a fair return of five percent on the invested sums. Renters were to be encouraged to form consumer cooperatives in order to lower the costs for food and heating materials. Associations were considered a central part in Huber's reform concept that ultimately was to lead to moral and social improvement of the working classes.[19]

Huber's article found an enthusiastic audience in Berlin where a couple of reform-minded citizens deliberated the founding of a social housing company for some time.[20] Carl Wilhelm Hoffmann, the royal architect (Landbaumeister) in Berlin, published in February 1847 a call for the founding of a *Berliner gemeinnützige Baugesellschaft*.[21] This association, Hoffmann argued, was to follow the model of the *Metropolitan Association for Improving the Dwellings of the Industrious Classes* in London. Hoffmann was convinced that Berlin needed a social housing company that would provide healthy and affordable housing for working-class families in order to stop the increasing speculation on the housing market that lead to dreadful housing conditions and unreasonable profits. He convinced fifty-two like-minded individuals to create this social housing company as a limited dividend housing company in November 1847.[22] The founders of this housing company read Huber's article on internal colonization and adopted some of its ideas for their housing enterprise and in fact invited Huber to take a position in its administration. Huber's pamphlet introduced the concept of renters' associations and, thus, provided for the merging of the Philanthropy and Five Percent model with the idea of self-administration, and the vision that renters should acquire their homes over time.

Following the model of London's limited dividend housing companies— the *Society for Improving the Condition of the Labouring Classes* and the *Metropolitan Association for Improving the Dwellings of the Industrious Classes*—the *Berliner gemeinnützige Baugesellschaft* (Berlin Mutual Building Company) was founded as a stock company. Wealthy and reform-minded citizens purchased shares (100 Thaler each) to the total amount of about 200,000 Thaler.[23] The investors were promised a steady return of four percent. Huber compared this return with the return offered by several railway companies and argued that, in contrast to risky private stock companies, this housing company would offer a guaranteed protection of the invested sums even in case of default, since the land and the buildings would not lose their value.

In contrast to London's limited dividend companies, this Berlin enterprise included renters associations. These associations would after thirty years— so at least the vision of the founders—become the collective owners of the apartment buildings, which each contained up to nineteen units. They were also in charge of establishing reading rooms and kindergartens. Last but not least, they organized meetings for renters to discuss problems and the future of this housing company on a regular basis. Trustees participated in these meetings and encouraged the participation of the renters in the administration of the housing association.

It is an irony of intercultural transfer that the modifications and mutations that occurred in this particular case proved to be unsuccessful. Huber's insistence on renters associations as well as the original plan of selling the tenements to its renters had to be abandoned already in the 1850s.[24] With these changes, the Berlin housing company became a "pure" limited dividend company that barely showed any difference from its London predecessors. However, the notion of bringing together philanthropy and self-help in this company was decades later taken up again in the formation of the savings and building cooperatives.

The *Berliner gemeinnützige Baugesellschaft* set an example that inspired similar enterprises in cities such as Frankfurt am Main.[25] In May 1860, five civic-minded members of Frankfurt's upper class published a call for the formation of a *gemeinnützige Baugesellschaft*.[26] Among these individuals was Johann Georg Varrentrapp, who like Huber traveled extensively across Western Europe in search of ideas for improving various aspects of social life. He was interested in prison reform, the health care and hygiene movement, waste disposal, and housing conditions.[27]

Following his 1838 voyage and several more visits to England, Varrentrapp engaged actively in prison reform (he favored the Pennsylvania system of solitary imprisonment), the hygiene movement, and housing reform.[28] Discussions at the First International Congress on Public Hygiene in Brussels in 1852 sparked his interest in the housing question. Following the congress, Varrentrapp traveled repeatedly to England and France to study the early forms of private social housing companies. He was most likely the primary instigator of the Frankfurt limited dividend housing company and possibly the major author of the *Aufforderung zur Gründung einer gemeinnützigen Baugesellschaft in Frankfurt am Main* (Call for the Creation of a Social Housing Enterprise in Frankfurt am Main). In this call for support, the authors argued that a limited dividend company would constitute a philanthropic enterprise like many others Frankfurt's citizens had already established (insane asylum, kindergarten, institute for the blind and deaf). However, in this case, instead of donating money, the participants were asked to buy shares that were to yield a four percent return. The main goal of the company was to limit speculation with housing property and instead support the provision of healthy and affordable housing. Attached to the call for support were the bylaws and a text by Varrentrapp in which he surveyed the attempts at social housing in various European countries (England, France, Belgium) and cities (Amsterdam, Groningen, Copenhagen, Basel, Bremen, Berlin). England and London were first in his presentation and Varrentrapp repeatedly pointed to the *Society for Improving the Condition of the Labouring Classes* as a model for the Frankfurt social housing company.[29] Varrentrapp succeeded in convincing a large number of Frankfurt's well-to-do citizens to purchase its 4000 shares for 425 marks each. According to the annual reports of 1868 to 1905, this housing company was very successful in keeping its promise to pay a four percent dividend each year and still accumulate enough capital to maintain and expand the building complexes. By 1909, the housing enterprise owned 524 apartments.[30]

The *gemeinnützige Baugesellschaft in Frankfurt am Main* (Mutual Building Company in Frankfurt am Main) followed its English predecessors closely from the onset and excluded the cooperative elements Huber had introduced to the Berlin company. It was, however, this combination of philanthropic support and self-help that would determine the production of social housing in Germany at the end of the nineteenth century. Although during the 1870s and 1880s a number of such limited dividend companies were founded all over Germany, the legal framework and economic conditions did not favor such enterprises and their widespread support. Instead, a new model of social housing—a hybrid between limited dividend company (philanthropy) and cooperative (self-help)—emerged as the dominant player in Germany's social housing sector.

After the German government introduced the principle of "limited liability" for all economic enterprises in 1889[31] and after the *Spar- und Bauverein Hannover* (Hanover Savings and Building Cooperative, founded in 1885) had set an example of how to combine the Five Percent Philanthropy with self-help did the social housing movement gain strength. Before 1885, most housing cooperatives were based on the idea of transferring the homes into the private property of its members. The most important such cooperative was the *Flensburger Arbeiterbauverein* (Workers' Housing Association Flensburg) founded in 1878. But these cooperatives, which were influenced by the model of the *Kopenhagen Arbeiterverein* (Kopenhagen Workers' Association), were not a suitable instrument for dealing with the housing problems of the lower classes.[32] Therefore, reform-minded citizens of the city of Hanover and workers who experienced the lack of affordable housing founded the *Spar- und Bauverein*. The founders of this new association turned their attention back to English models and attempted to integrate, as Huber had championed, the concepts of cooperative association (self-help) with philanthropic assistance. However, in contrast to Huber and Hoffmann's *Berliner gemeinnützige Baugesellschaft*, the Hanover enterprise was founded on three innovative tenants: (1) it did not produce housing units which could be bought by its members over time; instead the buildings were to remain in the possession of the cooperative indefinitely; (2) it combined self-help (each renter had to be a member of the cooperative and was expected to purchase at least one share of 300 marks) with financial assistance from wealthy citizens (who were allowed to purchase multiple shares) by merging the housing cooperative with a credit union; and (3) it adopted the legal provision of limited liability and, thus, limited the liability of shareholders to the amount of their shares (300 marks).[33]

The establishment of a credit union in conjunction with the housing cooperative provided for an economic solution in which individual wealthy citizens were encouraged to invest their money into social housing associations. The contributions of such wealthy individuals were significant for the economic well-being of such associations, as the example of the Hanover cooperative proves. In 1900 its members had purchased shares for 583,510.23 marks, while wealthy citizens had deposited 659,922.68 marks with the credit union of this association.[34] As A. Grävell points out in his history of the German cooperative movement, many cooperatives founded on the model of the Hanover housing cooperative allowed in their regulations for individuals to purchase multiple shares of 100–300 marks each. Such rules enabled private citizens to acquire shares of up to 40,000 marks at a guaranteed return of four percent, and it provided these housing cooperatives with sufficient funding for the production of affordable and healthy working-class housing.[35] It set an example for all German cities and soon sparked imitation in Berlin, Göttingen, Leipzig, and Dresden.[36] The number of housing cooperatives increased, according to Rudolf Albrecht, from 28 with about 2,000 members in 1888 to 764 with about 140,000 members in 1908. Those cooperatives owned property (land and buildings) valued at more than 200 million marks by 1908.[37] And in contrast to British and American limited dividend companies, these savings and housing associations were, at least until World War II, even more successful in guaranteeing as steady return of four percent.[38]

Until the early 1920s, the German housing cooperatives were dominated by wealthy burghers who run these associations and limited the influence of its members to an absolute minimum. Only after World War I, with the general democratization of German society, did these associations become institutions of self-help in which workers/tenants took over the administration of those associations and increasingly assumed financial responsibility for both the shares and the savings deposited with the credit unions.[39] Such emancipating goals were not part of the "Philanthropy and Five Percent" inspired housing reform in England or in the United States.

From Five Percent to Seven Percent Philanthropy and Social Control

About thirty years after Huber had visited London and more than twenty years after the *Berliner gemeinnützige Baugesellschaft* was established as the result of a successful intercultural transfer of a social housing model from London to Berlin, American social reformers became interested in European social housing experiments. In contrast to Huber who championed the ideas of "Philanthropy and Five Percent" at a time when this concept was still new and untested, American observers in the 1870s had the advantage to study an already established system of philanthropic housing companies in London. However, at this time London's social housing companies were the most advanced and most reliable examples of social housing in Western Europe. Social reformers in continental Europe still observed the English developments, arguing that the housing problem in German cities was not yet as bad as in London, and focused on either associations that were aimed at tenants who would acquire the homes built for them or on factory villages as for instance in the case of Alfred Krupp.[40] For American observers from Boston and New York who were faced with large numbers of poor immigrants in an urban environment these were not useful solutions. They were interested in social housing projects that provided affordable and healthy housing in multi-story tenement buildings in an urban environment at a profitable return. London was the best place for finding ideas and models that could suit the needs and the potential of Boston and New York.

The first to travel to London was the eminent Boston physician Henry Ingersoll Bowditch who went to the British metropolis in 1870 and stayed there for the summer to study its various social housing projects.[41] When Bowditch arrived in London he was overwhelmed by the large number of social housing enterprises. Shaftesbury's *Society for Improving the Condition of the Labouring Classes*, which had been among Huber's objects of observation, had become one among several thriving social housing companies. In addition, the model of "Philanthropy and Five Percent" had received competition from two other concepts: (1) the concept of pure philanthropy (housing trust) and (2) Octavia Hill's house management system.[42] This multiplicity of social housing concepts and the large number of social housing companies forced Bowditch to make a selection and to compare the selected models with regards to a possible transfer from London to Boston. It is interesting to note that neither Bowditch nor any of the American social reformers who followed in his footsteps seemed to pay any serious interest to the model of cooperation as Huber had done. Only Canadian housing reformers developed some interest in the mixing of philanthropy and self-help after the turn of the nineteenth century.[43]

Bowditch focused his attention on four distinct models for social housing: (1) pure philanthropy (*Peabody Trust*); (2) "Philanthropy and Five Percent" (*Improved Industrial Dwelling Company*); (3) the *Jarrow Building Company*, which was organized along the lines of a cooperative that enabled its tenants to purchase their homes over time; and (4) Octavia Hill's house management system.[44] While Bowditch dismissed the *Peabody Trust* as too philanthropic and paid little attention to the *Jarrow Building Company*, he focused his attention at the concept of Sydney Waterlow's *Improved Industrial Dwelling Company* and Octavia Hill's system of friendly rent collecting. Writing about Peabody's famous housing trust, Bowditch immediately recognized that it could not serve as inspiration for social reform back in Boston. "The percentage for rents on the original outlays is so small that no capitalist would desire to employ his surplus funds without greater gain. We must look in other directions for plans and successful experiments in which philanthropy and capital joins hands."[45] Bowditch shared with Huber the desire to combine improving the housing conditions of the deserving poor with philanthropy and a profitable investment for capitalists. Both, Bowditch and Huber, also shared the belief that workers/tenants needed material and moral improvement. While for Huber education and association were the tools to improve the moral and ethical character of working-class families, Bowditch found a more direct and with the everyday life experience of working-class families interfering method in Octavia Hill's friendly visiting scheme. It was Hill's fundamental conviction "that the poor needed example, tuition, inspiration and guidance in their everyday lives more than they needed charity."[46] Bowditch found her concept of employing ladies of higher social standing to collect the rent directly from the renters on a weekly basis very appealing since he and his fellow Bostonian social reformers believed that the poor Irish immigrants needed strict guidance and moral improvement.[47] Such improvement seemed to be feasible if such ladies were endowed with the power to give advice with regards to the conditions of the apartment and to the general social life of the family.

When Bowditch returned to Boston, he convinced 163 wealthy Bostonians to form the *Boston Cooperative Building Company*, which was capitalized at $200,000 and limited to seven percent dividends. Inspired by Bowditch and headed by Martin Brimmer (1829–1906), this social housing enterprise combined the concept of "Philanthropy and Five Percent" with Hill's house management system.[48] In his *Letter from the Chairman of the State Board of Health* that was published as part of the *Second Annual Report of the State Board of Health of Massachusetts* and in various annual reports of the Boston *Cooperative Building Company*, Bowditch continuously publicized Octavia Hill's system of friendly rent collecting and applied central aspects of this system to the business practice of the *Boston Cooperative Building Company*.[49]

While the concept of limited dividend companies (in Berlin and Frankfurt with a four percent return and in Boston with a seven percent return promise) seemed to dominate on both sides of the Atlantic, German and American social reformers had very different visions with regards to the moral and intellectual improvement of the tenants. Although everyone agreed that moral and intellectual improvement was necessary, Huber and Bowditch envisioned different paths toward success. While Huber believed in the possibility for moral and ethical improvement of the renters and even participated in this project,[50] Bowditch and his fellow Bostonian reformers were from the outset rather skeptical toward the renters of one of its most troubled project, the Lincoln Building, which served as an experiment in the application of Hill's management system. In its *Third Annual Report* the board of directors already cautioned by warning: "It is, however, ... felt that the experiments in London and Boston must necessarily differ very materially from one another" because of "the difference between the characteristics of the English race, with which Miss Hill had chiefly to deal, and those of the Celtic family with which the committee was to come in contact."[51] Whereas German social reformers seem to have trusted in the possibility of moral improvement, American social reformers displayed racial stereotypes and resorted to a much more rigid approach toward moral improvement than their German counterparts.

Further, the interest promised to investors in Boston was two percent higher than that of London's limited dividend companies (seven instead of five percent).[52] Bowditch had argued that the margin of profit had to be higher in Boston since the overall profit margin in the United States was higher than in England during the 1870s.[53] However, the *Boston Cooperative Building Company* rarely reached its goal of paying a seven-percent return to its investors. A seven-percent return was paid only between 1871 and 1875, but between 1876 and 1889 "dividends were stopped or reduced to three percent and earnings were invested." In the 1890s dividends reached between five and six percent.[54] On paper London's "Philanthropy and Five Percent" had become "Philanthropy and Seven Percent" but in reality, the returns lagged behind that goal for years. It should be noted that this failure to produce the promised seven-percent return did not cause shareholders to sell their shares and to look for better investment possibilities. In fact, none of the limited dividend housing companies went bankrupt because the investor-philanthropists withdrew their support in response to the lower interest paid on their shares. The shareholders hold on to their shares and even left them to their children upon death. Although German and American social reformers had sincerely hoped to produce a working business model for the provision of social housing, the shareholders seemed to have defeated this goal by behaving not like investors but like philanthropists who did not care about the return. Furthermore, the obvious difficulties of producing a seven-percent return might also explain the lack of imitation. Protagonists of the "Philanthropy and Five Percent" concept always argued that such companies' main goal was to set an example and to induce individuals who were only marginally interested in social welfare projects to invest in such projects.[55] Huber continuously compared the interest of the *Berliner gemeinnützige Baugesellschaft* to that offered by railway companies and he further suggested that capital invested in the housing company would be much safer than risky investments in companies that could fail.[56] It might have been much safer than investments in other stock companies such as railway or shipping companies, but it was not always as profitable as investments in such enterprises.[57]

Casting a Wider Net: American Observers in Germany

After the early encounters of German and American social reformers and philanthropists with London's social housing companies and initial intercultural transfers of these concepts which in the process of transfer had been modified and transformed, cross-cultural observation and transfer continued up until World War I. American social reformers such as Alfred Treadway White[58] and Elgin R. L. Gould (1860–1915) as well as their German counterparts, as for instance Wilhelm Ruprecht (1858–1943)[59] and Paul Felix Aschrott (1856–1927),[60] continued to travel to London in search for inspiration and concepts for providing better housing for lower-class families. In this process, London's various housing companies were praised as effective solutions and turned into models that should be emulated in various cities that faced the same challenges of industrialization and urbanization. The reports of these observers often read as if the authors wanted to sell a specific social housing concept to its reading audience. The argument often went beyond passionate interest on the side of the author and entered the realm of manipulation. Ruprecht and Aschrott, for instance, argued that London's limited dividend companies always reached their goal of guaranteeing a five-percent return when in reality they rarely did.[61]

At the end of the nineteenth century, the American focus also shifted from a narrow fixation on London to a focus on Europe. Since many philanthropists all over Western Europe had adopted London's ways of dealing with the housing of working-class families, American observers such as Gould embarked on research trips to study the success of London-inspired social housing companies in various cities on the continent with a particular focus on German cities. In contrast to earlier observers, this second generation of housing reformers publicized their findings widely by producing detailed descriptions of all aspects of social housing companies with regards to their architecture, their economic set up, the hygienic standards, and the social characters of the tenants. The most extensive such survey of 443 pages plus 136 plans has been produced by Elgin Gould in 1895 with his book *The Housing of the Working People*. In 1887 Gould went to Europe on an extensive study mission to compile available data on social housing companies in Great Britain, Germany, France, Austria, Holland, Sweden, Belgium, and Denmark. Chapter IX (model block buildings) with 149 pages and chapter X (model small houses) with 79 pages are the most extensive and dominating parts of Gould's treatise. In chapter IX, Gould limited his description of American social housing companies to the two cities of New York and Boston. The two big companies he discussed, the *Improved Dwellings Company of New York* (founded by White) and the *Boston Cooperative Building Company* (founded by Bowditch), were both inspired by London models and took a lead in American housing reform. The main part of this chapter was dedicated to English and German social housing companies (both limited dividend companies and housing trusts). The case of housing companies in German cities such as Berlin, Leipzig, and Hanover was of particular interest to Gould since these housing companies had been the result of intercultural transfer.

During his stay in Germany, Gould visited the *Berliner gemeinnützige Baugesellschaft*, *Meyer's Housing Trust* in Leipzig, and the *Spar- und Bauverein* in Hanover.[62] All of these housing companies had been founded under the direct influence (first-hand experience through travel, influence of travelers on wealthy individuals who had the financial means to realize social housing projects, and second-hand information based on reading travel accounts and observing other "translations" of "foreign" housing models) of various social housing companies in London. Gould, who had already sufficient knowledge about London's social housing models, was, nevertheless, very interested in the study of these German transfers and "translations" of those London models. In his description of the *Berliner gemeinnützige Baugesellschaft*, which was based upon the "Philanthropy and Five Percent" model, Gould harshly criticized this enterprise since it "was organized on a purely philanthropic basis."[63] It is not clear whether he misunderstood the workings of this limited dividend company (since he later championed the concept of limited dividend companies) or if he thought the margin of profit was simply too small (only four percent). *Meyer's Housing Trust* in Leipzig was an impressive sight for Gould although he did not share Herrmann Julius Meyer's conviction that the only way for solving the housing problem was to create housing trusts. Following the model of the *Peabody Trust* in London, Meyer had donated nearly 19 million marks for the creation of this housing trust.[64] While these two enterprises did not present anything new to Gould, the *Spar- und Bauverein* in Hanover was certainly an unprecedented novelty to him. According to his description this "company is a cooperative society with limited liability. Shares have a value of 300 marks ($71.40), and are payable in weekly installments of 30 pfennigs (7 cents). The rate of annual dividend paid upon share capital since the society was founded has been 4 per cent."[65] Even though Gould realized that this housing company included a savings bank, which was an integral part of the organization's concept of joining self-help and philanthropic assistance, he did not further analyze this new model for the provision of social housing.

Although the study of German social housing companies offered to Gould no new models—he chose to dismiss the *Spar- und Bauverein* as a viable model— the study of these companies offered Gould some insight into the process of intercultural transfer. Gould was able to compare the modifications and symbiosis that occurred in the process of transferring social housing companies from one economic, social, and cultural space to another. In contrast to earlier housing reformers, Gould also had the advantage of being able to investigate the original models in London and to compare them to social housing companies that had been created in different settings all over Western Europe and even back home in New York and Boston. He could rely on an extensive body of statistical information with regards to the financing schemes, the rent levels, and the tenement population as well as the architectural concepts of social housing enterprises. American and German social reformers were equally concerned with the type of tenant who should be the target of social reform and with the best way to create a closed environment for the nuclear family.

In his description of the German social housing projects, Gould constantly pointed to the various ways to ensure that each family living in an apartment house would be isolated from the other tenants in order to create and protect a private sphere for this family. An "open apartment" structure would, in the eyes of nineteenth-century housing reformers on both sides of the Atlantic, lead to increased social intercourse between the tenants of one building, promiscuity, and social decay. "We have learned by experience," stated the *Third Annual Report of the Boston Co-operative Building Company*, "that such tenements as this which has common corridors, common water rooms, and, above all, common privies, are a disgrace to modern civilization, and public nuisances, inasmuch as they encroach upon the family relations, tend to make them impure, and thereby sap the very foundations of the State."[66] The creation of a "closed apartment" with a separate hallway, an entrance door that could be locked, no communal facilities (bathroom etc.) and the limitations of the number of apartments which would share the same stairway were essential to the protection of the family and a stable society. *Meyer's Housing Trust* in Leipzig seemed, in the eyes of Gould, to set the right architectural example. Writing about this housing trust, Gould pointed out that each "of the tenements ... has a private hallway adjoining the main corridor and staircase. One door from a tenement opens directly to the corridor and stairway. Corridors are too small to allow promiscuous mingling. The private hallway of each tenement is considered another means of preserving the independence and isolation of the individual family."[67]

Philanthropists and housing reformers alike were also discussing the various ways of administrating social housing projects. Wherever Gould went in Great Britain and Germany, he often discovered that German reformers had, with few exceptions, adopted Octavia Hill's house management system. However, some companies such as the *Berliner gemeinnützige Baugesellschaft* and the *Spar- und Bauverein* in Hanover experimented with cooperative forms of management in which the renters were integrated into the administration of the buildings they inhabited. In the case of the Berlin company "porters, janitors, and other assistants are usually selected from among the oldest tenants, who are generally functionaries. They receive no salary, nor are they granted reduced rentals. They gladly assume the duties of keeping order, lighting the halls, etc., for the honor of holding the position. A small gratuity, usually 30 marks ($7.14), is given to them at Christmas."[68]

Furthermore, reformers were also discussing the target of housing reform. Not every lower-class family was considered fit for inclusion in the social housing reform. On both sides of the Atlantic, reformers and philanthropists spoke of the upper strata of the working-class as the intended target of reform. However, it was often a problem to identify those worthy of social assistance. German social reformers decided to define the desired audience of social housing companies by establishing wage limits for those who would be allowed to live in social housing projects. In the case of the *Berliner gemeinnützige Baugesellschaft*, individuals "having a yearly income under 500 marks ($119) or over 3,000 marks ($714) are ruled out as tenants."[69] In the case of *Meyer's Housing Trust* the restrictions were even tighter: it admitted only individuals with yearly incomes between 800 and 1800 marks as renters.[70]

While Berlin, Leipzig, and Hanover served not as sources of new and original models of social housing, American social reformers considered them as laboratories, in which foreign models of social housing were tested for their use within a different social and economic setting. Leipzig proved to Gould that it was possible and desirable to transfer social housing models between different urban spaces. While earlier American social reformers in Boston and New York displayed enormous skepticism that British standards of living in apartment buildings could be introduced into American cities with their large numbers of Irish immigrants, Gould was clearly convinced that such concepts were fully compatible with the American situation. Since the best example is always to translate theory into practice, Gould decided to prove that European-style housing companies could be replicated within American society. In 1896, Gould together with Robert Fulton Cutting, the president of the *Association for Improving the Condition of the Poor*, convinced 410 wealthy New Yorkers to found the *City & Suburban Homes Company*, which followed both British and German models. It was organized as a limited dividend company with about 410 shareholders. The apartment buildings provided self-contained apartments for its renters, which were accessible from staircases and closed toward other apartments. "Every apartment is a complete home in itself."[71] To avoid long hallways and, thus, more contact between renters, larger complexes were subdivided into smaller houses with multiple entrances and staircases for a limited number of apartments. Following Meyer's concept of "isolation of the renter family" the buildings of the *City & Suburban Homes Company* displayed an architectural design that limited social contacts between renters to a bare minimum. Female rent collectors were in charge of collecting the rent on a weekly basis. They used this opportunity to visit with the renters and to inspect the apartments often offering advice. In the self-description of the *City & Suburban Homes Company* the intercourse of the rent collectors with the renters "often becomes cordial and helpful in a social way. ... Advice is often asked regarding the arrangement of furniture, or choice of color in painting the rooms, care of children and on other domestic themes."[72]

Intercultural Transfer and Philanthropy

Studying intercultural transfer and philanthropy across the Atlantic in the nineteenth century poses a potential challenge to the role and importance of the nation state. It might be true that the nation state remained a "weighty actor" as some have claimed. By setting legal limits to migration and trade, by regulating elementary and higher education and by encouraging industrial development, nation states had a decisive impact on shaping the face of modern societies. However, as important as the nation state as an analytic category might be, it should not come into the way of investigating the contexts, interconnections, and similarities that characterized the Atlantic world in the nineteenth century. The transfer of models for social housing across the British Channel and across the Atlantic Ocean occurred not between nation states, but between cities and towns. The initiative for this transfer did not originate from state or local governments but from private citizens who were concerned with the common good. Agents of intercultural transfer were essential to the observation and learning processes involved in the creation of philanthropic networks that connected cities on both sides of the Atlantic Ocean regardless of national belonging. In fact, New York's housing reformers preferred to look to Europe instead to Boston for inspiration and guidance.

The actual transfer of models for urban organization happened in many ways: (1) Agents of intercultural transfer kept travel diaries and, according to outside sources, made a point of repeatedly discussing within their social circles their encounters with institutions they wished to have replicated in their home towns. (2) Agents of intercultural transfer published articles in newspapers and journals and some even wrote books. Such an approach provided for a wide distribution of ideas about urban institutions that could spark imitation back home by individuals who have not even traveled abroad. (3) Agents of intercultural transfer concerned with social problems (housing, slums, city planning) often already belonged to a voluntary group of citizens who were interested in ideas and models and where willing to implement these models without much time delay. In the case of Bowditch and Gould, both formed limited dividend housing companies after their return to create social housing projects inspired by European models. That assured the realization of the ideas and concepts they had encountered. Although Gould still published the findings of his journey (1895), the time delay between observation (1887)—forming a model—and implementation (1896) had been less than ten years. Since in some cases agents of intercultural transfer could rely on a group of volunteers and philanthropists, it was not always necessary to publicize their observations. It was possible to distribute the knowledge about models for urban organization by direct discussion and engagement.

In the process of intercultural transfer, agents of intercultural transfer created models for replication by universalizing and selecting characteristics of the observed institution. The model also often incorporated aspects of several institutions that were observed. Gould's model for social housing in New York City represented the combination of different even contrasting architectural and organizational models from London and Leipzig. The model created in intercultural transfer, thus, is the sum of ideas and impressions collected and selected by agents of intercultural transfer in the process of observation. Since intercultural transfer is closely connected to memory and processes of memorization, they are subjective in nature and do not lead to the creation of a simple duplicate in the receiving society. The very nature of intercultural transfer poses a serious challenge to the historian since transfers are not obvious and can only be explored by leaving the iron cage of the nation state behind. Fortunately, agents of intercultural transfer left notes and diaries that allow us to delve into the transatlantic dimension of nineteenth-century life.

Notes

1. Daniel T. Rodgers, *Atlantic Crossings: Social Politics in a Progressive Age*, Cambridge and London: The Belknap Press of Harvard University Press, 1998; Axel R. Schäfer, *American Progressives and German Social Reform 1875–1920: Social Ethics, Moral Control, and the Regulatory State in a Transatlantic Context*, Stuttgart: Franz Steiner Verlag, 2000.
2. Rodgers, *Atlantic Crossings*, 70.
3. For Wright see: James Leiby, *Carroll Wright and Labor Reform: The Origin of Labor Statistics*, Cambridge: Harvard University Press, 1960.
4. Wright considered the collection of statistical data a necessary precondition and an integral part of social reform. From his appointment as chief of the bureau of labor for Massachusetts, Wright engaged in large-scale sociological studies focusing first on Massachusetts, later on the United States, and finally on a comparative level with European societies. The scope of his sociological investigations included: the education and employment of the young, the conditions of workingmen's families, illiteracy, profits and wages, the relation of intemperance to pauperism and crime, divorce, cooperation and profit sharing, prices and cost of living, factory legislation, etc. No such statistical work had existed before and his studies were used as textbooks in colleges and attracted attention in Europe. See the Special Reports of the Commissioner of Labor, he arranged to be published. Among these volumes were: *A Report on Marriage and Divorce in the United States, 1867 to 1886 Including an Appendix Relating to Marriage and Divorce in Certain Countries in Europe* by Carroll Davidson Wright (First Special Report, 1891); *Compulsory Insurance in Germany Including an Appendix Relating to Compulsory Insurance in Other Countries in Europe* by John Graham Brooks (Fourth Special Report, 1895); *The Housing of the Working People* by Elgin R. L. Gould (Eighth Special Report, 1895); and *Coal Mine Labor in Europe* by Carroll Davidson Wright (Twelfth Special Report, 1905).
5. David Ward, "Population Growth, Migration, and Urbanization, 1860–1920," in: Thomas F. McIlwraith and Edward K. Muller (eds.), *North America: The Historical Geography of a Changing Continent*, Lanham, Boulder, New York, Oxford: Rowman & Littlefield Publishers, 2001, 285–305; Lawrence J. Vale, *From the Puritans to the Projects: Public Housing and Public Neighbors*, Cambridge and London: Harvard University Press, 2000, 51–62.
6. Gerald Daly, "The British Roots of American Public Housing," in: *Journal of Urban History* 15, 4 (1989): 417.
7. Susannah Morris, "Private Profit and Public Interest: Model Dwelling Companies and the Housing of the Working Classes in London, 1840–1914" (D.Phil. thesis, University of Oxford, 1998).
8. Quoted after Susannah Morris, "Market Solutions for Social Problems: Working-Class Housing in Nineteenth-Century London," in: *Economic History Review* LIV, 3 (2001): 528; Susannah Morris, "Changing Perceptions of Philanthropy in the Voluntary Housing Field in Nineteenth- and Early-Twentieth-Century London," in: Thomas Adam (ed.), *Philanthropy, Patronage, and Civil Society: Experiences from Germany, Great Britain, and North America*, Bloomington: Indiana University Press, 2004, 144ff.
9. Kathleen Woodroofe, *From Charity to Social Work in England and the United States*, Toronto: University of Toronto Press, 1962, 92–93.
10. Thomas Bender, *Rethinking American History in a Global Age*, Berkeley: University of California Press, 2002.

11 Patricia Clavin, "Defining Transnationalism," in: *Contemporary European Review* 14, 4 (2005): 421–39. See also: Gunilla-Friedericke Budde, Sebastian Conrad, and Oliver Janz (eds.), *Transnationale Geschichte: Themen, Tendenzen und Theorien*, Göttingen: Vandenhoeck & Ruprecht, 2006.

12 Michel Espagne and Michael Werner, "Deutsch-Französischer Kulturtransfer im 18. und 19. Jahrhundert. Zu einem neuen interdisziplinären Forschungsprogramm des C. N. R. S.," in: *Francia* 13 (1985): 502–10; Michel Espagne and Matthias Middell (eds.), *Von der Elbe bis an die Seine: Kulturtransfer zwischen Sachsen und Frankreich im 18. und 19. Jahrhundert*, Leipzig: Leipziger Universitätsverlag 1993; Matthias Middell (ed.), *Kulturtransfer und Vergleich* (special issue of *Comparative* 10, 1 (2000). See also: Michael Werner and Bénédicte Zimmermann, "Vergleich, Transfer, Verflechtung: Der Ansatz der Histoire croisée und die Herausforderung des Transnationalen," in: *Geschichte und Gesellschaft* 28, 4 (2002): 607–36; Hartmut Kaelble, "Herausforderungen an die Transfergeschichte," in: Barbara Schulte (ed.), *Transfer lokalisiert: Konzepte, Akteure, Kontexte*, Leipzig: Leipziger Universitätsverlag, 2006, 7–12; Kirsten Belgum, "Reading Alexander von Humboldt: Cosmopolitan Naturalist with an American Spirit," in: Lynne Tatlock and Matt Erlin (eds.), *German Culture in Nineteenth-Century America: Reception, Adaptation, Transformation*, Rochester: Camden House, 2005, 107–27.

13 It took George Ticknor, for instance, 32 years to realize his dream of the Boston Public Library, which was based upon the model of the Royal Saxon Library in Dresden. See: Thomas Adam, *Buying Respectability: Philanthropy and Urban Society in Transnational Perspective, 1840s to 1930s*, Bloomington and Indianapolis: Indiana University Press, 2009, 31–38; Thomas Adam, "Cultural Baggage: The Building of the Urban Community in a Transatlantic World," in: Thomas Adam and Ruth Gross (eds.), *Traveling between Worlds: German-American Encounters*, College Station: Texas A&M University Press, 2006, 87–93.

14 Michel Espagne, "Kulturtransfer und Fachgeschichte der Geisteswissenschaften," in: Middell, *Kulturtransfer und Vergleich*, 45.

15 Morris, "Philanthropy in the Voluntary Housing Field in London," 24–38; John Nelson Tarn, *Five Per Cent Philanthropy: An Account of Housing in Urban Areas between 1840 and 1914*, Cambridge: Cambridge University Press, 1973, 15ff.

16 Victor Aimé Huber, "Die Wohnungsnot," in: K. Munding (ed.), *V. A. Hubers Ausgewählte Schriften über Socialreform und Genossenschaftswesen*, Berlin: Verlag der Aktien-Gesellschaft Pionier, 1894), 594; Morris, "Philanthropy in the Voluntary Housing Field in London," 25.

17 Rudolf Elvers, *Victor Aimé Huber: Sein Leben und Wirken* vol. 2, Bremen: C. Ed. Müller, 1874, 210–11; Victor Aimé Huber, "Die Wohnungsreform," in: *V. A. Hubers Ausgewählte Schriften*, 1051–53; Tarn, *Five Per Cent Philanthropy*, 16–17.

18 Elvers, *Huber*, 302. Huber made the argument, perhaps for nationalist purposes, that the German cooperative movement developed without English influences. See: Victor Aimé Huber, *Die genossenschaftliche Selbsthülfe der arbeitenden Klassen*, Elberfeld: N. L. Fridrichs, 1865, 44. For Huber's interest in English cooperatives and his propagation of these ideas see: Victor Aimé Huber, *Ueber die cooperativen Arbeiterassociationen in England: Ein Vortrag, veranstaltet von dem Central-Verein für das Wohl der arbeitenden Klassen, gehalten am 23. Februar 1852*, Berlin: Wilhelm Hertz, 1852 and his *Sociale Fragen: V. Die Rochdaler Pioniers: Ein Bild aus dem Genossenschaftswesen*, Nordhausen: Ferd. Förstemanns, 1867.

19 Victor Aimé Huber, *Über innere Colonisation. Aus d. Janus*, Heft. VII. VIII., besonders abgedruckt zum Besten des Berliner Handwerkervereins, Berlin: Justus Albert Wohlgemuth 1846, 34–36, 41ff.; Elvers, *Huber*, 193–97.

20 Michael A. Kanther and Dietmar Petzina's claim that Huber's text in fact sparked the founding of the first German limited dividend company, the *Berliner gemeinnützige Baugesellschaft*, seems to be exaggerated. See: Michael A. Kanther and Dietmar Petzina, *Victor Aimé Huber (1800–1869): Sozialreformer und Wegbereiter der sozialen Wohnungswirtschaft*, Berlin: Duncker & Humblot, 2000, 75. In his book about the founding of this company, Edmund Krokisius does not even mention Huber. See: Edmund Krokisius, *Die unter dem Protektorat Seiner Majestät des Kaisers und Königs Wilhelm II. stehenden Berliner gemeinnützige Bau-Gesellschaft und Alexandra-Stiftung 1847 bis 1901*, Berlin: Ferd. Dümmler Verlagsbuchhandlung, 1901, 10. Carl Wilhelm Hoffmann mentions Huber's influence in his treatment of the founding of this company. See: Carl Wilhelm Hoffmann, *Die Wohnungen der Arbeiter und Armen I. Heft: Die Berliner Gemeinnützige Bau-Gesellschaft*, Berlin: E. H. Schroeder, 1852, 20.
21 Carl Wilhelm Hoffmann, *Die Aufgabe einer Berliner gemeinnützigen Baugesellschaft*, Berlin: Hayn, 1847.
22 Hoffmann, *Die Wohnungen der Arbeiter und Armen*, 19–24; Krokisius, *Berliner gemeinnützige Bau-Gesellschaft*, 12–13.
23 The bylaws of this company can be found in: Hoffmann, *Die Wohnungen der Arbeiter und Armen*, 37–57. For the starting of this company see also: Dr. Gaebler, *Idee und Bedeutung der Berliner gemeinnützigen Baugesellschaft*, Berlin: Commissions-Verlag von Carl Heymann, 1848.
24 Elvers, *Huber*, 272–77; Huber, "Die Wohnungsreform," 1062–65; Kanther and Petzina, *Victor Aimé Huber*, 75–79; Walter Vossberg, *Die deutsche Baugenossenschafts-Bewegung*, Halle a. S. 1905, 8–9.
25 For the development of this company until the turn of the century see: Krokisius, *Berliner gemeinnützige Bau-Gesellschaft*.
26 Institut für Stadtgeschichte Frankfurt am Main, "Aufforderung zur Gründung einer gemeinnützigen Baugesellschaft in Frankfurt am Main," 1860.
27 Dr. E. Marcus, "Dr. Georg Varrentrapp," in: *Jahresbericht über die Verwaltung des Medizinalwesens der Stadt Frankfurt a. M. 1886*: 264ff.; Alexander Spiess, "Georg Varrentrapp gestorben den 15. März 1886," in: *Deutsche Vierteljahresschrift für öffentliche Gesundheitspflege* 18 (1886): XIff.
28 Spiess, "Georg Varrentrapp"; Marcus, "Dr. Georg Varrentrapp," 264–66; Georg Varrentrapp, *Tagebuch einer medicinischen Reise nach England, Holland, und Belgien*, Frankfurt am Main: Franz Varrentrapp, 1839; Georg Varrentrapp, *Ueber Pönitentiarsysteme, insbesondere über die vorgeschlagene Einführung des pensylvanischen Systems*, Frankfurt am Main: Franz Varrentrapp, 1841; Georg Varrentrapp, *De l'emprisounement individuel sous le rapport sanitaire et des attaques dirigées contre lui par M. M. Charles Lucas et Leon Faucher*, Paris: Guillaumain 1844; Georg Varrentrapp, *Ueber Entwässerung der Städte, über Werth und Unwerth der Wasserclosette, über deren angebliche Folgen: Verlust werthvollen Düngers, Verunreinigung der Flüsse, Benachtheiligung der Gesundheit*, Berlin: Hirschwald, 1868.
29 Institut für Stadtgeschichte Frankfurt am Main, "Aufforderung zur Gründung," 4–6, 20–30; *Die Gemeinnützige Bautätigkeit in Frankfurt am Main*, Frankfurt am Main: Verlag des Vereins für Förderung des Arbeiterwohnungswesens und verwandte Bestrebungen, 1915, 22–25; Henriette Kramer, "Die Anfänge des sozialen Wohnungsbaus in Frankfurt am Main, 1860–1914," in: *Archiv für Frankfurts Geschichte und Kunst* 1978: 135–38.
30 Institut für Stadtgeschichte Frankfurt am Main, Magistratsakten MA T 2054.
31 *Reichsgesetzblatt* no. 11: "Gesetz, betreffend die Erwerbs- und Wirthschaftsgenossenschaften vom 1. Mai 1889." For Huber's observations of the English situation in the 1850s,

see: Victor Aimé Huber, *Reisebriefe aus England im Sommer 1854*, Hamburg: Agentur des Rauhen Hauses, 1855, 462–64.

32   Rudolf Albrecht, *Die Aufgabe, Organisation und Tätigkeit der Beamten-Baugenossenschaften im Rahmen der deutschen Baugenossenschafts-Bewegung*, Stuttgart: Ferdinand Enke, 1911, 38–39.

33   Wilhelm Ruprecht, "Gesunde Wohnungen," in: *Göttinger Arbeiterbibliothek* 1, 6 (1896): 81–96; F. Bork, "Der Spar- und Bauverein, E.G.m.beschr. Haftpflicht in Hannover," in: *Die Spar- und Bau-Vereine in Hannover, Göttingen und Berlin. Eine Anleitung zur praktischen Betätigung auf dem Gebiete der Wohnungsfrage* (Schriften der Centralststelle für Arbeiter-Wohlfahrtseinrichtungen no. 3), Berlin: Carl Heymann, 1893, 1–93.

34   A. Grävell, *Die Baugenossenschafts-Frage: Ein Bericht über die Ausbreitung der gemeinnützigen Bauthätigkeit durch Baugenossenschaften, Aktienbaugesellschaften, Bauvereine etc. in Deutschland während der letzten 12 Jahre*, Berlin: Im Selbstverlage des Centralverbandes städtischer Haus- und Grundbesitzer-Vereine Deutschlands, 1901, table II b no. 83.

35   Grävell, *Die Baugenossenschafts-Frage*, 117. See also table II b.

36   *Die Spar- und Bau-Vereine in Hannover, Göttingen und Berlin*.

37   Albrecht, *Die Aufgabe, Organisation und Tätigkeit der Beamten-Baugenossenschaften*, 41.

38   Thomas Adam, *125 Jahre Wohnreform in Sachsen: Zur Geschichte der sächsischen Baugenossenschaften, 1873–1998*, Leipzig: Antonym, 1999, 134, 143–44.

39   Adam, *125 Jahre Wohnreform*, 136–37.

40   Renate Kastorff-Viehmann, "England, Frankreich, Preußen: Programme für den Arbeiterwohnungsbau im Industriegebiet im 19. Jahrhundert," in: *Westfälische Forschungen* 44 (1994): 140–51; Renate Kastorff-Viehmann, *Wohnungsbau für Arbeiter: Das Beispiel Ruhrgebiet bis 1914*, Aachen: Klenkes, 1981, 153–59; Joachim Schlandt, "Die Kruppsiedlungen – Wohnungsbau im Interesse eines Industriekonzerns," in: Hans G. Helms and Jörn Janssen (eds.), *Kapitalistischer Städtebau*, Neuwied and Berlin: Luchterhand, 1970, 95–108; Lothar Gall, *Krupp: Der Aufstieg eines Industrieimperiums*, Berlin: Siedler 2000, 219–20.

41   *The National Cyclopedia of American Biography* vol. 8, New York: James T. White 1924, 214; *Biographical Encyclopaedia of Massachusetts of the Nineteenth Century*, New York: Metropolitan Publishing and Engraving Co. 1879, 303–6; John C. Rand (ed.), *One of a Thousand: A Series of Biographical Sketches of One Thousand Representative Men Resident in the Commonwealth of Massachusetts A D 1888–89*, Boston: First National Publishing Company, 1890, 68–69. *The Harvard Graduates Magazine* I (1892–1893): 38–43.

42   Thomas Adam, "Transatlantic Trading: The Transfer of Philanthropic Models between European and North American Cities during the Nineteenth and early Twentieth Centuries," in: *Journal of Urban History* 28, 3 (2002): 328–51.

43   Adam, *Buying Respectability*, 79–85; Thomas Adam, "Philanthropic Landmarks: The Toronto Trail from a Comparative Perspective, 1870s to the 1930s," in: *Urban History Review* 30, 1 (2001): 17–18.

44   Henry I. Bowditch, "Letter from the Chairman of the State Board of Health, concerning Houses for the People, Convalescent Homes, and the Sewage Question," in: *Second Annual Report of the State Board of Health of Massachusetts January 1871*, Boston: Wright & Potter, State Printers, 1871: 182.

45   Bowditch, "Letter from the Chairman," 198.

46   Enid Gauldie, *Cruel Habitations: A History of Working-Class Housing 1780–1918*, London: Allen & Unwin, 1974, 214.

47   *Third Annual Report of the Boston Co-Operative Building Company*, Boston: W. L. Deland, 1874: 13.

48 *The First Annual Report of the Boston Co-operative Building Co. with the Act of Incorporation and By-Laws*, Boston: W. L. Deland 1872; Elgin R. L. Gould, *The Housing of the Working People*, Washington: Government Printing Office, 1895, 200–207; David M. Culver, "Tenement House Reform in Boston, 1846–1898" (PhD thesis Boston University 1972), 145–64; Christine Cousineau, "Tenement Reform in Boston, 1870–1920: Philanthropy, Regulation, and Government Assisted Housing" (working paper presented at the Third National Conference on American Planning History November 30–December 2, 1989 in Cincinnati), 6–8; Joseph Lee, *Constructive and Preventive Philanthropy*, New York: The Macmillan Company, 1902, 70–71; David P. Handlin, *The American Home: Architecture and Society, 1815–1915*, Boston and Toronto: Little, Brown and Company 1979, 252–63. Lawrence J. Vale mentions this company only briefly in his account of Boston public housing. See: Vale, *From the Puritans to the Projects*, 63–64.
49 Bowditch, "Letter from the Chairman," 212–17; *Seventeenth Annual Report of the Boston Co-Operative Building Company*, Boston: Press of L. Barta & Co., 1888, 18. For the transfer of Octavia Hill's ideas to the US see: Daphne Spain, "Octavia Hill's Philosophy of Housing Reform: From British Roots to American Soil", in: *Journal of Planning History* 5, 2 (2006): 106–25. For the global spread of Hill's ideas see: Thomas Adam, *Intercultural Transfers and the Making of the Modern World, 1800–2000*, New York: Palgrave Macmillan, 2012, 40–59.
50 Elvers, *Victor Aimé Huber*, 276.
51 *Third Annual Report of the Boston Co-Operative Building Company*, 13.
52 *The First Annual Report of the Boston Co-operative Building Co.*, 10.
53 This assessment is confirmed by Susannah Morris in her article "Market Solutions for Social Problems," 537–38.
54 Robert Treat Paine, "The Housing Conditions in Boston," in: *The Annals of the American Academy of Political and Social Science* XX (1902), Philadelphia 1902: 125.
55 Marcus T. Reynolds, *The Housing of the Poor in American Cities. The Prize Essay of the American Economic Association for 1892*, Baltimore: Press of Guggenheim, Weil & Co., 1893, 107.
56 *V. A. Hubers Ausgewählte Schriften*, 1181–82.
57 See in contrast: Morris, "Market Solutions for Social Problems," 537–38.
58 Richard Plunz, *A History of Housing in New York City: Dwelling Type and Social Change in the American Metropolis*, New York: Columbia University Press, 1990, 89–93; Gould, *The Housing of the Working People*, 177–86.
59 Wilhelm Ruprecht, *Die Wohnungen der arbeitenden Klassen in London. Mit besonderer Berücksichtigung der neueren englischen Gesetzgebung und ihrer Erfolge*, Göttingen: Vandenhoeck & Ruprecht, 1884.
60 Paul Felix Aschrott, "Die Arbeiterwohnungsfrage in England," in: Verein für Socialpolitik (ed.), *Die Wohnungsnoth der ärmeren Klassen in deutschen Großstädten und Vorschläge zu deren Abhülfe*, Leipzig: Duncker & Humblot, 1886, 97–146.
61 Morris, "Market Solutions for Social Problems," 538; Ruprecht, *Die Wohnungen der arbeitenden Klassen in London*, 105–6; Aschrott, "Die Arbeiterwohnungsfrage in England," 133.
62 I decided not to use Gould's translations of the original German company names since they are often times erroneous.
63 Gould, *The Housing of the Working People*, 289.
64 Thomas Adam, "Stiften in deutschen Bürgerstädten vor dem Ersten Weltkrieg: Das Beispiel Leipzig," in: *Geschichte und Gesellschaft* 33, 1 (2007): 46–72.

65 Gould, *The Housing of the Working People*, 308.
66 *Third Annual Report of the Boston Co-operative Building Company*: 14–15.
67 Gould, *The Housing of the Working People*, 293.
68 Gould, *The Housing of the Working People*, 290.
69 Gould, *The Housing of the Working People*, 290. For average workers income see: Thomas Adam, "How Proletarian Was Leipzig's Social Democratic Milieu?" in: James Retallack (ed.), *Saxony in German History: Culture, Society, and Politics, 1830–1933*, Ann Arbor: The University of Michigan Press, 2000, 259–62; Thomas Adam, *Arbeitermilieu und Arbeiterbewegung in Leipzig 1871–1933*, Cologne, Weimar, Vienna: Böhlau Verlag, 1999, 68–77.
70 Heinrich Geffken and Chaim Tykocinski, *Stiftungsbuch der Stadt Leipzig*, Leipzig: Bär & Hermann, 1905, 686.
71 *Fourth Annual Report of the City and Suburban Homes Company*, New York, 1900: 5.
72 *Third Annual Report of the City and Suburban Homes Company*, New York, 1899: no page number.

Bibliography

Primary Sources

Albrecht, Rudolf. *Die Aufgabe, Organisation und Tätigkeit der Beamten-Baugenossenschaften im Rahmen der deutschen Baugenossenschafts-Bewegung*. Stuttgart: Ferdinand Enke, 1911.

Aschrott, Paul Felix. "Die Arbeiterwohnungsfrage in England." In: *Die Wohnungsnoth der ärmeren Klassen in deutschen Großstädten und Vorschläge zu deren Abhülfe*, edited by the Verein für Socialpolitik. Leipzig: Duncker & Humblot, 1886, 97–146.

Biographical Encyclopaedia of Massachusetts of the Nineteenth Century. New York: Metropolitan Publishing and Engraving Co., 1879.

Bork, F. "Der Spar- und Bauverein, E.G.m.beschr. Haftpflicht in Hannover." In: *Die Spar- und Bau-Vereine in Hannover, Göttingen und Berlin. Eine Anleitung zur praktischen Betätigung auf dem Gebiete der Wohnungsfrage* (Schriften der Centralststelle für Arbeiter-Wohlfahrtseinrichtungen no. 3). Berlin: Carl Heymann, 1893, 1–93.

Bowditch, Henry I. "Letter from the Chairman of the State Board of Health, concerning Houses for the People, Convalescent Homes, and the Sewage Question." In: *Second Annual Report of the State Board of Health of Massachusetts January 1871*. Boston: Wright & Potter, State Printers, 1871: 182–243.

Brooks, John Graham. *Compulsory Insurance in Germany Including an Appendix Relating to Compulsory Insurance in Other Countries in Europe*. Washington D.C.: Government Printing Office, 1895.

Elvers, Rudolf. *Victor Aimé Huber: Sein Leben und Wirken* vol. 2. Bremen: C. Ed. Müller, 1874.

The First Annual Report of the Boston Co-operative Building Co. with the Act of Incorporation and By-Laws, Boston: W. L. Deland, 1872.

Fourth Annual Report of the City and Suburban Homes Company. New York, 1900.

Gaebler, Dr. *Idee und Bedeutung der Berliner gemeinnützigen Baugesellschaft*. Berlin: Commissions-Verlag von Carl Heymann, 1848.

Geffken, Heinrich and Chaim Tykocinski. *Stiftungsbuch der Stadt Leipzig*, Leipzig: Bär & Hermann, 1905.

Die Gemeinnützige Bautätigkeit in Frankfurt am Main. Frankfurt am Main: Verlag des Vereins für Förderung des Arbeiterwohnungswesens und verwandte Bestrebungen, 1915.

Gould, Elgin R. L. *The Housing of the Working People*. Washington: Government Printing Office, 1895.

Grävell, A. *Die Baugenossenschafts-Frage: Ein Bericht über die Ausbreitung der gemeinnützigen Bauthätigkeit durch Baugenossenschaften, Aktienbaugesellschaften, Bauvereine etc. in Deutschland während der letzten 12 Jahre*. Berlin: Im Selbstverlage des Centralverbandes städtischer Haus- und Grundbesitzer-Vereine Deutschlands, 1901.

The Harvard Graduates Magazine I (1892–1893).

Hoffmann, Carl Wilhelm. *Die Aufgabe einer Berliner gemeinnützigen Baugesellschaft*. Berlin: Hayn, 1847.

Hoffmann, Carl Wilhelm. *Die Wohnungen der Arbeiter und Armen I. Heft: Die Berliner Gemeinnützige Bau-Gesellschaft*. Berlin: E. H. Schroeder, 1852.

Huber, Victor Aimé. "Die Wohnungsnot," in: *V. A. Hubers Ausgewählte Schriften über Socialreform und Genossenschaftswesen*, edited by K. Munding. Berlin: Verlag der Aktien-Gesellschaft Pionier, 1894, 593–627.

Huber, Victor Aimé. "Die Wohnungsreform," in: *V. A. Hubers Ausgewählte Schriften über Socialreform und Genossenschaftswesen*, edited by K. Munding. Berlin: Verlag der Aktien-Gesellschaft Pionier, 1894, 1051–68.

Huber, Victor Aimé. *Sociale Fragen: V. Die Rochdaler Pioniers: Ein Bild aus dem Genossenschaftswesen*. Nordhausen: Ferd. Förstemanns, 1867.

Huber, Victor Aimé. *Die genossenschaftliche Selbtshülfe der arbeitenden Klassen*. Elberfeld: N. L. Fridrichs, 1865.

Huber, Victor Aimé. *Reisebriefe aus England im Sommer 1854*. Hamburg: Agentur des Rauhen Hauses, 1855.

Huber, Victor Aimé. *Ueber die cooperativen Arbeiterassociationen in England: Ein Vortrag, veranstaltet von dem Central-Verein für das Wohl der arbeitenden Klassen, gehalten am 23. Februar 1852*, Berlin: Wilhelm Hertz, 1852.

Huber, Victor Aimé. *Über innere Colonisation*. Aus d. Janus, Heft. VII. VIII., besonders abgedruckt zum Besten des Berliner Handwerkervereins. Berlin: Justus Albert Wohlgemuth, 1846.

Institut für Stadtgeschichte Frankfurt am Main, "Aufforderung zur Gründung einer gemeinnützigen Baugesellschaft in Frankfurt am Main" 1860.

Institut für Stadtgeschichte Frankfurt am Main, Magistratsakten MA T 2054.

Krokisius, Edmund. *Die unter dem Protektorat Seiner Majestät des Kaisers und Königs Wilhelm II. stehenden Berliner gemeinnützige Bau-Gesellschaft und Alexandra-Stiftung 1847 bis 1901*. Berlin: Ferd. Dümmler Verlagsbuchhandlung, 1901.

Marcus, Dr. E. "Dr. Georg Varrentrapp." *Jahresbericht über die Verwaltung des Medizinalwesens der Stadt Frankfurt a. M. 1886*: 262–85.

The National Cyclopedia of American Biography vol. 8. New York: James T. White, 1924.

Paine, Robert Treat. "The Housing Conditions in Boston." *The Annals of the American Academy of Political and Social Science* 20 (1902): 123–36.

Rand, John C. (ed.), *One of a Thousand: A Series of Biographical Sketches of One Thousand Representative Men Resident in the Commonwealth of Massachusetts A D 1888–89*. Boston: First National Publishing Company, 1890.

Reichsgesetzblatt no. 11: "Gesetz, betreffend die Erwerbs- und Wirthschaftsgenossenschaften vom 1. Mai 1889."

Reynolds, Marcus T. *The Housing of the Poor in American Cities. The Prize Essay of the American Economic Association for 1892*. Baltimore: Press of Guggenheim, Weil & Co., 1893.

Ruprecht, Wilhelm. *Die Wohnungen der arbeitenden Klassen in London. Mit besonderer Berücksichtigung der neueren englischen Gesetzgebung und ihrer Erfolge*. Göttingen: Vandenhoeck & Ruprecht, 1884.

Ruprecht, Wilhelm. "Gesunde Wohnungen." *Göttinger Arbeiterbibliothek* 1, 6 (1896): 81–96.
Seventeenth Annual Report of the Boston Co-Operative Building Company. Boston: Press of L. Barta & Co., 1888.
Spiess, Alexander. "Georg Varrentrapp gestorben den 15. März 1886." *Deutsche Vierteljahresschrift für öffentliche Gesundheitspflege* 18 (1886): III–XXIV.
Third Annual Report of the Boston Co-Operative Building Company, Boston: W. L. Deland, 1874.
Third Annual Report of the City and Suburban Homes Company. New York 1899.
Varrentrapp, Georg. *Tagebuch einer medicinischen Reise nach England, Holland, und Belgien.* Frankfurt am Main: Franz Varrentrapp, 1839.
Varrentrapp, Georg. *Ueber Pönitentiarsysteme, insbesondere über die vorgeschlagene Einführung des pensylvanischen Systems.* Frankfurt am Main: Franz Varrentrapp, 1841.
Varrentrapp, Georg. *De l'emprisounement individuel sous le rapport sanitaire et des attaques dirigées contre lui par M. M. Charles Lucas et Leon Faucher.* Paris: Guillaumain, 1844.
Varrentrapp, Georg. *Ueber Entwässerung der Städte, über Werth und Unwerth der Wasserclosette, über deren angebliche Folgen: Verlust werthvollen Düngers, Verunreinigung der Flüsse, Benachtheiligung der Gesundheit.* Berlin: Hirschwald, 1868.
Wright, Carroll Davidson. *Coal Mine Labor in Europe.* Washington D.C. Government Printing Office, 1905.

Secondary Sources

Adam, Thomas. *Intercultural Transfers and the Making of the Modern World, 1800–2000.* New York: Palgrave Macmillan, 2012.
Adam, Thomas. *Buying Respectability: Philanthropy and Urban Society in Transnational Perspective, 1840s to 1930s.* Bloomington and Indianapolis: Indiana University Press, 2009.
Adam, Thomas. *Arbeitermilieu und Arbeiterbewegung in Leipzig 1871–1933.* Cologne, Weimar, Vienna: Böhlau Verlag, 1999.
Adam, Thomas. *125 Jahre Wohnreform in Sachsen: Zur Geschichte der sächsischen Baugenossenschaften, 1873–1998.* Leipzig: Antonym, 1999.
Adam, Thomas. "Stiften in deutschen Bürgerstädten vor dem Ersten Weltkrieg: Das Beispiel Leipzig." *Geschichte und Gesellschaft* 33, 1 (2007): 46–72.
Adam, Thomas. "Cultural Baggage: The Building of the Urban Community in a Transatlantic World." In: *Traveling between Worlds: German-American Encounters*, edited by Thomas Adam and Ruth Gross. College Station: Texas A & M University Press, 2006, 79–99.
Adam, Thomas. "Transatlantic Trading: The Transfer of Philanthropic Models between European and North American Cities during the Nineteenth and early Twentieth Centuries." *Journal of Urban History* 28, 3 (2002): 328–51.
Adam, Thomas. "Philanthropic Landmarks: The Toronto Trail from a Comparative Perspective, 1870s to the 1930s." *Urban History Review* 30, 1 (2001): 3–21.
Adam, Thomas. "How Proletarian Was Leipzig's Social Democratic Milieu?" In: *Saxony in German History: Culture, Society, and Politics, 1830–1933*, edited by James Retallack. Ann Arbor: The University of Michigan Press, 2000, 255–70.
Belgum, Kirsten. "Reading Alexander von Humboldt: Cosmopolitan Naturalist with an American Spirit." In: *German Culture in Nineteenth-Century America: Reception, Adaptation, Transformation*, edited by Lynne Tatlock and Matt Erlin. Rochester: Camden House, 2005, 107–27.

Bender, Thomas. *Rethinking American History in a Global Age*. Berkeley: University of California Press, 2002.
Budde, Gunilla-Friedericke, Sebastian Conrad, and Oliver Janz (eds.), *Transnationale Geschichte: Themen, Tendenzen und Theorien*. Göttingen: Vandenhoeck & Ruprecht, 2006.
Clavin, Patricia. "Defining Transnationalism." *Contemporary European Review* 14, 4 (2005): 421–39.
Cousineau, Christine. "Tenement Reform in Boston, 1870–1920: Philanthropy, Regulation, and Government Assisted Housing." (working paper presented at the Third National Conference on American Planning History November 30–December 2, 1989 in Cincinnati).
Culver, David M. "Tenement House Reform in Boston, 1846–1898" (PhD thesis, Boston University, 1972).
Daly, Gerald. "The British Roots of American Public Housing." *Journal of Urban History* 15, 4 (1989): 399–434.
Espagne, Michel. "Kulturtransfer und Fachgeschichte der Geisteswissenschaften." In: *Kulturtransfer und Vergleich* (special issue of *Comparative* 10, 1), edited by Matthias Middell. Leipzig: Leipziger Universitätsverlag, 2000: 42–61.
Espagne, Michel and Matthias Middell (eds.), *Von der Elbe bis an die Seine: Kulturtransfer zwischen Sachsen und Frankreich im 18. und 19. Jahrhundert*. Leipzig: Leipziger Universitätsverlag, 1993.
Espagne, Michel and Michael Werner, "Deutsch-Französischer Kulturtransfer im 18. und 19. Jahrhundert. Zu einem neuen interdisziplinären Forschungsprogramm des C. N. R. S." *Francia* 13 (1985): 502–10.
Gall, Lothar. *Krupp: Der Aufstieg eines Industrieimperiums*. Berlin: Siedler, 2000.
Gauldie, Enid. *Cruel Habitations: A History of Working-Class Housing 1780–1918*. London: Allen & Unwin, 1974.
Handlin, David P. *The American Home: Architecture and Society, 1815–1915*. Boston and Toronto: Little, Brown and Company, 1979.
Kaelble, Hartmut. "Herausforderungen an die Transfergeschichte." In: *Transfer lokalisiert: Konzepte, Akteure, Kontexte*, edited by Barbara Schulte. Leipzig: Leipziger Universitätsverlag, 2006, 7–12.
Kanther, Michael A. and Dietmar Petzina. *Victor Aimé Huber (1800–1869): Sozialreformer und Wegbereiter der sozialen Wohnungswirtschaft*. Berlin: Duncker & Humblot, 2000.
Kastorff-Viehmann, Renate. "England, Frankreich, Preußen: Programme für den Arbeiterwohnungsbau im Industriegebiet im 19. Jahrhundert." *Westfälische Forschungen* 44 (1994): 121–55.
Kastorff-Viehmann, Renate. *Wohnungsbau für Arbeiter: Das Beispiel Ruhrgebiet bis 1914*. Aachen: Klenkes, 1981.
Kramer, Henriette. "Die Anfänge des sozialen Wohnungsbaus in Frankfurt am Main, 1860–1914." *Archiv für Frankfurts Geschichte und Kunst* 56 (1978): 123–90.
Lee, Joseph. *Constructive and Preventive Philanthropy*. New York: The Macmillan Company, 1902.
Leiby, James. *Carroll Wright and Labor Reform: The Origin of Labor Statistics*. Cambridge: Harvard University Press, 1960.
Middell, Matthias, ed. *Kulturtransfer und Vergleich* (special issue of *Comparative* 10, 1). Leipzig: Leipziger Universitätsverlag, 2000.
Morris, Susannah. "Private Profit and Public Interest: Model Dwelling Companies and the Housing of the Working Classes in London, 1840–1914" (D.Phil. thesis, University of Oxford, 1998).
Morris, Susannah. "Changing Perceptions of Philanthropy in the Voluntary Housing Field in Nineteenth- and Early-Twentieth-Century London." In: *Philanthropy, Patronage, and*

Civil Society: Experiences from Germany, Great Britain, and North America, edited by Thomas Adam. Bloomington: Indiana University Press, 2004, 138–60.

Morris, Susannah. "Market Solutions for Social Problems: Working-Class Housing in Nineteenth-Century London." *Economic History Review* 54, 3 (2001): 525–45.

Plunz, Richard. *A History of Housing in New York City: Dwelling Type and Social Change in the American Metropolis*. New York: Columbia University Press, 1990.

Rodgers, Daniel T. *Atlantic Crossings: Social Politics in a Progressive Age*. Cambridge and London: The Belknap Press of Harvard University Press, 1998.

Schäfer, Axel R. *American Progressives and German Social Reform 1875–1920: Social Ethics, Moral Control, and the Regulatory State in a Transatlantic Context*. Stuttgart: Franz Steiner Verlag, 2000.

Schlandt, Joachim. "Die Kruppsiedlungen – Wohnungsbau im Interesse eines Industriekonzerns." In: *Kapitalistischer Städtebau*, edited by Hans G. Helms and Jörn Janssen, Neuwied and Berlin: Luchterhand, 1970, 95–108.

Spain, Daphne. "Octavia Hill's Philosophy of Housing Reform: From British Roots to American Soil." *Journal of Planning History* 5, 2 (2006): 106–25.

Tarn, John Nelson. *Five Per Cent Philanthropy: An Account of Housing in Urban Areas between 1840 and 1914*. Cambridge: Cambridge University Press, 1973.

Vale, Lawrence J. *From the Puritans to the Projects: Public Housing and Public Neighbors*. Cambridge and London: Harvard University Press, 2000.

Vossberg, Walter. *Die deutsche Baugenossenschafts-Bewegung*. Halle a. S. 1905.

Ward, David. "Population Growth, Migration, and Urbanization, 1860–1920." In: *North America: The Historical Geography of a Changing Continent*, edited by Thomas F. McIlwraith and Edward K. Muller. Lanham, Boulder, New York, Oxford: Rowman & Littlefield Publishers, 2001, 285–305.

Werner, Michael and Bénédicte Zimmermann. "Vergleich, Transfer, Verflechtung: Der Ansatz der Histoire croisée und die Herausforderung des Transnationalen." *Geschichte und Gesellschaft* 28, 4 (2002): 607–36.

Woodroofe, Kathleen. *From Charity to Social Work in England and the United States*. Toronto: University of Toronto Press, 1962.

Chapter 3

CULTURAL EXCURSIONS: THE TRANSNATIONAL TRANSFER OF MUSEUMS IN THE TRANSATLANTIC WORLD

Abstract: American art museums emerged from the intercultural transfers of concepts for art collecting and art exhibition, funding mechanisms, and architectural solutions from Europe in the second half of the nineteenth century. English and German museums in particular informed American observers who searched of organizational models and inspiration. George Fisk Comfort obtained the role of an agent of intercultural transfer in the field of art museums. During his extensive travels in Germany, he visited and observed the creation of art museums and the founding of art associations as supporting institutions for these museums. He provided the knowledge he amassed to the circle of museum enthusiasts in New York. The Metropolitan Museum of Art emerged from this knowledge transfer. At the core of this transfer was the introduction of the German art association to American art museum funding. After American museums were founded, these museums attracted visitors and observes from the European continent. The most prominent visitor was the German museum director Adolf Bernhard Meyer. His report about museum in the United States provided a comprehensive text that informed museum reform in North America and Europe. The transfer of models for art museums was, thus, not a one-way street but worked in both directions, And Woldemar von Seidlitz' claim that the museum association that he found in New York was an original American idea shows that the origins of transfer were often quickly forgotten and for strategic reasons often obscured by those involved in the transfer process.

This ch apter was first published in *The Museum is Open: Towards a Transnational History of Museums 1750–1940*, edited by Andrea Meyer and Bénédicte Savoy, Berlin and Boston: De Gruyter 2014, 103–16.

Introduction

From the 1820s, wealthy Americans made the cities of the German Confederation their favored destination for purposes of education and enjoyment. Among the American visitors were students such as George Ticknor and John Lothrop Motley who attended the University of Göttingen as well as intellectuals and politicians such as Washington Irving, James Fenimore Cooper, and George Bancroft who came for the benefits of the rich cultural and social life in cities such as Dresden and Berlin.[1] Industrialization had made some Americans very rich. The number of millionaires in the United States rose slowly but steady from just 20 in 1850 to more than 4,000 by 1892 and approximately 16,000 by 1916.[2] While these individuals had amassed incredible riches, they often lacked the social graces which supposedly come with wealth.[3] German cities provided these newly rich a source and training ground in social manners and helped newly rich Americans to acquire social etiquette and cultural education. Dresden's royal court and the city's nobility was very open and welcoming to all wealthy American visitors who made that city the prime destination for educated Americans and those who aspired to become part of the High Society. In the last third of the nineteenth century the daughters of newly rich Americans were even married to titled, but poor European noblemen. These contacts from visiting to marrying contributed to the creation of a bourgeois-noble transatlantic upper class that embraced the value system of the European nobility and introduced European pre-modern traditions and concepts into American society.[4] Stays of six to twenty-four months in Dresden were not uncommon for American visitors who enjoyed a favorable exchange rate and a city in which accommodation and participation in cultural life was quite affordable.[5] Yet, Dresden was also an eminent cultural center with its gallery of paintings where the famous *Sistine Madonna* by Raphael is on display. Among art experts and connoisseurs, Dresden— affectionately called the "Florence on the Elbe"—was considered to be the most impressive place of art north of the Alps.

The Founding of the Metropolitan Museum of Art in New York City

After decades of having to cross the Atlantic in order to enjoy a rich cultural life, New York's High Society became impatient with the quality of urban life in the New World. At the end of the 1860s members of the exclusive Union League Club took a lead in the creation of the Metropolitan Museum of Art. Many of its members were men with colonial (Dutch and English) names such as Stuyvesant, Beekman, Rhinelander, and Winthrop (the so-called

Knickerbocker families). They claimed that their ancestors were among the first Europeans to reach the shores of the New World. They belonged to New York's leading circles and had made their money in real estate and banking.[6] To ensure the social exclusivity of this political and social club, membership requirements limited access. Candidates for admission had to "be proposed by one member, seconded by another, and bulletined, before reference to the committee whose business it [was] to investigate as to qualifications or eligibility. At every monthly meeting of the club, it [was] the duty of this body to report upon the names of candidates submitted to its consideration, after which the members vote[d] by ballot upon names thus recommended."[7] The Grand Tour to Europe for cultural education was a shared experience among its members.

After John Jay suggested the establishment of a Metropolitan Art Museum in New York City in his speech given to Americans in Paris celebrating the ninetieth anniversary of American independence in 1866,[8] William Cullen Bryant, a founding member of the Union League Club, became involved in the attempts made by this club to popularize such an enterprise among his peers. He accepted George P. Putnam's invitation to preside over a meeting on November 23, 1869 in the Theatre of the Union League Club to which all individuals interested in establishing an art museum were invited.[9] Some three hundred members of the Union League Club, the National Academy of Design, the New York Historical Society, the Century, the Manhattan, and other social clubs, attended this meeting. In his introductory speech, Bryant reminded his fellow citizens that in terms of cultural life and atmosphere New York City could not compete with even the tiniest European city or kingdom:

> Yet beyond the sea there is the little kingdom of Saxony, which, with an area less than that of Massachusetts, and a population but little larger, possesses a Museum of the Fine Arts marvelously rich, which no man who visits the continent of Europe is willing to own that he has not seen. There is Spain, a third-rate power of Europe and poor besides, with a museum of Fine Arts at her capital, the opulence and extent of which absolutely bewilder the visitor. I will not speak of France or of England, conquering nations, which have gathered their treasures of art in part from regions overrun by their armies; nor yet of Italy, the fortunate inheritor of so many glorious productions of her own artists. But there are Holland and Belgium, kingdoms almost too small to be heeded by the greater powers of Europe in the consultations which decide the destinies of nations, and these little kingdoms have their public collections of art, the resort of admiring visitors from all parts of the civilized world.[10]

His emotional speech was followed by an enthusiastic but informed talk about art museums and the organizing principles of art collections by George Fisk Comfort, an 1857 graduate of Wesleyan College who had spent nearly five years (1860–1865) in Europe.[11] He traveled extensively from Trieste to Turkey, Greece, Italy, Spain, Austria, France, Belgium, Holland, Germany, and Great Britain. Not much is known about his travels or about how much time he spent in each country and which universities and museums he visited. However, we know from his letters and notes that he spent years in Germany. In a letter to Reverend John Makan (Allegheny College) in 1866, Comfort stated that he had spent "nearly five years in traveling through most of the classic lands of ancient and medieval art, studying the monuments and museums, and devoting nearly half of my time to formal study in the German universities."[12]

In his speech, Comfort pointed to the museums in Kensington and Berlin as possible models for the Metropolitan Museum of New York City:

> The Kensington Museum has been organized within twenty years, and it contains a large number of casts of works of sculpture and architecture and many works of art that are owned by wealthy people in England, left there as loans for the inspection of the public without cost. They may be reclaimed by them or their heirs, but probably the larger portion will be given or bequeathed to the museum. This museum also contains a large collection of works, illustrating the application of the arts to industry. And there are schools connected with the museum—it is an institution of science as well.[13]

As this passage shows, Comfort favored the connection between the display of artistic work and artistic education. More importantly, he was very concerned with the property rights of the artistic works. And although the Kensington Museum provided some inspiration for the founding of the Metropolitan Museum,[14] Comfort's eyes were fixed on the museums in Berlin and other German cities. He continued his speech with high praise for the museums of Berlin as the largest and most impressive cultural institutions of his day:

> The foundation of the old museum building was laid in the year 1828; and the building was finished some four years after. The foundation of the new museum building was laid in the year 1852, and was finished two or three years after. This building contains today the largest collection of casts of works of Sculpture of any museum in the world. There is no place where a person can study to more advantage the progress of

Sculpture, from its first appearance in Egypt down to its appearance in Greece and through the middle ages, and through the modern times, than he can in Berlin, and by all means of this valuable collection of casts. The casts that are in that museum, if I am rightly informed, cost about 300,000 thalers, which is equivalent to about 300,000 dollars in our present paper money.[15]

Comfort learned to appreciate both museums during his stay in that city between 1863 and 1865, "where he pursued his studies in the University, the Academy of Fine Arts and the Royal Library. He was received in social circles of leading artists, critics, connoisseurs and the professors of art and archeology of that great literary capital of the world, as Cornelius, Kaulbach, Lepsius, Waagen, Gerhart, Piper, von Ranke and others."[16] In the aforementioned letter to Makan, Comfort pointed out that he had "paid much attention to the organization of academies of art and museums of art."[17] While he studied in Berlin, Comfort visited art museums in Nuremberg, Munich, Leipzig, Dresden, Posen, and Bremen in order to collect information about the organization of art institutions and the objects shown.[18]

Traveling to these cities, Comfort encountered a rich, cultural urban life which included art museums, private art exhibitions, and art associations. As Manuel Frey pointed out, by 1850 nearly every German city had its own art association (Kunstverein).[19] Wealthy citizens founded these associations to organize art exhibitions, support artists, and create art museums independent of royal/ducal control. Within the context of nineteenth-century German society, art associations represented the drive for bourgeois emancipation from a feudal monopoly over art. By establishing their own art scene burghers claimed a leading position within urban society, and by financing artistic endeavors, they proved their economic power and their desire to produce a new culture. Such art associations represented a collective approach to philanthropy, since they could easily bring together several hundred members. The Leipzig Kunstverein, for example, received support from close to one thousand members as early as 1837. Membership in these art associations was often divided into various classes according to social status and the willingness to participate in the funding of the association. In the case of the Leipzig art association two classes had been established: the class of shareholders (Aktionäre) who paid three Taler a year and the class of subscribers (Abonnenten) who paid one Taler and eight Groschen a year.[20]

Influenced by what he experienced in Germany, Comfort

expressed himself as 'overwhelmingly impressed by the vast gulf, wider and deeper than the Atlantic Ocean, that separated the institutions and conditions of education and culture in continental Europe from those in America', speaking especially of that time, the early sixties. And he felt impelled to dedicate his life, as far as his circumstances should permit, to awaking a more active interest in higher culture, especially in esthetic and artistic lines, in his native country, particularly by establishing institutions, as schools and museums, for promoting and diffusing artistic education and culture in the people at large.[21]

His handwritten *Address before the Syracuse Chamber of Commerce regarding a Museum of Fine Arts* (1897) not only provides some details about what Comfort encountered in Germany but also gives a plan for the establishment of a fine arts museum. In this address, Comfort emphasized the importance of museums for attracting visitors from other countries. He noted that most American travelers after having arrived in Hamburg or Bremen immediately left for Dresden or Munich. Dresden attracted a large number of cultured men because of its famous art galleries. Large colonies of wealthy, transient residents from Russia, Great Britain, and the United States sprang up in the capital of Saxony. Comfort reminded his audience that "the possession of Raphael's *Sistine Madonna* alone, perhaps the most pleasing and popular picture in the world, gives luster to the fame of the city of Dresden, and adds to the material wealth of the city."[22]

Although Comfort was very impressed by the exceptional collection of the Dresden art gallery, he recognized that it would not inspire similar institutions in the United States, since a nobility was absent and wealthy men of his days were little inclined to dedicate enormous amounts of money toward an art museum. In a letter to George P. Putnam, chairman of the organizing committee of the Metropolitan Museum, Comfort suggested several German museums (Gotha, Berlin, Nuremberg) as possible models, but he mentioned the Leipzig museum of art before all others.[23] He probably visited the Leipzig museum during his stay in Germany. It was opened to the public in December of 1858—two years before Comfort arrived in Europe—and displayed the paintings, casts, and statutes purchased by the Leipzig art association. While the museum building had been financed by silk merchant Heinrich Adolf Schletter, the members of the art association had donated the art objects displayed in the museum.[24]

Comfort recommended forming a membership organization, the American version of the German art association, to collect financial and material support from wealthy New Yorkers. At the initial meeting in November 1869, a Provisional Committee of fifty prominent New York citizens was formed. Within this committee a subcommittee of thirteen men under Putnam's leadership was appointed to prepare the constitution of the Metropolitan Art

Museum Association. In May 1870, this association was incorporated, and its constitution published.

The structure of this new association adopted some features from the German art associations and some features from the social clubs of New York City. Similar to the Union League Club, membership in the Metropolitan Art Museum Association was initially limited to 250. Those who aspired to become members had to be nominated by the trustees. Only if two-thirds of the members approved the nomination did the aspirant become a member.[25] This procedure was evidently copied from the Union League Club to ensure that only New York's well-established families could gain access. However, the new art association was even more exclusive. While membership in the Union League Club was limited in numbers and restricted to Knickerbocker families, it was sufficient that a new member was proposed by one existing member and seconded by another member. Neither of the two clubs required two-thirds of its members to approve. The nomination and election procedure would ensure the exclusion of newer families from this exclusive art association.[26]

The founding of an art association, which was in fact an association not of artists but of philanthropists who pledged to support the arts, was reminiscent of Leipzig's art association, which differed from other German art associations in the social/occupational profile of its membership. While the Dresden art association had a large number of artists among its members, the Leipzig art association was nearly exclusively an organization of wealthy citizens who were interested in the promotion and the funding of art. Less than seven percent of the members of Leipzig's art association had been artists. With five percent, New York's art association had an even lower share.[27] In Leipzig and in New York City, the primary goal was to establish an art museum and to create a membership organization that would provide the financial basis for running it. Similar to Leipzig, the organizational committee in New York City decided to establish more than one membership class. However, while the Leipzig organizers thought that two classes were sufficient, New York's organizers insisted on three. For a contribution of $1,000, one could become a Patron of the Museum, for $500 one became a Fellow in Perpetuity, and for $200 one was entitled to be a Fellow for Life.[28] While German art associations were intended to provide a platform for bourgeois emancipation from feudal domination and the abolishment of class differences, art associations in the United States reflected the desire of the wealthy to create distinction and status among themselves. German and American art associations were, however, linked by their striving toward cultural domination and the exercising of power over cityscapes and urban populations by the bourgeoisie.

While German art museums and their art associations provided the inspiration for the organizational structure of the Metropolitan Museum of Art, the Kensington Museum provided concepts about what to collect and how to arrange the collections. This becomes evident in the decision to include applied art in the collections of the museum. A pamphlet about the future plans for the Metropolitan Museum published in March 1871 announced: "Officers of the Museum desire[d] especially to begin at an early day the formation of a collection of industrial art, of objects of utility to which decorative art has been applied, ornamental metalwork, carving in wood, ivory, and stone, painted glass, glass vessels, pottery, enamel, and all other materials."[29] While the creation of such collections in Germany was just underway and often resulted in the creation of separate applied arts collections and museums, the founders of the Metropolitan Museum attempted in a catch-all approach to combine the art museum (collection of paintings and busts) with the museum of applied arts (collection of industrial produced objects).[30]

Comfort's chief concerns were teaching, collaboration with artistic education and integration of the museum into higher education. The Berlin museum, which was built in close proximity to the Academy of Fine Arts, impressed Comfort deeply. He had very fond memories of his education in Berlin where he could easily "go after the lecture and see the works of which the lecturer has spoken" in the museum, which was built just around the corner. Recalling his experience, Comfort told the individuals interested in founding the Metropolitan Museum of Art in his speech for the first meeting in November 1869: "The Museum of Berlin is used as an appendage to the University and the professors of the University of Ancient and Modern Art take their classes from the University building to the Museum building, and there standing before the work of art can show its good points and the position that it occupies in the History of Art." Following the Berlin model of connecting museum and university, Comfort suggested locating the Metropolitan Museum of Art "in close proximity to a great university." Furthermore, he thought that it would be desirable to provide the museum with "a few rooms in which lectures could be given from time to time for the general public." Sharing the believe that education of the masses would ultimately lead to the betterment of society, Comfort argued that such "an institution [...] would also indirectly stimulate and foster an increased interest on the part of our people in favor of a good municipal government."[31]

The Professionalization of Intercultural Transfer

The organizational structure of the Metropolitan Museum of Art became a model for many museums founded in the United States and Canada. New York City, with its museums, occupied a central place within the transatlantic network of urban communities and cultural life. It essentially functioned as a translation and transmission station for the import of museum models from Europe up until World War I. While the transfer of such models was initially an occupation for wealthy dilettantes, it turned into a professional business after 1900. Museum directors and academics visited selected museums and investigated their architecture, collection principles, and financing schemes. After their return, they delivered a written report to the board of trustees. The prime example of this new approach is the survey of American museums by Adolf Bernhard Meyer, the director of the Royal Zoological, Anthropological, and Ethnographical Museum in Dresden.

Meyer was sent by the authorities of the Royal Saxon Collections of Art and Science in 1899 "to visit the museums and kindred institutions of the United States so far as they relate to museum affairs, and to pay special attention to the preservation of the collections from fire."[32] Because of the large number of American museums and the limited time available, Meyer decided to visit only the Eastern part of the country (New York, Albany, Buffalo, Chicago, Washington, Philadelphia, Boston, and Cambridge). His observations were published after his return to Germany under the title *Über Museen des Ostens der Vereinigten Staaten von Nord-Amerika* in 1900/01. This volume includes information on architecture and building costs, the size and character of the collections; the financing schemes for the purchase of art objects and for the maintenance of the museums, opening times and entrance fees and concepts of educational schemes targeted at the general population. The educational work organized and carried out by American museums impressed Meyer the most. He admired the concepts regarding the integration of children into museum education—a tradition absolutely alien to Germany. Meyer reported that in "the large museums, a section may generally be found specially adapted to the comprehension of children." Furthermore, direct "efforts are made to induce pupils of both sexes to visit the museums by offering prizes for essays adapted to the different classes."[33]

Public lectures to popularize science were an integral part of the educational work provided by American museums, such as the American Museum of Natural History in New York City. Summarizing his experience, Meyer emphasized that

> Americans assign a leading part in the activity of their museums to the exhibition collections, which they arrange for wide circles of the educated, half educated, and uneducated classes. At the same time, they foster the interests even of little children, and try to stimulate the older ones by offering prizes; they make the museums contribute directly to the cause of education by series of lectures, by popular publications, and

by lending collections; and they keep the doors of their museums open to everybody from morning till evening.[34]

The opening times were of particular concern to Meyer. While the Metropolitan Museum of Art was opened at "7, 8, 9, or 10 in the morning till 6,"[35] the Green Vault in Dresden, for instance, was open only between 9 and 2.[36] Furthermore, while American museums attempted to invite as many visitors as possible and to make the collections accessible to the average person, German museums tended to treat the visitor as intruders and provided little help for understanding the cultural and artistic objects on display. In short, German museums were meant to educate the intellectual visitor while American museums were meant to entertain both the educated and the uneducated person. Obviously, Meyer was very much in favor of the attempts to work with children in museums, but he was also skeptical whether "all this could be adapted to German conditions."[37]

This report written in German and intended to provide a material basis for the reorganization of German museums influenced the practical work in museums in Germany less than it did in North America. Four years after Meyer's report was published in Germany, the Smithsonian Institution included in its Annual Report for 1903 a translation of Meyer's account on American museums together with an account about European museums, which Meyer had published in 1902.[38] These two texts provided the North American reader with a comprehensive survey of American, British, French, and Belgian museums and became a reference point for organizers of museums across the North American continent.

However, Meyer's critical remarks about the state of German museums should not make one believe that Americans could no longer find inspiration in Europe. American museum makers were, even after 1900, still intrigued by the ways their European counterparts created and maintained museums. When the board of trustees of the Museum of Fine Arts in Boston decided to construct a new museum building in 1902, it appointed a commission to collect information on architectural aspects of European museums. Samuel D. Warren, Edward Robinson, R. Clipston Sturgis, and Edmund M. Wheelwright spent three months (January 2, 1904 to April 2, 1904) on the continent "to study European museums, and, hopefully, discover excellencies of detail that might be anthologized in the future Boston design."[39] These four Bostonians searched for architectural ideas concerning how to arrange the collection, how to effectively light the exhibitions and how to provide an entrance hall, which invited visitors. They toured ninety-five museums in Italy, Germany, Switzerland, Holland, Belgium, and England, looking at the general character of the museum architecture, exterior landscape, lighting, the size of the galleries, the arrangement of paintings and sculptures, and the technologies of heating and ventilation. However, the board of trustees was also concerned with the tasks and purposes of an art museum regarding the education of the general public and the provision of study collections. To discuss these issues, the board of trustees included in its four-volume report *The Museum Commission in Europe* articles and essays written by several European authorities on museums.[40] This collection included an essay by Ernst Grosse, professor of the history of art at Freiburg University, on the aims and arrangements of German museums of fine arts, and an article written by Alfred Lichtwark, director of the Kunsthalle in Hamburg, about the faults of existing museum buildings and his visions for future buildings.[41]

The Bostonian observers seemed to be very impressed by the New Grand Ducal Museum in Darmstadt: "In its general features it was found the most suggestive as embodying ideas that had been under consideration in the study of the proposed Boston building." Evaluating the Darmstadt museum, the Bostonian visitors remarked: "It would appear that the architect had here sought to give expression to the reasonable theories recently advanced by museum authorities, which are based upon the principle that the collections should be arranged upon a system which permits the public to see them with the least confusion of mind and the minimum of fatigue; to this end objects should be grouped in well-defined departments, and each class of objects should have the method of lighting suited to its best display." The organization of the Darmstadt museum into separate and autonomous departments impressed the visitors very much. The "Mediaeval and Renaissance Department is, in fact, a separate Historical Museum, a diminutive model of that at Zürich, and presents an interesting example of the historic-picturesque arrangement as opposed to the scientific dispositions of the older museums."[42]

The architectural plans for the new building of the Museum of Fine Arts followed this concept of departmentalization. The building was divided into "segments to contain departments structurally separate, each constituting a museum complete in itself, with a well-defined circuit for the visitor." This is captured in Samuel D. Warren's description of the museum: "The building may be described as a group of museums under one roof, the space in each devoted to collections compactly arranged and two rooms for study being approximately equal to the gallery space [...]."[43] The reports printed and published by the Museum of Fine Arts provided an English translation of the newest German academic and artistic discussions on the purposes and aims of museums. These translations benefited not only the Boston enterprise but also museums in the United States in general.

Conclusion

The transatlantic transfer of cultural and intellectual concepts and ideas has never been a one-way street. Transfer always occurred in both directions and in some cases involved objects that have been repeatedly exchanged. In this process of multiple transfers, the origin of the objects became obscured and the object gained universality in its application. In 1913, Woldemar von Seidlitz, advisor to the Royal Art Museum in Dresden, published an essay in the German journal *Museumskunde* in which he provided an overview of *Museumsvereine* (museum patrons associations) in Germany, France, and Great Britain. These associations were, according to Seidlitz, phenomena of the late nineteenth century and originated with the Metropolitan Art Museum Association in 1870. Seidlitz' essay delivered a detailed description of the New York museum association and of subsequent museum associations in Lübeck (1880), Amsterdam (1883), Krefeld (1883), Berlin (1897), Paris (1897), Frankfurt am Main (1899), Celle (1900), London (1903), Munich (1905), Stuttgart (1906), Leipzig (1909), Breslau (1910), Dresden (1911), and Halle (1912).[44] The existence of earlier versions of such museum associations and their influence on the emergence of similar institutions in North America was either disregarded by or unknown to Seidlitz. It is the irony of history that Seidlitz looked to the United States for ideas regarding the reorganization of Germany's museums and that he propounded the Metropolitan Art Museum Association as a model for Germans when in fact the New York art association had been inspired by earlier art associations in cities such as Leipzig.

Notes

1. Konrad Jarausch, "American Students in Germany, 1815–1914. The Structure of German and U.S. Matriculants at Göttingen University," in: Henry Geitz, Jürgen Heideking, Jurgen Herbst (eds.), *German Influences on Education in the United States to 1917*, Washington D.C and Cambridge: Cambridge University Press, 1995, 195–212; Carl Diehl, *German Scholarship 1770–1870*, New Haven and London: Yale University Press, 1978; Jurgen Herbst, *The German Historical School in American Scholarship. A Study in the Transfer of Culture*, Ithaca: Cornell University Press, 1965; Anja Becker, "For the Sake of Old Leipzig Days ... Academic Networks of American Students at a German University, 1781–1914," Ph.D. thesis, University of Leipzig, 2006; Eberhard Brüning, "'Saxony Is a Prosperous and Happy Country' American Views of the Kingdom of Saxony in the Nineteenth Century," in: Thomas Adam and Ruth Gross (eds.), *Traveling between Worlds. German-American Encounters*, College Station: Texas A&M Press, 2006, 20–50; Ashley Sides, "'That Humane and Advanced Civilization' Interpreting Americans' Values from their Praise of Saxony, 1800–1850," in: Thomas Adam and Nils H. Roemer (eds.), *Crossing the Atlantic. Travel and Travel Writing in Modern Times*, College Station: Texas A&M Press, 2011, 11–49; Thomas Adam and Gisela Mettele

(eds.), *Two Boston Brahmins in Goethe's Germany. The Travel Journals of Anna and George Ticknor*, Lanham et al.: Lexington Books, 2009.

2   Olivier Zunz, *Philanthropy in America. A History*, Princeton and Oxford: Princeton University Press, 2012, 8.

3   Judith Martin, *Star-Spangled Manners*, New York and London: W. W. Norton & Company, 2003.

4   Sven Beckert, *The Monied Metropolis. New York City and the Consolidation of the American Bourgeoisie, 1850–1896*, Cambridge: Cambridge University Press, 2001.

5   Nadine Zimmerli, "'The Rendezvous of all Nations:' Cosmopolitan Encounters in the German City of Dresden before World War I," Ph.D. thesis, University of Wisconsin-Madison, 2011.

6   Will Irwin, Earl Chapin May, and Joseph Hotchkiss, *A History of the Union League Club of New York City*, New York: Dodd, Mead, 1952, 24.

7   Francis Gerry Fairfield, *The Clubs of New York. With an Account of the Origin, Progress, Present Condition and Membership of the Leading Clubs, an Essay on New York Club Life*, New York: Henry L. Hinton, Publishers, 1873, 114–15.

8   Winifred E. Howe, *A History of the Metropolitan Museum of Art. With a Chapter on the Early Institutions of Art in New York*, New York: Gilliss Press, 1913, 100–101; Leo Lerman, *The Museum. One Hundred Years and the Metropolitan Museum of Art*, New York: Viking, 1969, 12.

9   William Cullen Bryant II, Thomas G. Voss (eds.), *The Letters of William Cullen Bryant. Volume V, 1865–1871*, New York: Fordham University Press, 1992, 344–45; Charles H. Brown, *William Cullen Bryant*, New York: Charles Scribner's Sons, 1971, 486.

10 Smithsonian Archives of American Art: *George Comfort Deposit Reel 4276 T 6814* (Microfilm): A Metropolitan Art Museum in the City of New York: Proceedings of a meeting held at the Theatre of the Union League Club, Tuesday Evening, November 23, 1869, New York: Printed for the Committee, 1869, 9.

11 Barabara Hall Cruttenden, "George Fisk Comfort. A Biography," M.A. thesis, Syracuse University, 1956.

12 Smithsonian Archives of American Art: *George Comfort Deposit Reel 4274 T 6812* (Microfilm): Letter from George Fisk Comfort to Reverend John Makan, dated April 14, 1866.

13 Smithsonian Archives of American Art: *George Comfort Deposit Reel 4276 T 6814* (Microfilm): A Metropolitan Art Museum in the City of New York: Proceedings of a meeting held at the Theatre of the Union League Club, Tuesday Evening, November 23, 1869, New York: Printed for the Committee, 1869, 15.

14 Steven Conn, *Museums and American Intellectual Life, 1876–1926*, Chicago and London: The University of Chicago Press, 1998, 195–97.

15 Smithsonian Archives of American Art: *George Comfort Deposit Reel 4276 T 6814* (Microfilm): A Metropolitan Art Museum in the City of New York: Proceedings of a meeting held at the Theatre of the Union League Club, Tuesday Evening, November 23, 1869, New York: Printed for the Committee, 1869, 15–16.

16 Syracuse University Archive, Comfort Family Papers Box 1: *George F. Comfort Biographical Material*, Dean Comfort's Departure.

17 Smithsonian Archives of American Art: *George Comfort Deposit Reel 4274 T 6812* (Microfilm): Letter from George Fisk Comfort to Reverend John Makan, dated April 14, 1866.

18 Syracuse University Archive, Comfort Family Papers Box 1: *George F. Comfort Biographical Material*, Sketch of my life (handwritten account by George Fisk Comfort).

19 Manuel Frey, *Macht und Moral des Schenkens. Staat und bürgerliche Mäzene vom späten 18. Jahrhundert bis zur Gegenwart*, Zwickau: Fannei & Walz, 1999, 66; James J. Sheehan, *Museums in the German Art World from the End of the Old Regime to the Rise of Modernism*, New York: Oxford University Press, 2000, 101–11.
20 Margaret Eleanor Menninger, "Art and Civic Patronage in Leipzig, 1848–1914," Ph.D. thesis, Harvard University, 1998, 90–91, 94–99; Anett Müller, *Der Leipziger Kunstverein und das Museum der bildenden Künste. Materialien einer Geschichte (1836–1886/87)*, Leipzig: Nouvelle Alliance, 1995, 44–51, 86–93.
21 Syracuse University Archive, Comfort Family Papers Box 1: *George F. Comfort Biographical Material*, Biographical Sketch of Dr. George F. Comfort, 4–5.
22 Smithsonian Archives of American Art: *George Comfort Deposit Reel 4276 T 6814* (Microfilm): Extracts from the Address of Professor Comfort before the Syracuse Chamber of Commerce regarding a Museum of Fine Arts, 15.
23 Howe, *A History of the Metropolitan Museum of Art*, 119.
24 Müller, *Der Leipziger Kunstverein*, 86–93.
25 Howe, *A History of the Metropolitan Museum of Art*, 116–17, 125.
26 Fairfield, *The Clubs of New York*, 57–83; Reginald T. Townsend, *Mother of Clubs. Being the History of the First Hundred Years of the Union Club of the City of New York 1836–1936*, New York: The Printing House of William Edwin Rudge, 1936, 9–24.
27 This number is based on my data bases for the membership of the Metropolitan Art Museum Association for 1876. The 1876 list is the first available membership list. *Sixth Annual Report of the Trustees of the Association for the Year Ending May 1, 1876*, 86–90. For Leipzig see: Müller, *Der Leipziger Kunstverein*, 46–47.
28 Howe, *A History of the Metropolitan Museum of Art*, 129–30.
29 Howe, *A History of the Metropolitan Museum of Art*, 134.
30 Conn, *Museums and American Intellectual Life*, 197; Menninger, "Art and Civic Patronage in Leipzig," 113–18.
31 Smithsonian Archives of American Art: *George Comfort Deposit Reel 4276 T 6814* (Microfilm): A Metropolitan Art-Museum in the City of New York (New York, 1869), 16.
32 Adolf Bernhard Meyer, "Studies of the Museums and Kindred Institutions of New York City, Albany, Buffalo, and Chicago. With Notes on Some European Institutions" (*Annual Report of the Board of Regents of the Smithsonian Institution, Showing the Operations, Expenditures, and Condition of the Institution for the Year ending June 30, 1903*), Washington: Government Printing Office, 1905, 321. The German version was published as Adolf Bernhard Meyer, *Über Museen des Ostens der Vereinigten Staaten von Nord-Amerika*, Berlin: A. Friedländer, 1900/01.
33 Meyer, "Studies of the Museums and Kindred Institutions," 325, 326.
34 Meyer, "Studies of the Museums and Kindred Institutions," 328.
35 Meyer, "Studies of the Museums and Kindred Institutions," 348.
36 Thomas Adam, "Philanthropic Landmarks in Toronto. The Toronto Trail from a Comparative Perspective, 1870s to the 1930s," in: *Urban History Review* 30, 1 (2001): 8.
37 Meyer, "Studies of the Museums and Kindred Institutions," 328.
38 Meyer, *Über einige europäische Museen und verwandte Institute*, Berlin: A. Friedländer 1902.
39 Walter Muir Whitehall, *Museum of Fine Arts Boston. A Centennial History* vol. 1, Cambridge: The Belknap Press of Harvard University Press, 1970, 179.
40 Museum of Fine Arts, Boston, *Communications to the Trustees III* (January 1905), *The Museum Commission in Europe* 4 vols., vol. 1, 6–7.

41 *The Museum Commission in Europe* vol. 1, 65–75, 85–88.
42 *The Museum Commission in Europe* vol. 3, 86.
43 Whitehall, *Museum of Fine Arts Boston*, 221.
44 Woldemar von Seidlitz, Museumsvereine, in: *Museumskunde* 9 (1913): 36–43.

Bibliography

Primary Sources

Adam, Thomas and Gisela Mettele, eds. *Two Boston Brahmins in Goethe's Germany. The Travel Journals of Anna and George Ticknor*, Lanham et al.: Lexington Books, 2009.

Bryant II, William Cullen and Thomas G. Voss, eds. *The Letters of William Cullen Bryant. Volume V, 1865–1871*. New York: Fordham University Press, 1992.

Fairfield, Francis Gerry. *The Clubs of New York. With an Account of the Origin, Progress, Present Condition and Membership of the Leading Clubs, an Essay on New York Club Life*. New York: Henry L. Hinton, Publishers, 1873.

Meyer, Adolf Bernhard. *Über Museen des Ostens der Vereinigten Staaten von Nord-Amerika*. Berlin: A. Friedlander, 1900/01.

Meyer, Adolf Bernhard. *Über einige europäische Museen und verwandte Institute*. Berlin: A. Friedlander, 1902.

Meyer, Adolf Bernhard. "Studies of the Museums and Kindred Institutions of New York City, Albany, Buffalo, and Chicago. With Notes on Some European Institutions." (*Annual Report of the Board of Regents of the Smithsonian Institution, Showing the Operations, Expenditures, and Condition of the Institution for the Year ending June 30, 1903*), Washington: Government Printing Office, 1905.

Museum of Fine Arts, Boston, *Communications to the Trustees III* (January 1905), *The Museum Commission in Europe*, 4 vols.

Seidlitz, Woldemar von. "Museumsvereine," *Museumskunde* vol. 9 (1913): 36–43.

Sixth Annual Report of the Trustees of the Association [Metropolitan Art Museum Association] for the Year Ending May 1, 1876.

Smithsonian Archives of American Art: *George Comfort Deposit Reel 4274 T 6812* (Microfilm): Letter from George Fisk Comfort to Reverend John Makan, dated April 14, 1866.

Smithsonian Archives of American Art: *George Comfort Deposit Reel 4276 T 6814* (Microfilm): A Metropolitan Art Museum in the City of New York: Proceedings of a meeting held at the Theatre of the Union League Club, Tuesday Evening, November 23, 1869. New York: Printed for the Committee, 1869.

Smithsonian Archives of American Art: *George Comfort Deposit Reel 4276 T 6814* (Microfilm): Extracts from the Address of Professor Comfort before the Syracuse Chamber of Commerce regarding a Museum of Fine Arts.

Smithsonian Archives of American Art: *George Comfort Deposit Reel 4276 T 6814* (Microfilm): A Metropolitan Art-Museum in the City of New York (New York, 1869).

Syracuse University Archive, Comfort Family Papers Box 1: *George F. Comfort Biographical Material*, Dean Comfort's Departure.

Syracuse University Archive, Comfort Family Papers Box 1: *George F. Comfort Biographical Material*, Sketch of my life (handwritten account by George Fisk Comfort).

Syracuse University Archive, Comfort Family Papers Box 1: *George F. Comfort Biographical Material*, Biographical Sketch of Dr. George F. Comfort.

Townsend, Reginald T. *Mother of Clubs. Being the History of the First Hundred Years of the Union Club of the City of New York 1836–1936*. New York: The Printing House of William Edwin Rudge, 1936.

Secondary Sources

Adam, Thomas. "Philanthropic Landmarks in Toronto. The Toronto Trail from a Comparative Perspective, 1870s to the 1930s." *Urban History Review* 30, 1 (2001): 3–21.
Becker, Anja. "For the Sake of Old Leipzig Days ... Academic Networks of American Students at a German University, 1781–1914." Ph.D. thesis, University of Leipzig, 2006.
Beckert, Sven. *The Monied Metropolis. New York City and the Consolidation of the American Bourgeoisie, 1850–1896*. Cambridge: Cambridge University Press, 2001.
Brown, Charles H. *William Cullen Bryant*. New York: Charles Scribner's Sons 1971.
Brüning, Eberhard. "'Saxony Is a Prosperous and Happy Country' American Views of the Kingdom of Saxony in the Nineteenth Century." In: *Traveling between Worlds. German-American Encounters*, edited by Thomas Adam and Ruth Gross. College Station: Texas A&M Press, 2006, 20–50.
Conn, Steven. *Museums and American Intellectual Life, 1876–1926*. Chicago and London: The University of Chicago Press, 1998.
Cruttenden, Barabara Hall. "George Fisk Comfort. A Biography," M.A. thesis, Syracuse University, 1956.
Diehl, Carl. *German Scholarship 1770–1870*. New Haven and London: Yale University Press, 1978.
Frey, Manuel. *Macht und Moral des Schenkens. Staat und bürgerliche Mäzene vom späten 18. Jahrhundert bis zur Gegenwart*, Zwickau: Fannei & Walz, 1999.
Herbst, Jurgen. *The German Historical School in American Scholarship. A Study in the Transfer of Culture*. Ithaca: Cornell University Press, 1965.
Howe, Winifred E. *A History of the Metropolitan Museum of Art. With a Chapter on the Early Institutions of Art in New York*. New York: Gilliss Press, 1913.
Irwin, Will, Earl Chapin May, and Joseph Hotchkiss, *A History of the Union League Club of New York City*. New York: Dodd, Mead, 1952.
Jarausch, Konrad. "American Students in Germany, 1815–1914. The Structure of German and U.S. Matriculants at Gottingen University." In: *German Influences on Education in the United States to 1917*, edited by Henry Geitz, Jürgen Heideking, Jurgen Herbst. Washington D.C and Cambridge: Cambridge University Press, 1995, 195–212.
Lerman, Leo. *The Museum. One Hundred Years and the Metropolitan Museum of Art*. New York: Viking, 1969.
Martin, Judith. *Star-Spangled Manners*. New York and London: W. W. Norton & Company, 2003.
Menninger, Margaret Eleanor. "Art and Civic Patronage in Leipzig, 1848–1914." Ph.D. thesis, Harvard University, 1998.
Müller, Anett. *Der Leipziger Kunstverein und das Museum der bildenden Kunste. Materialien einer Geschichte (1836–1886/87)*. Leizpig: Nouvelle Alliance, 1995.
Sheehan, James J. *Museums in the German Art World from the End of the Old Regime to the Rise of Modernism*. New York: Oxford University Press, 2000.
Sides, Ashley. "'That Humane and Advanced Civilization.' Interpreting Americans' Values from their Praise of Saxony, 1800–1850." In: *Crossing the Atlantic. Travel and Travel Writing*

in Modern Times, edited by Thomas Adam and Nils H. Roemer. College Station: Texas A&M Press, 2011, 11–49.

Whitehall, Walter Muir. *Museum of Fine Arts Boston. A Centennial History* vol. 1. Cambridge: The Belknap Press of Harvard University Press, 1970.

Zimmerli, Nadine. "'The Rendezvous of all Nations'" Cosmopolitan Encounters in the German City of Dresden before World War I," Ph.D. thesis, University of Wisconsin-Madison, 2011.

Zunz, Olivier. *Philanthropy in America. A History*. Princeton and Oxford: Princeton University Press, 2012.

Chapter 4

THE INTERCULTURAL TRANSFER OF FOOTBALL: THE CONTEXTS OF GERMANY AND ARGENTINA

Abstract: Historians of sport have paid little attention to the ways in which modern sports such as football were transferred from its place of origin to receiving cultures around the globe. While it is recognized that this ball game emerged in nineteenth-century English public schools, little is known about the transformations this game underwent in becoming modern-day German football and modern-day Argentine football. Applying the model of intercultural transfer, this chapter will investigate the process of the transfer of this ball game from English public schools to German and Argentine high schools. The emergence of football and its transfer across the world was carried out by teachers and students and it was part of educational reform since this game offered an alternative to the traditional ways of imposing discipline. Discipline did not come from an outside force such as the teacher but from the rules of the game. This game, further, encouraged teamwork in order to achieve victory and offered sons of middle-class families an introduction into the mechanisms of the capitalist market. The introduction of football into urbanizing cultures was also part of social hygiene debates and many of the protagonists of this game were also involved in social reform debates about improving the quality of living in modern cities. The application of the intercultural transfer paradigm to the global dispersion of football also shows the advantages of this paradigm over traditional nation-focused approaches. In nation-centered approaches to the history of football, attention is paid nearly exclusively to the relationship between this sport and the construction of national cultures and identities. Its global and transnational character is easily overlooked. Applying a horizontal instead of a vertical approach to the study of football reveals its close relationship with school reform and the role of football in advancing student-centered forms of learning in a global setting.

This chapter was first published in *Sport in Society: Cultures, Commerce, Media, Politics* 20, 10 (2017): 1371–89.

Introduction

Football is undoubtedly a global phenomenon. Yet, historians have studied the emergence of football nearly exclusively within the narrow framework of nation states and with an eye on the construction of national cultures and national identities.[1] While such an approach certainly enriched our understanding of the construction of national identities and the place of sports within it, it ignored the causes and the context for the global spread of football and its integration into local (but not national) cultures and social milieus across the globe.

Football was born as a modern sport at English public schools in the 1860s. While it was British and non-British teachers and students who transferred the game into high schools across continental Europe and South America, it was soldiers and a few administrators who brought the game to the British colonies in Africa and Asia.[2] In continental Europe and in South America, the introduction of football was intended to improve education and contribute to school reform. After it was introduced as a teaching subject to make education more attractive and to create self-discipline among students, football quickly became a popular pastime for high-school students. This transfer was followed by the nationalization of the sport which was reinvented as an intrinsic element of national identities such as the Argentine and German identity. Its English roots were increasingly obscured and national narratives that constructed Argentine and German roots of football were invented. In the course of the twentieth century, international football matches pitted national teams against each other, and the game often took on overtly nationalistic tones. The matches were portrayed in terms of war and national honor. This nationalistic climate stripped football of its transnational and global roots. The hiding of these transnational roots went hand in hand with the internationalization of football that resulted in international matches and even the creation of international football organizations.[3]

To force the history of football into the straitjacket of the nation state and to ignore the intercultural transfer of football in the nineteenth century that connected high schools at localities as far away as Rio de Janeiro and Buenos Aires with the public school at Eton artificially creates borders where there were none. It further removes the game of football from the transnational context of school reform and the discourse about urban hygiene in the last decades of the nineteenth century in which football was just one aspect among others. This chapter will tell the story of football not from a comparative point of view but from the point of intercultural transfer studies.[4] The focus is on the intercultural transfer of football from English public schools to high schools in Buenos Aires (Argentina) and Braunschweig (Germany). It will explore the reasons which made this game so attractive to nineteenth-century educators and social reformers and it will, further, discuss the integration of football into urban subcultures that were defined by economic aspects in the case of Argentina and by politic orientations in the case of Germany. Historians of football have all too often overlooked the deep divisions in nineteenth-century societies which resulted in the creation of these subcultures. Football became part of these subcultures rather than of a national or even regional culture. In the case of Germany, a Socialist football culture emerged side by side to a Conservative football culture. This division was forcefully destroyed only in 1933 with Adolf Hitler's ascension to power and the destruction of the Socialist subculture.

The Concept of Transnational History and Intercultural Transfer Studies

This chapter builds upon the concept of transnational history which represents a counter-model to the paradigm of national history.[5] Rather than seeing history as a function of nation states and only in its national variants, transnational history considers history as a universal and global project. The concept of intercultural transfer is based upon the fundamental belief that humans live in an interconnected world. Instead of researching and writing the history of a particular phenomenon within the confines of a given nation state, transnational history encourages historians to follow a particular phenomenon wherever it leads us. The space of our account is not determined by the imagined and constructed spaces ascribed to particular nations,[6] but rather by the transfer of the game of football which created its own space. Within this space of football, different "provinces" emerged since the game and its rules were modified in the process of intercultural transfer.[7] These provinces were defined by particular football rules and practices. They grew over time and "annexed" neighboring provinces through the creation of rules and regulations that could be accepted in several places since football relied on the need to have an opposing team for a football match. The need to facilitate such matches increased the desire to create standards for the game that extended beyond a particular locality or province of football. One should not, however, infer that the necessity to stage matches automatically led to the creation of national football spaces and international matches. The example of Germany in particular will make very clear that the spaces that emerged from the standardization of football rules did not always result in national spaces, but rather in spaces that were defined by sociopolitical conditions and which did not coincide with national spaces.

Processes of the transfer of material and immaterial goods between different cultures have increasingly been studied by historians in the last three decades. However, historians have all too hastily employed a terminology of copying, influencing and modeling to label these processes. Many historians still embrace concepts of diffusion—of which the notion of Americanization is the most prominent—to conceptualize such transfers.[8] Yet, neither of the terms of copying or modeling nor the idea of diffusion grasps the complexity of the processes of intercultural transfer. They mistake transfers to be one-way roads; they wrongly strip the receiving culture of all agency; and they wrongly infer that the product transferred and received in the receiving culture is identical to the product in the giving culture. Such concepts simply cannot explain the conundrum of the modern world that the world becomes more similar and more dissimilar at the same time.[9]

If we study intercultural transfers closely and attentively, we will see that phenomena transferred from one culture to another experienced significant mutations and transformations that occurred in the process of transfer and which were determined by the actions of the agents of transfer as well as the needs and expectations of the receiving culture. Intercultural transfers occurred because of a need to fill a perceived gap in the receiving culture. Transfers were often accompanied by a discourse in which the giving culture was described as being superior. However, the giving culture had no or a very limited role in the process of transfer beyond presenting a phenomenon for selection. Agents of transfers almost always came from the receiving culture and had some connection to the giving culture. The phenomenon selected for transfer experienced significant transformations and it was made to fit into the receiving society by members of that society. The fitting into the receiving society was often done in ways that the origins of the transferred phenomenon were almost obscured, and members of the receiving culture began to believe over time that this phenomenon had always been part of their culture and history.[10]

The Intercultural Transfer of Football and the Nationalization of Football

The transfer of football was closely connected with educational reform and involved the activities of teachers and students who acted on their own volition and not on the orders of governments and states. The individuals involved in the intercultural transfer of football were later stylized as founding fathers of this sport for their respective nations. These founding fathers and the introduction of football became the subject of elaborate myths, and legends were created. In the case of Argentina, it was Alexander Watson Hutton

(1853–1936) who was embraced as the founding father of Argentine football. Born in Glasgow (Scotland), Hutton graduated from the University of Edinburgh and then moved to Buenos Aires in 1882 in order to become the headmaster of St. Andrews School. This high school was an educational institution for English families living in Argentina. In 1884, he founded with the English High School his own educational institution, which served the English community of that growing capital.[11]

In the case of Brazil, the story of introduction is more complicated and involves English as well as German actors. However, most accounts credit two individuals—Charles Miller and Oscar Cox—with the introduction of this sport. Charles William Miller (1874–1953), who was born to Scottish–English parents living in Brazil, was sent to school in Southampton (England). When he returned to his home country to work for the Sao Paulo Railway Company in 1894, he brought a football with him to Sao Paulo. Oscar Cox (1880–1931), who was also born to English parents living in Brazil, was sent to attending a high school in Lausanne (Switzerland). It was here that he first experienced playing football. Upon his return to Rio de Janeiro, he brought the ball game with him.[12]

Traditional accounts of German football credit Konrad Koch (1846–1911) with introducing football to Germany. Koch began upon graduation from the University of Leipzig in 1868, a career as a teacher of the classic languages at the *Gymnasium Martino-Katharineum* in Braunschweig. Here, he has been said to have introduced the game of football into the school curriculum.[13] Yet the sources of Koch's knowledge of the game and its various versions are unclear. Koch never traveled to England. He did not participate in the everyday life of an English colony of which there were so many across Southern and Central Germany, such as in the cities of Stuttgart and Dresden. Little is known about his university education, which he obtained at the universities at Göttingen, Berlin, and Leipzig. His major subjects were theology and Latin and Greek philology. His only contact with English culture and education was a thesis he wrote in the field of pedagogy about Thomas Arnold. It seems that this thesis caused Koch to become interested in the inclusion of sports into the highschool curriculum.[14]

Koch claimed, according to Kurt Hoffmeister, to have learned about football from reading various reports of German travelers such as J. A. Voigt, Karl Hillebrand, and Ludwig Wiese who observed the English school system during their travels in England in the 1850s and the 1870s.[15] However, these travel reports, presumably utilized by Koch, did neither provide extensive descriptions of ball games at public schools nor did they embrace these games as a model for German education. Wiese in particular wrote with great dismay about the practice of games among English high-school students. He even suggested that engaging in these games led to a disproportional strengthening of arm muscles at the expense of muscle formation in legs. To improve the health of young students, Wiese advocated the introduction of gymnastics into English high-school curricula rather than the introduction of sports into German high school curricula.[16]

It seems more likely that Koch who had also enjoyed reading Thomas Hughes book *Tom Brown's Schooldays* found a more favorable account of sports in this particular book. The first German translation of Hughes' book was produced by Ernst Wagner, who also authored a report about the English school system that appeared in 1864.[17] However, Wagner seemed to have shared Wiese's attitude with regard to the place of sports in school education. Instead of providing a favorable account of the inclusion of sport into English school curricula, Wagner cited in his book several English manufacturers and entrepreneurs who praised gymnastics and military exercises for preparing students for the industrial workforce. Gymnastics and military exercises improved, according to the cited statements made by English industrialists, the ability of individuals for collaboration and conformity. Both characteristics appeared, according to Wagner's account, highly desirable among English businessmen.[18] In his annotated translation of *Tom Brown's Schooldays*, Wagner inserted in the chapter that provided the famous description of a football game at Rugby a lengthy footnote explaining the rules of football as it was presumably played at Rugby. In this footnote, Wagner wrongfully insisted that players were allowed to use only their feet to kick the ball. The use of hands was, according to Wagner, ruled out.[19]

Miller and Cox were—just as Koch—born and grew up in the space to which they transferred football. They had been born in Brazil but because of their parents who had migrated from England to South America, they had a connection to England. They were also raised within English language and culture and sent to obtain education in Europe. In contrast to Koch who never traveled abroad and who obtained his education in his home country, Miller and Cox had first-hand experience of the game in a place other than their place of birth. And while Miller experienced football in its English cradle, Cox witnessed already the first wave of intercultural transfer that brought the game to the European continent. Miller's actions, thus, resulted in a primary transfer of football. Cox's advocacy for football upon his return from Lausanne to Rio de Janeiro represented a secondary transfer of football.

The story of Hutton's introduction of football to the English high schools of Buenos Aires differs markedly from the other two transfers. Hutton—in contrast to Koch, Miller and Cox—did not grow up in the place—here Buenos Aires—to which he introduced football. Instead he grew up in Scotland and migrated to Argentina after he finished his university training. Hutton made that city his new home and continuously taught at English high schools of that city. However, he did not bring the game to indigenous students but to the English enclave in Buenos Aires. His goal was not the introduction of football to Argentine society but to the English schools in Buenos Aires.

These three cases represent three different types of contact: (1) The first type of contact was established through the reading of travel reports that contained observations of the English educational system, written by non-English observers who belonged to the receiving society. In this case, the agent of intercultural transfer had no direct first-hand encounter with football in its place of origin. (2) The second type of contact was arranged through travel as part of the education of the individual who also acted as agent of intercultural transfer. In this case, the agent had a direct first-hand experience with the game at its birthplace or a secondary location to which it had already successfully been transferred. (3) The third type of contact was established through relocation of the agent of intercultural transfer, who was a member of the giving society, from the giving society to the receiving society. While such relocation and the origin of the agent in the giving society in particular prove almost always detrimental to the success of the transfer of a phenomenon from one society to another, it can in rare and exceptional cases such as this one facilitate such a transfer.

Foreign roots and the involvement in the creation of a national sport of individuals who were not members of the receiving society were either written out of history or reinvented by increasingly nationalistic accounts of this sport. The English roots of German football, to take just one prominent example, were already hidden by Konrad Koch who saw them as an obstacle to the acceptance of football in an increasingly nationalistic German culture. Over time, these agents of intercultural transfer became the subject of the formation of legends. They were turned into the founding fathers of national sports and they became the center of stories about the beginnings of football in their respective countries. In some cases, they even were made the focus of popular movies such as the movie *Escuela de Campeones* (School of Champions), made in Peron-era Argentina in 1950, and the German movie *Der Ganz Grosse Traum* (Lessons of a Dream), made in the post-national era in 2011.

Escuela de Campeones reflects the stereotypical national re-interpretation of the birth of football in any particular nation. Made in the Peron era, it was to provide the Argentine audiences with a patriotic reading of their glorious history and to bolster national identity and self-confidence. The story is severely tweaked in that Hutton does not appear as an English outsider but rather as an agent of the Argentine state. Instead of acting on his own, Hutton is shown asking the minister of education Domingo Sarmiento (who had previously been president of that country from 1868 to 1874) for permission to found his new high school in 1884 and to introduce football into the curriculum of that school. The deal is sealed with a handshake between Sarmiento and Hutton. This symbolic scene places the English High School within the context of the development of the Argentine school system. Rather than understanding Hutton's school as an extension of the English school system replicated in Argentina, it becomes the first successful Argentine public school.

Further, after a tragic accident—an English student is killed during a game against the team from St. Andrews (the first English high school at which Hutton taught when he moved to Buenos Aires)—the fate of Hutton's school seems to be in peril. It causes the English students to leave the school, which forced Hutton to consider closing his school. Abandoned by the English, the survival of the school is saved by Diego Brown who brings a dozen boys of Hispanic origin whom he calls "sons of Argentina." Not only did the admission of these boys into Hutton's school keep the school open but it was their participation in the football team that earned the English High School its decade-long dominance. The movie, thus, reinvents Hutton as an agent of the nascent Argentine nation and his school as the beginning of the national school system which is populated with Argentine rather than English pupils.

The German film *Der Ganz Grosse Traum*, made six decades later and in an environment in which nation states and national master narratives have lost some of their attraction, does neither hide the English roots of the game nor the English influence that clashed with the nationalist climate at German high schools in the Wilhelmine Empire. The story is focused exclusively on Koch who is portrayed as a rebellious teacher who refused to use corporal punishment to discipline students and instead tried to make learning fun. He is, further, reinvented as an English teacher who had just returned from his training in Great Britain and who is in charge of introducing modern languages to the high school in Braunschweig. The football was part of his luggage when he arrived in Braunschweig.

These stories about the arrival of football in any national culture were often from the beginning worked into the national (hi)stories under construction. The English origins of football were in the process increasingly written out of history. The intercultural transfer of football from English to German high schools occurred after all in the last third of the nineteenth century and, thus, at a time, when national history and identities took increasingly root within the German population. Foreign ideas were not necessarily welcomed and phenomena such as football had to be disguised as a truly German invention. Koch felt compelled to argue in his book *Die Geschichte des Fußballs im Altertum und in der Neuzeit* (The History of Football in Antiquity and Modern Times) that football was not an English game, but that it had been played across continental Europe already in the Middle Ages.[20] He, further, argued that no nation could claim to have invented football but that it was rather an European phenomenon, in which Germans had participated already in earlier centuries. Koch had realized that he needed to win over German nationalists to secure the success of football in German society.[21] This tendency to write out of history the English origin of that sport and instead portray the sport of football as a game that originated within the space claimed as cradle of the German nation reflects a main characteristic of the model of intercultural transfer. While the modern world is based upon intercultural transfers that reflected the interconnected nature of the human experience, these connections were often hidden by agents of transfer in order to facilitate the smooth transfer of practices such as football across hardening national borders.[22]

In order to turn the English game of football into a German game, Koch had to translate and, thereby, reinvent the rules of the game. He also needed to create a terminology for this new game, which initially combined the rules of rugby from the Public School at Rugby and association football from the Public School at Eton since Koch decided to adopt the rules of the Public School at Marlborough, which represented a mix of both.[23] Koch initially favored, according to his colleague August Hermann, rules that allowed the use of hands in order to propel the ball. However, since his colleagues preferred the game that favored kicking the ball over throwing the ball, Koch gave in and developed rules that prohibited the use of hands in the game.[24] In 1875, Koch published his first set of rules for playing football at the high school in Braunschweig. The game was, according to these rules, created as a winter game. During the winter season, students met for bi-weekly games. The playing field had two goals on opposite sides and it was the purpose of the game for each team to hit the ball above the goal line (which was 3.5 m above the ground). The players were allowed to use only their feet to hit the ball. The ball could only be handled if it was thrown back to the goal of the defending team. Koch introduced the *Abseits* rule according to which all players of one team had to be between their goal line and the ball. No player was allowed to be in front of the ball. And Koch insisted on fair play. All beating and tripping was banned. Games lasted for one hour with a change of sides after 30 minutes. The team with the highest number of points was declared as victor. Victory was determined by the number of points each team had reached. Twenty points were given for hitting the ball over the goal line but between the two supporting pillars. Five points were awarded for each attempted goal. The game introduced in Braunschweig represented a combination of the football played at Rugby (shape of goals) and the football played at Eton (kicking of the ball).[25]

In order to Germanize the game, Koch attempted to translate all technical terms from English into German. Team was translated with *Gespielschaft* (group of friends). The team captain was translated with *Spielkaiser* (game emperor), which reflected an overzealously monarchical and nationalist attitude, which might not have been received well since emperor could refer only to one person at the head of the state. Halfback was translated with *Markmann*, Offside with *Abseits*, and Tripping with *Beinstellen*. Some of these translations caught on quickly such as *Abseits*; others were translated multiple times before a term was found that appealed to a broad audience. The goal was, for instance, first translated as *Mal* which referred to a border marking. After a net was added to the goal posts, it was replaced with *Tor* (gate). And *Gespielschaft* which reminded too much of harmony and gymnastics was finally replaced by *Mannschaft*.[26]

While individuals such as Koch and Hutton certainly played an important role in popularizing the sport of football in their respective countries and took key roles in establishing norms, regulations and teams, they were not solely responsible for the intercultural transfer of football. Koch acted together with other individuals who had, in contrast to him, first-hand knowledge of the game of football and both educators were not the only ones who introduced the game to a particular culture. Industrialization, trade and shipping, and travel played an important part in the intercultural transfer of football. In Germany, it was the English colonies that had sprung up in cities such as Karlsruhe, Baden-Baden, Stuttgart, and Dresden where rugby and football was first played in the 1860s and 1870s.[27] The ball game often remained, however, an activity within these English communities and did not transfer into the surrounding society. William Cail, who became president of the Rugby Football Union in 1892, reminisced: "My recollections then carry me to the valley of the Neckar, where many of us English lads, some from the public schools finishing education at Stuttgart, some at the schools at Cannstatt used to meet weekly and play our Rugby game, …"[28]

Industrialization caused the mobility of many English laborers, engineers, miners and their families around the globe and games such as football traveled with them. The introduction of football into a receiving culture from these English expatriates was hard since the representatives of the giving culture supposedly had strange rules and spoke an even stranger language. Only after these rules had been translated and thereby nationalized—as in the case of Koch—did the game of football have success in being accepted from among the members of the receiving culture. The intercultural transfer of football into a culture was, however, not the action of a single individual. It was also not a one-time event. Football was introduced several times in several places by members of the giving and receiving culture. Multiple versions of the sport—rugby and association football—were introduced and presented to a particular culture. These transfers occurred within the English diaspora that included English communities in cities such as Stuttgart and Buenos Aires and it facilitated the transfer of this game from within the spaces created by the English diaspora into their surrounding urban environments.

Even if one ignores the multiple entry points of football into German society,[29] it can hardly be contended that Koch could claim sole responsibility for bringing football to Braunschweig. He acted in concert with a number of individuals that included his father-in-law Friedrich Reck as well as his teacher colleague August Herrmann and the owners of the firm of Dolffs & Helle. In 1874, Koch had married Margarethe Wecke whose mother remarried after the death of her first husband. Her second husband was the military physician and social reformer Friedrich Reck (1827–1878). During his service in the military from 1855 to 1868, Reck had traveled to England repeatedly and witnessed ball games.[30] It was Reck who brought football to Koch's attention and encouraged him to introduce the game into the school curriculum.[31] It was, further, Koch's colleague August Hermann (1835–1906)—since 1864 the instructor for gymnastics at the high school in Braunschweig—who brought the first football ball to Braunschweig. Hermann's sister-in-law Marie Tolle was the director of an exclusive girl's school in Braunschweig, which educated girls from well-off families from Germany, England, and France. Tolle traveled frequently to London and Paris in order to recruit new students. Her travels to London and the students she brought to her institute seem to have facilitated the transfer of knowledge about football to Braunschweig. Hermann, further, provided a home to English students in his own house. In an article for the *Zeitschrift für Turnen und Jugendspiel* (Journal for Gymnastics and Games for the Youth), Herrmann wrote that he received instructions in the game's rules from one of the students living in his house after the latter was sent a football from England.[32]

Koch also relied on the production of football and other gear needed for the game from the firm of Dolffs & Helle (founded in Braunschweig in 1865). This firm was the first enterprise in Northern Germany to import (since 1883) and later produce footballs. It advertised its services as "German Cricket and Football Industry." By 1887, it supplied products to 297 schools, and gymnasts' associations in the Duchy of Braunschweig and in Northern and Western Germany. A mutual relationship developed between Koch and this enterprise since his articles and books often carried its advertisements. These advertisements, published in connection with Koch's texts and independently of them, always contained references to Koch's rules and regulations of football.[33]

Koch's role in the process of intercultural transfer of football might have been rather limited since the ball was supplied by his colleague, the inspiration came from his father-in-law, and Koch had never traveled to England. Yet, he still managed to secure an important position for himself in the transfer process. Herrmann and Reck's contributions to this transfer were largely forgotten because of Koch's publishing activities. While he acknowledged Reck's importance by dedicating to him his book *Geschichte des Fußballs im Altertum und in der Neuzeit* and referring to the fact that it was Reck who had inspired the introduction of football in Braunschweig, it was Koch who had written the rules and created the technical language of football in German.[34]

In contrast to Koch, Hutton had first-hand knowledge of the game from his days as a student in public school and university. It seems that he did not rely on the participation of other individuals in the transfer process. And while Koch sought to translate and nationalize football, Hutton embarked on an opposite course of action. He did not translate the football rules into Spanish since he envisioned the game as a teaching tool for the students at his English High School. Football initially remained within the confines of the English colony of Buenos Aires. In 1893 football had spread, however, from Hutton's school to other English schools in the city. Several football teams had emerged, and Hutton decided to create the *Argentine Football League*. This league was initially limited to students from the English schools and the clubs and the league were dominated by English speakers.[35]

The Role of Football in Educational and Social Reform

The model of intercultural transfer suggests that transfers resulted from a perceived gap in a given society, which agents of this society sought to fill by transferring an idea from another society that was perceived and described as superior to the receiving society. Football proved to be attractive to German educators and social reformers in Wilhelmine Germany because it offered an alternative to the discipline enforced upon students with brutal force from the outside. It also provided an outlet for activities in an urbanized world in which the distance between nature and human experience steadily increased. And it offered a way to introduce students to competition and teamwork that was needed in a capitalist economy.

In the case of Germany, it was, further, the crisis of gymnastics that provided an opening for the introduction of football. Gymnastics as it had been developed by Friedrich Ludwig Jahn at the beginning of the nineteenth century in the context of the creation of a German identity was turned into a school subject by Adolf Spiess (1810–1858) in subsequent decades. Based upon Jahn's exercises, which stressed harmony and conformity, Spiess developed what he called "free gymnastics." These free exercises were activities that did not require any apparatus—i.e. marching exercises. School gymnastics was strictly organized and run in a quasi-military style. There was no space for individual agency or spontaneity. Students were forced to march in formation and to exercise in formation. One might imagine that such activities were not too attractive to young students. Reck was very critical of the practice of gymnastics in Braunschweig's schools and warned that the young men should not be burdened with military exercises and discipline before they entered military service.[36]

Since gymnastics had lost much of its appeal in the general population, Reck advocated the introduction of sport as an alternative form of physical activity. Sport games such as football had the advantage that they included competition and that they were oriented toward winning a game. Gymnastics did not know either. Victory in football was clearly established since the goals were openly counted. Games appealed to students because it gave them freedom and self-determination and at the same time encouraged collaboration between the members of a team. Football provided an option to create discipline among students that was not imposed by the teacher but a discipline that was created by the impersonal rules of the game and the necessity to work together in achieving victory over the opposing team. Students were not forced to work together to strike a goal; they decided to work together to achieve victory.[37]

Gymnastics might have been part of the project to create a national body through the integration of individuals into the group—the national body—and by focusing on exercises in which each gymnast moved in the prescribed and identical way as the others. Games such as football, by contrast, reflected a capitalist order in which competition and winning were emphasized. This appealed especially to the entrepreneurial middle class, which saw football as an opportunity to prepare their sons for their future business life.

Older interpretations of the success of football in modern society put forward by Norbert Elias and Eric Dunning stressed the significance of civilizing people but paid insufficient attention to the context of educational reform and completely ignored the context of social reform.[38] This flawed interpretation emerged from narrow theoretical premises as well as from the limited framework of the nation. If one focuses on one nation only, the story of that nation's football can only be told in a vertical and, thus, chronological direction. It starts out within high schools and colleges but moves quickly to football clubs and the history of organizations and matches. The role of educators as agents of transfer and of education as the proper framework for the emergence of football is largely marginalized.[39]

The horizontal approach of intercultural transfer studies, by contrast, allows us to research the introduction of football into multiple societies on a horizontal perspective and, thus, compare the context of football's introduction into various cultures and the entry points. Such an approach reveals the significance of educational reform for the acceptance of football and the key role of educators in the creation of national football cultures. From Koch to Hutton, the founding fathers of football across continental Europe and South America had either been professors or students who encountered football in their training. The introduction of football was in general closely related to school reform and it is safe to assume that educational reform was aside from Great Britain's leading economic and imperial position the precondition for football's global spread.

It all began with the reforms introduced at the Public School at Rugby by Thomas Arnold (1795–1842). English public schools had originally been founded by public benefactors for the education of poor boys. In the course of the nineteenth century, these schools turned into educational institutions for the aristocracy and gentry. Rugby stood somewhat out from these schools because it had a low proportion of children from titled families. Common to these schools was also the fagging system, which allowed older students to haze younger students who were forced into serving older students. Arnold sought, after he became headmaster of Rugby in 1828, to reform the fagging system not by getting rid of it—that proved impossible—but by regulating it. He introduced a system of indirect rule in which student prefects exercised power in place of headmasters. It was this concept of self-government of the students which attracted educators in continental Europe such as Koch to become interested in Arnold's reforms and the place of games within it. Koch wrote, when he was a student at the University of Leipzig, a thesis about Arnold and his pedagogical concept, which stressed self-determination of the students as well as a balance between physical and intellectual activities.[40]

Since Arnold outlawed the traditional aristocratic pastimes of hunting, shooting, and fishing, which had been firmly embedded in the leisure time activities of Rugby students and which had resulted in countless complaints from local farmers and residents, he needed to fill the void created with a new activity. Arnold found this new activity in the games of cricket and football, which had been embraced by students across the British Islands for some time. Ball games offered to Arnold and to the students a game that supported the hierarchies among students. It provided a new leisure time activity, and it also introduced new learning opportunities.[41]

Since the Public School at Rugby was still seeking its place in the educational landscape of public schools, there was also an incentive to develop a distinguished game. Teachers and students developed a form of football that was distinct from older forms of that game played on the streets of English towns and villages for centuries. They embraced the oval ball and H-shaped goals. In 1845, *The Laws of Football as Played at Rugby School*, which emphasized carrying and handling the ball, provided the first codified rules of this new game. These rules stipulated that all students had to participate in the game.

They, further, ruled out the use of bats and sticks. Players were allowed to propel the ball only with their body.[42] In response, the Public School at Eton developed a game with rules that stipulated that hands were allowed to touch the ball only "to stop the ball, or touch it when behind. The ball must not be carried, thrown or struck by the hand."[43] Rugby and association football were, thus, born.

The introduction of football in England, Germany, and Argentina was intrinsically linked with educational reform. It was further linked to the urban hygiene discourse that emerged because of accelerated urbanization in the Atlantic World at the end of the nineteenth century. Towns and cities in Germany and Argentina experienced significant population growth, which went hand in hand with an alienation of inhabitants from their surrounding nature. Many city dwellers did never leave the city and spent too much time in closed spaces (factories, apartments, pubs, and schools). Even German gymnastics was no longer taught and practiced outside but in specifically built gymnasiums.

Football emerged at the same time at which urban spaces were closed toward playful activities through the growth of the city and police ordinances limiting the activities of city dwellers. Local city ordinances increasingly banned games and play in the city's streets. In the city of Braunschweig, for instance, a Police Ordinance of 1872 outlawed throwing balls and various games on sidewalks throughout the city. Playing football on a military exercise field outside the old city provided an outlet for the desire to play a game within the urban environment.[44]

Football was foremost an urban phenomenon. The creation of football fields occurred at about the same time at which modern cities created public parks, and provided land for urban garden plots to preserve and recreate nature within overbuild and overpopulated cities. These football fields were of course as artificial as the nature in the public parks, which were created by city planners and landscape architects and cared for by gardeners. And yet, they still offered a scenery that was different from the busy roads and places of the modern city. In the case of Germany, it was the highly urbanized regions in Northern and Western Germany that provided specifically designed public spaces for football games. Of the 117 towns with more than 2000 inhabitants in the Kingdom of Saxony, 66 (=56%) had one or more football fields in the early 1890s. In the case of Bavaria, by contrast, it was only 40 out of 144 towns (=28%).[45]

The direct connection between the discourse about improving urban hygiene and football is made in Reck's writings. Reck was an ardent urban reformer for whom the introduction of football into the curriculum of Braunschweig's high schools was part of a much larger reform project of modern life. He authored many articles about topics that included diseases caused by urban living conditions, water quality, and the need to improve urban waste disposal systems.[46] His interest in football fit into the frame of his concern for the well-being of urban dwellers and in general into the improvement of the living conditions of urban populations. The introduction of sports into modern urban cultures was, thus, not only part of educational reforms but it also coincided with debates about improving the health conditions in cities and the reform of human life in modern society by the transnational lifestyle reform movement.

Football and Social Divisions in Society

Equally absent from most stories of football within a given national context is the integration of that game into existing socio-economic and sociocultural milieus. In both countries, Argentina and Germany, the legends about the creation of football as a national pastime focus on the introduction of football into high schools that were reserved for students who came from middle- and upper-class families. This is, however, only half of the story since in both countries two different traditions of football and two different football cultures emerged: one football culture for the middle and upper classes and one football culture for the working class. In Argentina, this division was even more solidified by the language division between the English-speaking upper class of the English enclave and the Spanish-speaking laborers.

While football, because of the introduction to elite schools—the English High School in Buenos Aires and the *Gymnasium* in Braunschweig—had the odor of being an elite phenomenon, the game also attracted young men from working-class backgrounds. Excluded from the elitist English schools, children of the poor neighborhoods in Buenos Aires played football on the city streets. Since this occurred outside of the school setting and without adult supervision, this variant of football was rougher and virtually unregulated. Winning the game superseded ideas of fair play. Playing football focused more on the individual than on the team.[47]

Football—English high-school football and Spanish street football—spread quickly throughout the city of Buenos Aires and drew in more and more young men. Hundreds of clubs emerged across the city and the country. The clubs formed at the elitist English high schools sought to dominate the emerging football culture by publishing binding football rules in Spanish in 1905 and by reviving the *Argentina Football League* which was Hispanicized (*Asociación Argentina de Football*). This association established itself as a national organization that sought to monopolize the game. It created clear rules about membership: (1) each club was required to have its own field and was not permitted to play on another club's field and (2) each club was further required to provide separate facilities for home and visiting teams including locker rooms and showers. These requirements proved to be a great challenge since space within the city was scarce and expensive. Clubs either had to move out to the suburbs or they had to expand their membership base to bring in funding for the acquisition of land with membership fees.[48]

The elitist football clubs' focus on fairness, amateurism, and enjoyment over victory was detrimental to the broadening of its membership and fan base. Such a game did simply not appeal to the broad masses and it failed to create a spectators' culture. A visitor observing a game played in one of the exclusive English clubs would be very disappointed since there was not much enthusiasm among players with regard to winning the match. The game was friendly and not confrontational, and the players appeared to be more interested in refreshments than in the game. The need to obtain funds for buying land, building stadiums, and constructing club facilities forced the elitist clubs to adopt the more aggressive football style developed by working-class clubs. Spectators asked to pay entrance fees had high expectations. They wanted to see an exciting game in which two opposing teams competed for victory. Amateurism was, therefore, slowly abandoned or circumvented by providing perks such as housing and paying for groceries to football players that drew in large crowds. As a result, differences between elite and working-class football slowly disappeared and football clubs and national leagues integrated English and Argentine traditions already after World War I.[49]

While social divisions in the case of Argentina were overcome rather quickly, Germany saw the growth and expansion of two parallel football cultures: one bourgeois and one working-class that co-existed up until 1933 when Socialist football clubs fell victim to the destruction of the Socialist subculture by the Nazis. The reason for the longer endurance of these divisions in the case of Germany was the political and ideological basis of this division. It was not simply a social division but because of the attempts of the Conservatives and Monarchists to exclude the Socialists from participation in political life a Bourgeois and a Socialist subculture was created that included societies and associations such as consumer and housing companies, mutual health insurance systems, adult education societies, and all kinds of leisure activity associations that provided all essential services for its members.[50]

In the 1880s, bourgeois football clubs emerged in many German cities including Berlin, Bremen, and Leipzig. Members and players were predominantly middle- and upper-class men. For nearly two decades, football remained a game of high school and university students who came from very wealthy families. However, even within bourgeois culture, football was at first not welcomed by the fathers of these students. The *Deutsche Turnerschaft*, which had been founded as a national organization in 1868 to spread gymnastics as it was created by Friedrich Ludwig Jahn, rejected the game of football because of its English roots and un-German character. The rejection of the new sport did, however, not deter young students from embracing it and, thereby, defy the norms of their fathers and grandfathers. In 1888, a football team was created within the *Allgemeiner Turnverein zu Leipzig*. This local gymnast association had been founded in 1845 and it belonged to the *Deutsche Turnerschaft*. The Leipzig football team introduced the members of the *Deutsche Turnerschaft* to the new game by playing a match against the London football team Orion at the annual *Turnfest*—a meeting of all members of the *Deutsche Turnerschaft*—in Munich in 1889. This early international match helped to popularize the game in Conservative circles and encouraged young gymnasts in other bourgeois gymnast associations to form football teams.[51]

One of the local branches of the *Deutsche Turnerschaft* that formed such a football team was located in Magdeburg. The Magdeburg football team managed to be included in the annual Sedan Celebrations, which were held each year on September 2 to celebrate Germany's victory over France in the Battle of Sedan in 1870. These celebrations brought together war veteran associations and the most Conservative circles of German society. The inclusion of football into these celebrations paved the way for football to be recognized as part of the bourgeois and monarchist culture. In the following years, sport teams were created as chapters of the *Deutsche Turnerschaft* in nearly every German city. These chapters of gymnast associations slowly transformed into independent sport associations as it happened in Leipzig in 1892. These sport associations were initially inclusive and embraced various ball games from football to tennis. The Leipzig sport association received its own playground in 1896. And from among the many sports played, football emerged quickly as the most favored game.[52]

The fact that the middle and upper classes embraced football turned this game into a bourgeois sport. Further, its focus on competition and winning increased the reluctance of Socialist leaders to accept football into the canon of physical activities appropriate for laborers young and old. The *Arbeiterturnerbund*, which had been founded in 1893 as a Socialist alternative to the *Deutsche Turnerschaft*, rejected football on ideological grounds. However, young laborers who were integrated into the Socialist subculture felt about gymnastics in the same way students from middle- and upper-class background had felt about it. Since Socialist leaders opposed football on the ground that it was foreign and elitist, young football players of working-class background were forced to create football clubs outside of the *Arbeiterturnerbund*. For the young sport enthusiasts involved in labor football this exclusion could come at a high price since sport injuries, which occurred quite frequently in football, were not covered by the health insurance provided to all members by the *Arbeiterturnerbund*. Only members of this organization were entitled to these benefits. Joining the bourgeois *Deutsche Turnerschaft* was an option but often not chosen because of the social and political distance between laborers and this bourgeois organization. And while bourgeois football teams had access to military drill grounds—the first games in Braunschweig were played on that city's *Exerzierplatz*—labor football teams were left with open grasslands outside of towns.[53]

The initial hope of the *Arbeiterturnerbund* leaders that its strict rejection of football would prevent the infiltration of working-class gymnastics by football eventually failed because field sports proved to be too attractive to young men of all social backgrounds. Football gained more and more ground among the young generation. The introduction and spread of football seemed to have been part of a conflict between the generation born before the founding of the German Empire and the generation that grew up in the 1880s and 1890s. The growth of labor football teams unaffiliated with the *Arbeiterturnerbund* seemed to endanger the future of labor gymnastics and finally forced that organization to change course. In 1912 the *Arbeiterturnerbund* opened its organization for football but the leadership imposed upon its teams the condition that they had to abstain from playing matches against bourgeois football teams that were affiliated with the *Deutsche Turnerschaft*. This ideologically motivated rule posed, of course, a significant challenge for a sport geared toward competition.[54]

The city of Leipzig, in particular, developed in the course of the 1920s into a center of sports within Germany. In 1921, the city was the home to about 50 football associations with a combined membership of 25,000 proletarian and bourgeois men and women. About 5500 of these 25,000 football players were organized within the *Arbeiterturnerbund* while the remaining 19,500 players were members of the *Deutsche Turnerschaft*. Teams of both subcultures developed their own infrastructure complete with their own football fields, tournaments, and publications. This division of German society into two opposing subcultures which also resulted in the creation of two independent football cultures ended only in 1933 with the closing and destruction of all Socialist organizations—including labor football teams—by the Nazis.[55]

Both Argentina and Germany saw the creation of two parallel football cultures, which were defined by social status and in the German case also by ideology. This division continued to exist in Germany for about two decades longer than in Argentina because of the entrenched social and political divisions between labor and bourgeoisie. And yet, in Argentina this division was not just a social division but was also a language division. While two football cultures co-existed in Germany without influencing each other, the style of Buenos Aires' street football was slowly integrated into the football culture developed within the elite football clubs creating an attractive game that turned football from a leisure time activity into a public spectacle for which people were willing to pay money.

Conclusion

Historians trained in national histories often raise the question for why we should forgo the old and proven ways of national history. Why should we embrace a transnational approach which requires the historian to become fluent in at least two languages and two national historiographies? They also charge that such a historical approach is in danger of losing its grounding since transnational history does not seem to have a space in the same way national history does. Transnational history is seen by its critics as turning history into an elusive chase of ideas that cross regions and borders and can hardly be captured. Yet, few historians seem to ask what our narratives miss out by limiting ourselves to the paradigm of national history and what our narratives could gain when we would embrace transnational approaches.

The example of football provides some insight into what is to be gained if we look beyond national variations of this sport and the role of this sport for the invention and perpetuation of national identities. The focus on the transfer of football across continents and oceans in the second half of the nineteenth century opens up new horizons and contexts in which this transfer occurred. Football was not just a sport that could be studied independently of social and cultural changes; it was a part of educational and social reform projects that were to improve urban life through bringing students out of unhealthy buildings onto fresh air. Football fields provided a way for social reformers to reconnect with nature albeit a nature that was artificially created.

Following the intercultural transfer of football around the globe also provides an innovative way at mapping history. Instead of creating maps that show political borders, we could imagine a map that represents the acceptance and rejection of this sport in nineteenth- and twentieth-century societies. This map would show the extent to which football was integrated into urban societies and also highlight the borders of its influence. These borders were as real and as constructed as the borders of nation states. Within the space created by football, different colors could highlight different traditions and different degrees of integration. Transnational history is certainly not a history without space. But space—national or transnational—is always constructed. Each circulating idea created a circulatory regime that appropriated a space defined, limited, and structured by this idea and its practitioners.[56]

Notes

1. Christiane Eisenberg (ed.), *Fußball, soccer, calcio: Ein englischer Sport auf seinem Weg um die Welt*, Munich: Deutscher Taschenbuch Verlag, 1997.
2. John S. Hill, John Vincent, and Matthew Curtner-Smith, "The Worldwide Diffusion of Football: Temporal and Spatial Perspectives," in: *Global Sport Business Journal* 2, 2 (2014): 1–27; Eisenberg, *Fußball*.
3. The terms "transnational" and "international" should not be confused since the first term points to connections of phenomena independent of the nation state while the second is based upon the existence of the nation state, which is seen as an organizing principle of human relations and history. See: Patricia Clavin, "Defining Transnationalism," in: *Contemporary European History* 14 (2005): 424–26.
4. Thomas Adam, *Intercultural Transfers and the Making of the Modern World, 1800–2000: Sources and Context*, New York: Palgrave Macmillan, 2012; Thomas Adam "New Ways to Write the History of Western Europe and the United States: The Concept of Intercultural Transfer," in: *History Compass* 11, 10 (2013): 880–92 (This article is reprinted as the first chapter in this book.); Michael Werner and Bénédicte Zimmerman, "Beyond Comparison: Histoire Croisée and the Challenge of Reflexivity," in: *History and Theory* 45, 1 (2006): 30–50.
5. Thomas Adam, "Transnational History: A Program for Research, Publishing, and Teaching," in: *Yearbook of Transnational History* 1 (2018): 1–10; Pierre-Yves Saunier, *Transnational History*, New York: Palgrave Macmillan, 2013; Adam "New Ways to Write the History."
6. Benedict Anderson, *Imagined Communities: Reflections on the Origin and Spread of Nationalism*, London and New York: Verso, 2006, 5–7; Eric J. Hobsbawn, *Nations and Nationalism since 1780: Programme, myth, reality* (Second Edition), Cambridge: Cambridge University Press, 1992, 14–45.
7. Adam, *Intercultural Transfers*.
8. Hill/Vincent/Curtner-Smith, "The Worldwide Diffusion of Football"; Everett M. Rogers, *Diffusion of Innovations*, New York, London, Toronto, Sydney, Tokyo, Singapore: The Free Press, 1995.
9. Rob Kroes, "American Empire and Cultural Imperialism: A View from the Receiving End," in: Thomas Bender (ed.), *Rethinking American History in a Global Age*, Berkeley, Los Angeles, London: University of California Press, 2002, 295–313; Daniel T. Rodgers, *Atlantic Crossings: Social Politics in a Progressive Age*, Cambridge and London: The Belknap Press of Harvard University Press, 1998, 1–7.
10. Adam, *Intercultural Transfers*, pp. 3–7.
11. Brandon Blakeslee, "How to Make a Foreign Idea Your Own: Argentine Identity And the Role Soccer Played In Its Formation" (MA thesis, The University of Texas at Arlington, 2014), 42–43. A rather superficial treatment can be found in: Aduardo P. Archetti "Argentinien," in: Eisenberg, *Fußball*, 149–70. See also: Tony Mason, *Passion of the People? Football in South America*. London: Verso, 1995.
12. Isabelle Rispler, "'Soccer is Our Mother': On the Intercultural Transfer of Soccer from Britain to Brazil" (Research Paper, The University of Texas at Arlington 2012). A rather superficial treatment can be found in: Waldenyr Caldas, "Brasilien," in: Eisenberg, *Fußball*, 171–84. See also: Mason, *Passion of the People?*
13. Kurt Hoffmeister, *Der Wegbereiter des Fußballspiels in Deutschland: Prof. Dr. Konrad Koch 1846–1911. Eine Biographie*, Braunschweig: Books on Demad GmbH, 2011; Malte

Oberschelp, *Der Fußball-Lehrer: Wie Konrad Koch im Kaiserreich den Ball ins Spiel brachte*, Göttingen: Verlag Die Werkstatt, 2010.

14 Hoffmeister, *Der Wegbereiter des Fußballspiels in Deutschland*, 12.

15 Hoffmeister, *Der Wegbereiter des Fußballspiels in Deutschland*, 80; J. A. Voigt, *Mittheilungen über das Unterrichtswesen Englands und Schottlands*, Halle: Eduard Anton, 1857; Karl Hillebrand, *Aus und über England*, Berlin: Robert Oppenheim, 1876; Ludwig Adolf Wiese, *Deutsche Briefe über Englische Erziehung* 2 vols., Berlin: Wiegandt und Grieben, 1852.

16 Wiese, *Deutsche Briefe über Englische Erziehung*, 174–75.

17 *Tom Brown's Schuljahre. Von einem alten Rugby-Jungen. Zur Darlegung des gegenwärtigen Standes der Erziehung in den oberen Classen Englands*, nach dem Englischen des " Th. Hughes", bearbeitet von Dr. Ernst Wagner, Gotha: Justus Perthes, 1867. Ernst Wagner, *Das Volksschulwesen in England und seine neueste Entwicklung*, Stuttgart: Verlag der J. B. Metzler'schen Buchhandlung, 1864.

18 Wagner, *Das Volksschulwesen in England und seine neueste Entwicklung*, 182–85.

19 *Tom Brown's Schuljahre*, 99.

20 Konrad Koch, *Die Geschichte des Fußballs im Altertum und in der Neuzeit*, Berlin: R. Gaertners Verlagsbuchhandlung, 1895 (reprint Münster: LIT Verlag 1983), 7.

21 Folko Damm, *Auf dem Weg zum Volkssport: Einführung und Verbreitung des Fußballs in Deutschland*, Norderstedt: GRIN Verlag, 2007, 23.

22 Adam, *Intercultural Transfers*, 6.

23 Koch, *Die Geschichte des Fußballs*, 41.

24 August Hermann, "Ergänzende und berichtigende Bemerkungen," in: *Zeitschrift für Turnen und Jugendspiel* 4 (1895): 132.

25 Konrad Koch, *Fußball. Regeln des Fußball-Vereins der mittleren Classen des Martino-Catharineums zu Braunschweig*, Braunschweig: D. Haering & Co., 1875; Kurt Hoffmeister, *Zeitreise durch die Braunschweiger Sportgeschichte*, Braunschweig and Norderstedt: Books on Demand, 2010, 18–19; Oberschelp, *Der Fußball-Lehrer*, 87–100.

26 Hoffmeister, *Der Wegbereiter des Fußballspiels in Deutschland*, 87–89; Damm, *Auf dem Weg zum Volkssport*, 23–25; Ph. Heineken, *Das Fußballspiel. Association und Rugby*, Hannover: Th. Schäfer, 1898 (reprint: 1993), 229–32.

27 Heineken, *Das Fußballspiel*, 236; Michael Broschkowski and Thomas Schneider, >>*Fußlümmelei*<< *Als Fußball noch ein Spiel war*, Berlin: TRANSIT, 2005, 30–33; Christiane Eisenberg, "Deutschland," in: Eisenberg, *Fußball*, 95–96.

28 Heineken, *Das Fußballspiel*, 236.

29 Ulrich Hesse-Lichtenberger, *Tor! The Story of German Football*, London: WSC Books, 2003, 19–27.

30 Hoffmeister, *Der Wegbereiter des Fußballspiels in Deutschland*, 27–29; Wilhelm Blasius, "Friedrich Reck. Nekrolog," in: *5. Jahresbericht des Vereins für Naturwissenschaft zu Braunschweig für das Vereinsjahr 1886 bis 1887*, Braunschweig: Friedrich Vieweg und Sohn, 1887: 127; Konrad Koch, "August Friedrich Reck, Dr. med. †," in: *Braunschweiger Tageblatt* November 9, 1878; Hermann, "Ergänzende und berichtigende Bemerkungen," 132.

31 Hoffmeister, *Der Wegbereiter des Fußballspiels in Deutschland*, 29; Koch, *Die Geschichte des Fußballs*, 3.

32 Hoffmeister, *Der Wegbereiter des Fußballspiels in Deutschland*, 34–35; Oberschelp, *Der Fußball-Lehrer*, 12.

33 Rat der Stadt Braunschweig (ed.), *Braunschweig*, Berlin: Deutscher Architektur- und Industrieverlag, 1921, 197; Oberschelp, *Der Fußball-Lehrer*, 29–30; Hoffmeister, *Der Wegbereiter des Fußballspiels in Deutschland*, 40, 82.

34 Koch, *Die Geschichte des Fußballs*, 3.
35 Blakeslee, "How To Make A Foreign Idea Your Own," 47. See also: Mason, *Passion of the People?*
36 Oberschelp, *Der Fußball-Lehrer*, 18–19; Christiane Eisenberg, *"English Sports" und deutsche Bürger. Eine Gesellschaftsgeschichte 1800–1939*, Paderborn, Munich, Vienna, Zurich: Schöningh 1999, 143; Hesse-Lichtenberger, *Tor!*, 16–18.
37 Wilhelm Hopf, "Wie der Fußball nach Deutschland kam," in: Koch, *Die Geschichte des Fußballs*, 49–53.
38 Norbert Elias, "The Social Constraint through Self-Constraint," in: Stephen Mennell and Johan Goudsblom (eds.), *Civilization, Power, and Knowledge*, Chicago: University of Chicago Press, 1998, 56; Eric Dunning and Kenneth Sheard, *Barbarians, Gentlemen, and Players, Second Edition: A Sociological Study of the Development of Rugby Football*, London and New York: Routledge, 2005; Patrick Murphy, Ken Sheard, and Ivan Waddington, "Figurational Sociology and its Application to Sport," in: Jay Coakley and Eric Dunning (eds.), *Handbook of Sports Studies*, London, Thousand Oaks, New Delhi: SAGE, 2000, 92–105. See also the contributions to the "Forum *European Sport and the Challenges of its Recent Historiography*" in: *Journal of Sport History* 38 (2 and 3) (2011).
39 Christopher Young, Anke Hilbrenner, and Alan Tomlinson, "European Sport Historiography: Challenges and Opportunities," in: *Journal of Sport History* 38 (2011): 181–87.
40 Hoffmeister, *Der Wegbereiter des Fußballspiels in Deutschland*, 12.
41 Dunnig/Sheard, *Barbarians, Gentlemen, and Players*, 69–86.
42 *The Laws of Football as Played at Rugby School*, Rugby: Crossley and Billington, 1862.
43 Graham Curry, "Football: A Study in Diffusion" (D.Phil. thesis, University of Leicester, 2001), 12.
44 Hoffmeister, *Zeitreise durch die Braunschweiger Sportgeschichte*, 17.
45 Viktor von Woikowsky-Biedau, "Über den Stand des Jugend- und Volksspiels in Deutschland 1892–1893," in: *Jahrbuch für Jugend- und Volksspiele* 3 (1894): 170.
46 Among his many publications are: *Bericht über die Gesundheitsverhältnisse der Stadt Braunschweig in den Jahren 1864 bis 1873 und die Cholera daselbst in den Jahren 1850 und 1855*, Braunschweig: Waisenhaus-Buchdruckerei, 1877; "Das Wasser als Nahrungsmittel und eine Vorrichtung, schlechtes Wasser zu verbessern," in: *Monatsblatt für öffentliche Gesundheitspflege* 1 (1878): 30–35; "Zur Beseitigung der Abfallstoffe," in: *Monatsblatt für öffentliche Gesundheitspflege* 1 (1878): 113–18. For a complete list see: Blasius, "Friedrich Reck," 130–31.
47 Blakeslee, "How To Make A Foreign Idea Your Own," 53.
48 Blakeslee, "How To Make A Foreign Idea Your Own," 53–54. See also: Mason, *Passion of the People?*
49 Blakeslee, "How To Make A Foreign Idea Your Own," 57–61.
50 Hartmann Wunderer, *Arbeitervereine und Arbeiterparteien: Kultur- und Massenorganisationen in der Arbeiterbewegung (1890–1933)*, Frankfurt am Main and New York: Campus Verlag 1980; Thomas Adam, *Arbeitermilieu und Arbeiterbewegung in Leipzig 1871–1933*, Cologne, Weimar, Vienna: Böhlau, 1999; Franz Nitsch and Lorenz Pfeiffer (eds.), *Die Roten Turnbrüder: 100 Jahre Arbeitersport*, Marburg: Schüren Presseverlag, 1995.
51 Jens Fuge, *Ein Jahrhundert Leipziger Fußball. Die Jahre 1883–1945*, Leipzig: Connewitzer Verlagsbuchhandlung, 1996, 7–9; Horst Sachse, *Fußball in und um Leipzig. Von den Anfängen bis 1945*, Leipzig: Leipziger Universitätsverlag, 2000, 10–12; Oberschelp, *Der Fußball-Lehrer*, 101–14; Koch, *Die Geschichte des Fußballs*, 42.

52 Koch, *Die Geschichte des Fußballs*, 46; Hoffmeister, *Der Wegbereiter des Fußballspiels in Deutschland*, 83–86.
53 Adam, *Arbeitermilieu und Arbeiterbewegung in Leipzig*, 122–30.
54 Adam, *Arbeitermilieu und Arbeiterbewegung in Leipzig*, 128–29.
55 Adam, *Arbeitermilieu und Arbeiterbewegung in Leipzig*, p. 131; Thomas Adam, "Sport und Politik in einer deutschen Grossstadt. Sozialdemokratischer und konservativer Fußball in Leipzig vom Kaiserreich bis zur nationalsozialistischen Machtergreifung," in: Thomas Höpel and Steffen Sammler (eds.), *Kulturpolitik und Stadtkultur in Leipzig und Lyon (18. – 20. Jahrhundert)*, Leipzig: Leipziger Universitätsverlag, 2004, 275–92.
56 This spatial concept is based upon Saunier, *Transnational History*, 58–79.

Bibliography

Primary Sources

Blasius, Wilhelm. "Friedrich Reck. Nekrolog". *5. Jahresbericht des Vereins für Naturwissenschaft zu Braunschweig für das Vereinsjahr 1886 bis 1887*. Braunschweig: Friedrich Vieweg und Sohn, 1887: 126–31.

Escuela de Campeopnes. Directed by Ralph Pappier (1950).

Der Ganz Grosse Traum. Directed by Sebastian Grobler (2011).

Hermann, August. "Ergänzende und berichtigende Bemerkungen." *Zeitschrift für Turnen und Jugendspiel* 4 (1895): 132–33.

Hillebrand, Karl. *Aus und über England*. Berlin: Robert Oppenheim, 1876.

Hughes, Thomas. *Tom Brown's Schuljahre. Von einem alten Rugby-Jungen. Zur Darlegung des gegenwärtigen Standes der Erziehung in den oberen Classen Englands*. Nach dem Englischen des "Th. Hughes," bearbeitet von Dr. Ernst Wagner. Gotha: Justus Perthes, 1867.

Koch, Konrad. *Fußball. Regeln des Fußball-Vereins der mittleren Classen des Martino-Catharineums zu Braunschweig*. Braunschweig: D. Haering, 1875.

Koch, Konrad. "August Friedrich Reck, Dr. med." *Braunschweiger Tageblatt*, November 9, 1878.

Koch, Konrad. *Die Geschichte des Fußballs im Altertum und in der Neuzeit*. Münster: LIT Verlag, 1983.

Rat der Stadt Braunschweig, ed. *Braunschweig*. Berlin: Deutscher Architektur- und Industrieverlag, 1921.

The Laws of Football as Played at Rugby School. Rugby: Crossley and Billington, 1862.

Voigt, J. A. *Mittheilungen über das Unterrichtswesen Englands und Schottlands*. Halle: Eduard Anton, 1857.

Wagner, Ernst. *Das Volksschulwesen in England und seine neueste Entwicklung*. Verlag der J. B. Metzler'schen Buchhandlung, 1864.

Wiese, Ludwig Adolf. *Deutsche Briefe über Englische Erziehung* 2 vols. Berlin: Wiegandt und Grieben, 1852.

Woikowsky-Biedau, Viktor von. "Über den Stand des Jugend- und Volksspiels in Deutschland 1892–1893." *Jahrbuch für Jugend- und Volksspiele* 3 (1894): 164–206.

Secondary Sources

Adam, Thomas. *Intercultural Transfers and the Making of the Modern World, 1800–2000*. New York: Palgrave Macmillan, 2012.

Adam, Thomas. *Arbeitermilieu und Arbeiterbewegung in Leipzig 1871–1933*. Cologne, Weimar, Vienna: Böhlau Verlag, 1999.
Adam, Thomas. "New Ways to Write the History of Western Europe and the United States: The Concept of Intercultural Transfer." *History Compass* 11, 10 (2013): 880–92.
Adam, Thomas. "Sport und Politik in einer deutschen Grossstadt. Sozialdemokratischer und konservativer Fußball in Leipzig vom Kaiserreich bis zur nationalsozialistischen Machtergreifung." In: *Kulturpolitik und Stadtkultur in Leipzig und Lyon (18. – 20. Jahrhundert)*. edited by Thomas Höpel and Steffen Sammler, Leipzig: Leipziger Universitätsverlag, 2004, 275–92.
Anderson, Benedict. *Imagined Communities: Reflections on the Origin and Spread of Nationalism*. London: Verso, 2006.
Archetti, Eduardo P. "Argentinien." In: *Fußball, soccer, calcio: Ein englischer Sport auf seinem Weg um die Welt*, edited by Christiane Eisenberg. Munich: Deutscher Taschenbuch Verlag, 1997, 149–70.
Blakeslee, Brandon. "How to Make a Foreign Idea Your Own: Argentine Identity and the Role Soccer Played in Its Formation." (MA thesis, The University of Texas at Arlington, 2014).
Broschkowski, Michael, and Thomas Schneider. *"Fußlümmelei" Als Fußball noch ein Spiel war*. Berlin: Transit, 2005.
Caldas, Waldenyr. "Brasilien." In: *Fußball, soccer, calcio: Ein englischer Sport auf seinem Weg um die Welt*, edited by Christiane Eisenberg. Munich: Deutscher Taschenbuch Verlag 1997, 171–84.
Clavin, Patricia. "Defining Transnationalism." *Contemporary European History* 14, 4 (2005): 421–39.
Curry, Graham. "Football: A Study in Diffusion." (D.Phil. thesis, University of Leicester 2001).
Damm, Folko. *Auf dem Weg zum Volkssport: Einführung und Verbreitung des Fußballs in Deutschland*. Norderstedt: GRIN Verlag 2007.
Dunning, Eric, and Kenneth Sheard. *Barbarians, Gentlemen, and Players, Second Edition: A Sociological Study of the Development of Rugby Football*. London: Routledge, 2005.
Eisenberg, Christiane, ed. *Fußball, soccer, calcio: Ein englischer Sport auf seinem Weg um die Welt*. Munich: Deutscher Taschenbuch Verlag, 1997.
Eisenberg, Christiane. *"English Sports" und deutsche Bürger: Eine Gesellschaftsgeschichte 1800–1939*. Paderborn: Schöningh, 1999.
Elias, Norbert. "The Social Constraint towards Self-Constraint." In: *Norbert Elias: Civilization, Power, and Knowledge*, edited by Stephen Mennell and Johan Goudsblom. Chicago: University of Chicago Press, 1998, 49–66.
Fuge, Jens. *Ein Jahrhundert Leipziger Fußball. Die Jahre 1883–1945*. Leipzig: Connewitzer Verlagsbuchhandlung, 1996.
Heineken, Ph. *Das Fußballspiel. Association und Rugby*. Hannover: Th. Schäfer, 1993.
Hesse-Lichtenberger, Ulrich. *Tor! The Story of German Football*. London: WSC Books, 2003.
Hill, John S., John Vincent, and Matthew Curtner-Smith. "The Worldwide Diffusion of Football: Temporal and Spatial Perspectives." *Global Sport Business Journal* 2, 2 (2014): 1–27.
Hobsbawm, Eric J. *Nations and Nationalism since 1780: Programme, Myth, Reality*. 2nd ed. Cambridge: Cambridge University Press, 1992.
Hoffmeister, Kurt. *Zeitreise durch die Braunschweiger Sportgeschichte*. Braunschweig: Books on Demand, 2010.

Hoffmeister, Kurt. *Der Wegbereiter des Fußballspiels in Deutschland: Prof. Dr. Konrad Koch 1846–1911. Eine Biographie.* Braunschweig: Books on Demad GmbH, 2011.

Hopf, Wilhelm. "Wie der Fußball nach Deutschland kam." In: *Die Geschichte des Fußballs im Altertum und in der Neuzeit* by Konrad Koch, edited by Wilhelm Hopf, 49–53. Münster: LIT Verlag, 1983, 49–53.

Kroes, Rob. "American Empire and Cultural Imperialism: A View from the Receiving End." In: *Rethinking American History in a Global Age*, edited by Thomas Bender. Berkeley: University of California Press, 2002, 295–313.

Mason, Tony. *Passion of the People? Football in South America.* London: Verso, 1995.

Murphy, Patrick, Ken Sheard, and Ivan Waddington. "Figurational Sociology and its Application to Sport." In: *Handbook of Sports Studies*, edited by Jay Coakley and Eric Dunning. London: Sage, 2000, 92–105.

Nitsch, Franz, and Lorenz Pfeiffer, eds. *Die Roten Turnbrüder: 100 Jahre Arbeitersport.* Marburg: Schüren Presseverlag, 1995.

Oberschelp, Malte. *Der Fußball-Lehrer: Wie Konrad Koch im Kaiserreich den Ball ins Spiel brachte.* Göttingen: Verlag Die Werkstatt, 2010.

Rispler, Isabelle. "'Football is Our Mother': On the Intercultural Transfer of Soccer from Britain to Brazil" (Research Paper, The University of Texas at Arlington, 2012).

Rodgers, Daniel T. *Atlantic Crossings: Social Politics in a Progressive Age.* Cambridge and London: Belknap Press of Harvard University Press, 1998.

Rogers, Everett M. *Diffusion of Innovations.* New York: Free Press, 1995.

Sachse, Horst. *Fußball in und um Leipzig. Von den Anfängen bis 1945.* Leipzig: Leipziger Universitätsverlag, 2000.

Saunier, Pierre-Yves. *Transnational History.* New York: Palgrave Macmillan, 2013.

Werner, Michael, and Bénédicte Zimmerman. "Beyond Comparison: Histoire Croisée and the Challenge of Reflexivity." *History and Theory* 45, 1 (2006): 30–50.

Wunderer, Hartmann. *Arbeitervereine und Arbeiterparteien: Kultur- und Massenorganisationen in der Arbeiterbewegung (1890–1933).* Frankfurt am Main: Campus Verlag, 1980.

Young, Christopher, Anke Hilbrenner, and Alan Tomlinson. "European Sport Historiography: Challenges and Opportunities." *Journal of Sport History* 38, 2 (2011): 181–87.

Chapter 5

INTERRELIGIOUS AND INTERCULTURAL TRANSFERS OF THE TRADITION OF PHILANTHROPY

Abstract: This chapter explores the transfer of patterns and institutions of philanthropy among Christianity, Islam, and Judaism in Europe and North America over the last two millennia. The teaching within these three religions provided instructions for philanthropic behavior—*zakat* and *sadaqa* in Arabic, *zedakah* in Hebrew, and philanthropy in English—that resulted in the formation of philanthropic institutions of the *waqf* in Islam, the *heqdesh* in Judaism, and the *foundation* in Christianity. These three institutions of philanthropy share significant communalities. And it is these communalities that have caused scholars to consider the possibility that these institutions did not emerge in isolation but from interreligious and intercultural transfer processes. This chapter, further, discusses the transformations of philanthropy within Christianity that were caused by the Protestant Reformation as well as the introduction of the voluntary association within Judaism and its appropriation by Christian women in the context of the Napoleonic Wars at the beginning of the nineteenth century.

This chapter was first published in *Charity in Jewish, Christian, and Islamic Traditions*, edited by Julia R. Lieberman and Michal Jan Rozbicki, Lanham, Boulder, New York, London: Lexington Books, 2017, 45–65.

Introduction

Scholars of religion and scholars of philanthropy agree that the tradition of philanthropy has been intrinsic to most of the world's cultures and religions. And while the giving and sharing of excess funds with individuals beyond the circle of family and friends might have been caused by a variety of motives, which were grounded in empathy and religion as well as in the desire to secure a particular social status, philanthropy appears to have been an anthropological condition that defines humanity and is as old as human civilization itself.[1] Our modern academic system with its high level of national specialization in the humanities and social sciences, however, appears to be ill-equipped to research a universal and complex phenomenon such as philanthropy. Researchers working on *waqfs* in the Islamic tradition and researchers working on the tradition of foundations in the Christian tradition rarely communicate with each other, and if specialists from these distinct fields meet in the same room for a conference, they often employ a different terminology that hides connections and common characteristics rather than revealing them.

The attempt made by Warren Ilchman, Stanley Katz, and Edward L. Queen to bring together scholars from different cultural and religious traditions is certainly a big step forward and helps us grasp the global and universal dimension of philanthropy.[2] Yet, even such projects result only in the presentation of case studies, in which each case from philanthropy in Judaism to philanthropy in Buddhism is presented independently of each other without exploring the connections between different religious contexts. Most scholars have failed to engage accounts of philanthropic traditions beyond their own specialized field that is defined by national borders rather than by the phenomenon under investigation.[3]

This state of affairs resulted from the institutional shortcomings of American universities and academic culture. Scholars are trained in national and regional fields rather than in the study of a (global) phenomenon. Graduate students are forced to settle for a field that is nationally and linguistically determined. The outcome is narrowly defined dissertations that focus on one limb of philanthropic activity that has been artificially cut off from the global and universal body of philanthropy. However, without studying the entire body of philanthropy, we will not be able to ascertain the particulars of philanthropy in a specific national, regional, or local context. Philanthropy is a phenomenon that simply cannot be forced into the straitjacket of the national paradigm since it lived from cross-cultural and cross-religious contacts and transfers.

American scholars are, further, misguided by the belief that philanthropy is a fundamentally American phenomenon that went hand in hand with the growth and expansion of civil society and democracy.⁴ Such a flawed paradigm severely hinders scholars to explore philanthropy in nondemocratic and authoritarian settings. A global focus reveals that philanthropy and democracy were not connected by a causal relationship, that the growth of American philanthropy occurred at the same time as that country democratized appears to have been a coincidence. The enormous growth of philanthropy in nineteenth-century Europe and North America was caused by the enormous accumulation of wealth created by the Industrial Revolution. This Industrial Revolution affected democratic and authoritarian states equally. Philanthropy, subsequently, flourished in both democratic and authoritarian systems and stabilized both types of political domination.⁵

This chapter will explore philanthropy not within the confines of any given nation or a given religion, but rather in its totality as a global and universal phenomenon of the Atlantic and Mediterranean world over the course of the last millennium. I seek to overcome the limitations of case studies as well as the limited value of comparative studies and instead employ the approach of intercultural transfer studies with their focus on the excavation of the hidden connections and transfers between cultures and societies. It will become clear to the reader that philanthropic institutions and practices in both branches of Christianity (Catholicism and Protestantism), Islam, and Judaism were not just similar, but that they were in fact related to and build upon each other because of the manifold contacts between these religions.⁶ To this end, this chapter discusses four zones of contact and zones of transition between these four religions: I will, first, discuss the creation of the *waqf* in relation to Christian precedents and the influence of the *waqf* on the emergence of Western European charitable trusts. Second, I will explore the transformation of charity in the context of the Protestant Reformation in sixteenth-century continental Europe. Third, I will discuss the emergence of female voluntary associations within Jewish culture and the appropriation of Jewish women's organized philanthropy by Christian women in the age of the Napoleonic Wars. Fourth, I will discuss the competition between Christian and Jewish donors for participation and dominance in urban philanthropy of the Western World at the end of the nineteenth century. Before I can begin my discussion of the intercultural transfers of philanthropy between Catholicism, Islam, Judaism, and Protestantism, it seems necessary to briefly introduce the concept of intercultural transfer.

The Concept of Intercultural Transfer

History as a discipline has been inextricably linked to the emergence of nation states and the construction of national identities. Since the inception of history as an academic discipline, history has been taught and written as national history. History has been linked to the project of the nation since it provided legitimacy to the nations constructed in the course of the nineteenth century. Nineteenth- and twentieth-century historians connected the modern nation with primordial people, thereby creating a genealogical lineage for nations such as the German, French, and English nation. By identifying historical predecessor who roamed the European forests millennia earlier, history also established claims to territory, since linkage to a certain group of people was identified with ownership of territory. Elusive battles such as the Battle in the Teutoburg Forrest became the focal point for national identities.[7]

In the process of creating national histories, historians were charged with identifying the characteristics that separated their national stories from others. History was driven by the search for uniqueness and authenticity. Connections and exchanges were considered signs of weakness and inferiority and, therefore, written out of history. This approach resulted in the creation of isolated narratives about cultures and societies with underlying claims of superiority over neighboring nations. The French nation appeared superior because of its revolution, the German nation, by contrast, claimed superiority because of the absence of a "bloody" revolution.[8]

The approach of intercultural transfer studies offers a nonnationalist and universal approach to the study of history. It is based upon the belief in an interconnected world. In this interconnected world, nothing developed in isolation. Even the most isolated system was still affected by movements and influences that originated far beyond its borders. The task of intercultural transfer studies is to discover the webs that connected phenomena in different cultures and the processes of transfer between these cultures.[9]

Intercultural Transfer Studies is a subfield of transnational history and contributes to the project of denationalizing, deterritorializing, and destating history.[10] It focuses on the processes by which a phenomenon became a global phenomenon that created its own space. This space is defined by the circulation of an idea rather than by political or geographical borders. This approach is grounded in cultural history and deals with the activities of individuals (agents of intercultural transfer) who act as citizens and not as agents of states or governments. The transfer of objects from one culture to another is directed by the receiving rather than the giving society. Caused by a feeling (not a reality) of inferiority and experiencing a gap, a receiving society selects an object presented by another society and individuals from the receiving society organize the transfer and integration of this idea into their society. The objects transferred always undergo mutations in the process. Nothing remains unchanged.[11]

The concept of intercultural transfers should not be confused with outdated concepts of diffusion such as Americanization.[12] Such concepts were based upon the faulty assumption that the transfer of American products and culture into other cultures makes these cultures more similar, yet, while other cultures might accept American products, they always reinvent them and develop their own language to refer to these objects. "American icons," as Rob Kroes has so keenly observed, "may have become the staple of a visual lingua franca that is understood anywhere in the world, yet their use can no longer be dictated solely from America."[13] The notion of Americanization can simply not explain the conundrum of the modern world: that the world becomes more similar and more different at the same time. The concept of intercultural transfer, by contrast, can make sense of these contradictory processes. Ideas and products are transformed in the process of transfer and made to fit into the receiving system. These ideas, thus, are global in reach but particular in their local expression.

The Shape of Philanthropy in Islam, Judaism, and Christianity: *Waqf*, *Heqdesh*, and Foundation

The claim that philanthropy is a universal anthropological phenomenon is rather uncontroversial since we find notions of obligation to help those in need in all major cultures, religions, and languages. Arabic, Hebrew, and English have terms that denote the provision of support for those in need. There is the concept of *zakat* and *sadaqa* in Arabic: *zakat* refers to obligatory alms and *sadaqa* refers to charity and philanthropy. In Hebrew, the term *zedakah* denotes the traditional Jewish community-oriented practice of philanthropy (the support of the poor to become self-sustaining). English knows the terms of charity and philanthropy. These obligations resulted over time in the creation of the institution of the *waqf*, *heqdesh*, and the foundation. All three institutional forms of philanthropy were based upon the donation of property and funds for charitable purposes. The existence of these notions and terms in different languages and cultures suggests for some scholars that the tradition of philanthropy in Judaism, Islam, Catholicism, and Protestantism were in fact related and resulted from frequent and intensive contacts between these religions.

Many scholars have noted that the institution of the *waqf*, *heqdesh*, and of the foundation (*piae causae*) show remarkable similarities.[14] (1) These three institutions were founded through the relinquishing of property by an individual who dedicated these properties to a particular purpose. The purposes included religious purposes and the funding of public services from social welfare to education. (2) With the act of the donation, the owner relinquished control over the institution that he created. (3) The institution created was put under the administration of a trustee selected by the donor. (4) Only the proceeds of the transferred property were to be used to realize the mission of this institution. The principle capital had to remain untouched. (5) These institutions were dedicated to God and envisioned as surviving the death of the founder.

The *waqf* and the pious foundation shared a further similarity. Both institutions provided the opportunity to limit the circle of beneficiaries to the descendants of the donor. The *waqf* and the foundations could come in two forms. The *waqf* could take the shape of the *waqf khairi*, which was a charitable foundation defined by its purpose or the service to be provided, or the *waqf ahli*, which was a family foundation, in which all proceeds of the property were to be provided to the descendants of the donor. The foundation could similarly either take the form of the charitable foundation, which provided social welfare to the poor, or the *fidei commissum*, in which the creator secured the transfer of property from one generation to subsequent generations. Through this institution that had been developed in Roman law descendants received only the use of the property but not its ownership. The *waqf ahli* and the *fidei commissum*, thus, shared significant similarities. In both institutions, "the founder designated property to relatives for a fixed period, or until their extinction, and nothing was given to the beneficiaries from the property other than beneficial use," and the principal property or fund could never be sold, given as a gift or inherited.[15]

Because of these similarities, scholars have suggested that these three institutions of philanthropy were in fact related and build upon each other. The institution of the *waqf*, as Timur Kuran pointed out,

> did not have to be developed from scratch because various ancient peoples—Persians, Egyptians, Turks, Jews, Byzantines, Romans, and others—had developed similar structures. Just as Islam itself did not emerge in a historical vacuum, so the first founders of Islamic trusts and the jurists who shaped the pertinent regulations almost certainly drew inspiration from models already present around them.[16]

Because *waqf* and *piae causae* shared so many similarities, scholars such as John Robert Barnes argued that the *waqf* emerged from the institution of the *piae causae*. Barnes suggested in his *Introduction to Religious Foundations in the Ottoman Empire* that was published in 1986 that *waqf* were built upon the model of the *piae causae* that had emerged during the fourth century in the Byzantine Empire. With the expansion of the Islamic Empire into the territories of the Byzantine Empire, Islamic society incorporated local practices and legal traditions. This merger resulted in the creation of the institution of the *waqf* from Byzantine precedents.[17]

While this explanation about the Byzantine Christian influence on the *waqf* might have been true for the *waqf khairi*, there was no precedent for the *waqf ahli* in Byzantine tradition. The *waqf ahli* might have been, by contrast, influenced by the *fidei commissum* developed in Roman law.[18] Barnes' argument is, as his critics noted, based upon logical reasoning and the belief that cultures develop through contacts, but not supported by direct literary evidence.[19] It is, therefore, not a surprise that Barnes' interpretation met with harsh criticism. Peter C. Hennigan warned, for instance, that we cannot deduce causation from correlation.[20] Also Claude Cahen reminded us that the *piae causae* could not have served as a model for the *waqf* because the Byzantine influence was restricted to Egypt and the existing *piae causae* in Egypt were abolished by Islamic rulers in the twelfth century and replaced with *waqfs*. These *waqfs* were based, according to Cahen, upon "ancient *waqf* in Arabia untouched by outside influence."[21]

Since the *waqf* shared many characteristics not only with the *piae causae* but also with the *heqdesh*, some scholars suggested that the formation of the *waqf* might have been influenced by this Jewish institution. There is, for Hennigan, no doubt that a transfer between Islamic and Jewish culture occurred, however, the evidence available proves only the influence of *waqfs* on *heqdesh* but not the other way around. Jewish documents about foundations in twelfth-century Cairo use the terminology of *waqf* rather than of *heqdesh*.[22]

While the suggestion that Christian and Jewish institutions had some influence on the emergence of the institution of the *waqf* were met with significant criticism, Sassanian influences in the creation of the *waqf* met with very little opposition.[23] The existence of two types of trusts—one for public purposes and one for private purposes—caused scholars to consider the Sassanian trust as a model for the creation of the *waqf khairi* and the *waqf ahli*. Hennigan contended that of "all the claims for the foreign origins of the *waqf*, the claim of Sassanian influence seems the most compelling."[24]

Scholars have also passionately discussed the influence of the *waqf* on the creation of the Christian and Western European institutions of the foundation and the charitable trust. Ann Van Wynen Thomas suggested in 1949 that

> it is not an idle contention to assume that the leaders of the Crusades against the Muhammadan world ... noted every branch and aspect of social and commercial relations of the infidels whom they attempted to conquer, and brought back to Western Europe, and particularly to England, at least a rudimentary knowledge of trusts, which they proceeded to apply and develop according to their own needs.[25]

Most scholars seem to agree that the creation of charitable trusts in England took off in the time of the Crusades. Such trusts were established by those Christian men who left for Palestine. To secure the well-being of their family and children, crusaders committed for the time of their absence and the possibility that they would not return their "property to a trustee to be kept for his children, the Franciscan Friars in England, or for other purposes."[26] The intensive cultural contact between Islam and Christianity in the time of the Crusades, as well as the striking similarities between the *waqf* and the charitable trust, caused scholars such as Henry Cattan to suggest that the English charitable trust was built upon the Islamic *waqf*.[27]

About thirty years later, George Makdisi expanded this argument by looking into the emergence of the modern university in Western Europe. Makdisi noted remarkable similarities between Islamic colleges and the first colleges in Paris and Oxford, which were based upon charitable bequests. The University College at Oxford was, for instance, founded in 1249 with a bequest made by William of Durham. These bequests were, according to Makdisi, different from earlier charitable foundations in the Byzantine and Roman tradition since they were not given to a previously existing legal person, but served to create a new legal person. This new type of foundation was, as Makdisi established, as alien to Roman law as it was to Byzantine law, but it was in fact "the only kind of foundation known to Islam."[28] Also, Monica Gaudiosi came in her study of the founding of Merton College at Oxford by Walter de Merton in 1274 to the conclusion that if the founding documents were "written in Arabic rather than Latin, the statutes could surely be accepted as a *waqf* instrument."[29] Monica Gaudiosi and Murat Çizakça, further, suggested that the Western European world, which had "lost all contact with the ancient world ... had to become acquainted with philanthropic endowments through the Islamic *waqf* system."[30] The English charitable trust, thus, appears to Cattan, Makdisi, and Gaudiosi as the result of intercultural and interreligious transfer that was probably facilitated by Franciscan Friars and a result of cultural contacts between Islam and Christianity in the times of the Crusades.

The discussion of the mutual influences in the emergence of the *waqf*, the *heqdesh*, and the charitable trust are overshadowed by the scholarly desire to establish originality and authenticity. Foreign influences in the formation of the *waqf*, the *heqdesh*, and the charitable trust seem, in the eyes of the scholars involved in these debates, to devalue these institutions. Mutual influence is perceived as a threat to diversity and independence of cultures and religions. Too many scholars prefer to believe that mutual influences were not essential to explaining the emergence of similar institutions in three different cultures. Norman Calder and Rudolph Peters, for instance, suggested in their legal studies "that it is not unusual for different societies to reach similar legal solutions to similar problems."[31] In addition, Gabriel Baer summarized the skeptical position with regards to transfers between Islam and Christianity that charity is such an elementary idea "that it is not surprising to find it in different legal system."[32]

Scholars should not confuse mutual influences and intercultural transfers with dependency and lack of originality. The suggestion that the creation of the *waqf* was based upon earlier institutions in other cultures does not suggest that the *waqf*, because of these influences, is somehow of lesser value. While the institution of the *waqf* was shaped through cultural contacts and the integration of "foreign" influences, it was still "sufficiently different from each of its pre-Islamic forerunners to be considered a distinctly Islamic tradition."[33] Nothing in world history developed in isolation. This includes the creation of many European institutions including charitable institutions. Cultural contacts occurred in contact zones and are often hard to prove because of the lack of documentation and because of the desire of the protagonists to hide such influences. Yet, coincidences are only coincidences if they are marginal and exceptional. When we have a large number of similarities among institutions of charity in cultures that were in constant contact, it is hard to believe that they did not share experiences and ideas. Peter Hennigan, who seemed to be quite skeptical of the suggestion that the *waqf* and the foundation developed in a process of mutual influences, suggested a composite theory in which what he calls "unconscious borrowing" might have occurred. The spread of Islam across North Africa and the Near East brought people and cultures with different backgrounds and diverse traditions into one empire. Roman, Byzantine, Persian, and Jewish legal traditions merged into one Islamic tradition that produced the *waqf* from local legal cultures.[34] If Hennigan's composite theory explains the emergence of the *waqf*, it could also explain the emergence of the charitable trust in Christian Western Europe. It seems to have emerged on the basis of Roman, Byzantine, and Islamic traditions in the same way in which the Islamic *waqf* emerged from local traditions of the territories that were integrated into the Islamic Empire. It is particularly interesting to note that both Christian and Islamic tradition share the idea that the circle of beneficiaries of foundations can be limited to the descendants of the donor.

The Transfer of the Philanthropic Tradition from Catholicism to Protestantism

Charitable trusts in continental Western and Central Europe grew quickly in number and in the land and property they owned. These trusts were, strictly speaking, endowments given to the Catholic Church, which was after all not just a recognized religious community but also a legal body, for their administration.³⁵ It has been estimated that between ten and thirty-three percent of all land in continental Western and Central Europe was, as a result, controlled by the church. Within the Holy Roman Empire, about 50 percent of all land was, at the eve of the Protestant Reformation, in the hands of the church.³⁶ Most authors overlook, however, that the church was not the only institution entrusted with charitable trusts (endowments). In the course of the fourteenth century, cities and universities increasingly became trustees of endowments created by individual burghers and noblemen, and *fidei commissum* (family foundations) became a popular tool of securing the socioeconomic position of noble families.³⁷

The Protestant Reformation challenged the established notion of charity and its institutionalized form of charitable trusts and endowments. Martin Luther, Huldrych Zwingli, and John Calvin rejected the Catholic conception of salvation, which suggested that giving for the poor through a bequest could cause God to forgive the donor's sins. Protestant reformers, thereby, challenged the traditional reasoning for creating charitable trusts, which had always been founded upon the concern for one's well-being in the afterlife. The acceptance of Luther's doctrine among many princes in North and Central Europe led to the closing of monasteries and the confiscation of Catholic property by these Protestant rulers. Since endowments given to the Catholic Church had been mixed into the general property of the church institution and, thereby, had become indistinguishable from church property, philanthropy became collateral damage in the expropriation of the Catholic Church. This confiscation of church and philanthropic properties had, however, unforeseen consequences, which in the end forced Luther to reverse his stance on charitable trusts.³⁸

The closing of church institutions in Protestant regions and a general insecurity about the use of a university degree in this rapidly changing society created a culture in which fewer and fewer young men entered college. This was a great concern for Protestant rulers and Luther since it led to a shortage of Protestant pastors and teachers. The significant drop in the college population in the early 1520s, when European universities lost more than two thirds of their students, caused Luther to reverse his opposition to the creation of charitable trusts.³⁹ In 1524, Luther published his famous call to establish schools. In this call, Luther encouraged rich citizens to endow these schools with funds that would offset the tuition required of students.⁴⁰ Luther went even further by urging rulers such as the Great Elector George the Pious of Saxony to use the riches taken from the Catholic Church to create scholarship funds for poor students. The most famous institution created in this context was the *Seminarum Philipinum*.⁴¹ Created by the Count of Hesse Philipp I in 1527, it provided room and board for sixty students of the newly founded University of Marburg. Duke Johann Friedrich of Saxony followed in 1545

Luther's advice to create an endowment with former church property, which was to provide scholarships for 150 young men from Saxony each year.[42]

These new Protestant endowments differed significantly from the Catholic tradition of giving. The creation of endowments was no longer guided by concerns for the afterlife. Charitable trusts were created because of a concern of the donor for his earthly life. Some scholars have interpreted this transition as the beginning of the secularization of philanthropy. While this might be too early, it definitely marked the interreligious transfer of charitable trusts from Catholicism to Lutheranism.[43] Protestant philanthropy differed from Catholic philanthropy with regards to the timing of the donation in the donor's life and with regards to the target of philanthropic support. More and more charitable trusts and endowments were created during the lifetime of the donor. Bequests at the deathbed, as it had been the rule in the Catholic tradition, became rather the exception. From the sixteenth century onward, educational philanthropy experienced a significant growth. High schools and colleges attracted endowments for professorships as well as for scholarship funds, which provided extensive scholarship aid to students in need. One could even speak of a competition in the sphere of educational philanthropy between Protestants and Catholics. Both sides sought to solidify their spheres of influence in society and secure religious control over the territories that were won over by either side.

The most prominent Protestant example was the *Gymansium zum Grauen Kloster* in Berlin (created in 1574). This high school attracted endowments from many alumni who followed in the footsteps of Sigismund Streit. Streit, a rich merchant living in Venice, left in 1760 an endowment that provided funding for teachers' salaries, scholarships for students, and the creation of a dormitory for twelve students. Streit's example caused many more alumni to contribute endowments to this high school. By 1902, the endowments of this high school totaled about one million marks and made it the richest high school in Germany.[44]

The most prominent Catholic example was with the *Gymnasial- und Stiftungsfonds zu Köln*, a centralized group of nearly 300 endowments for Catholic students attending that city's high schools. The first endowment dates back to 1422. It was the endowment of 1800 Gold Gulden provided by the physician Johann Wesebeder for the creation of a fund that was to provide four scholarships to high-school students who attended one of the three *Gymnasiums* of his home town. In the following decades and centuries, many fellow citizens followed Wesebeder's example and created similar endowments that provided tuition scholarships and stipends to students in need. Six endowments were added until 1500. From 1501 to 1600 another 48 were donated. The period from 1601 to 1700 saw the addition of 120 endowments, and in the time from 1701 to 1800, another 45 endowments were added, bringing their total to 220. By 1891, it administered a total of 282 endowments with combined assets of more than seven million marks. These endowments made available scholarship aid of more than 250,000 marks annually. The donors of these endowments decreed that the circle of potential recipients of scholarship aid from these endowments was to be limited to the members of specific Cologne families who had to belong to the Catholic faith. It was the clear intention of these donors to use philanthropy in an effort to prevent the spread of the Lutheran faith in their Catholic region.[45]

Having survived the Protestant Reformation, charitable trusts were under attack again in the period of the Enlightenment. Anne Robert Jacques Turgot, a leading French economist, contributor to the *Encyclopedia*, and minister of finance under Louis XVI, led the charge against charitable trusts which he identified as evil. In his article for the *Encyclopedia* on foundations, Turgot argued that endowments and foundations first created problems which they then promised to address.[46] Charitable trusts for the poor did, for instance, not encourage the poor to overcome poverty. More importantly, foundations were not controlled by the state even though they infringed on the state's authority. Turgot demanded that foundations and endowments be closed and confiscated by the French state. His ideas seem to have contributed to the first law in France that limited the space for philanthropy and charity in 1749. They also influenced the decision to abolish foundations and endowments in 1791 in the course of the French Revolution. The philanthropic property was transferred to the state, thus, making France a society without foundations and trusts but not, as Kathleen D. McCarthy has shown, without voluntary associations.[47]

The Appropriation of Jewish Women's Philanthropic Activities by Christian Women

While Turgot saw endowments and foundations as a danger to the state and society, voluntary associations could, for Turgot, play important roles in society. These associations were, in contrast to foundations, not intended to outlive their founder. They were, further, created not just by one individual but by a group of individuals. They were sporadic and focused on a particular task. Their lifespan was short, in contrast to foundations that were created for eternity, since they were to exist only until they had fulfilled their task.[48]

Associations played from a very early point onward an important role in Jewish charities but not in Christian or Islamic tradition. In Christian tradition, associations entered the stage only in the second half of the eighteenth century before they assumed significant positions in nineteenth-century society.[49] Jewish communities across Europe saw, by contrast, the formation of voluntary associations for the care of the sick and for the burial of their dead already in the fourteenth century. The first sick care associations (*Bikur Holim*) emerged in Spain in the early fourteenth century. These fraternities organized the visitation of the sick, the provision of food and medicine, and they supported the family of the sick person if they fell onto hard times. The *Bikur Holim* society in Perpignan was among the first such association that emerged in Western Europe.[50]

By the end of the sixteenth century, voluntary sick care associations had become important aspects of Jewish life across Europe.[51] These voluntary associations, which were removed from religious practices that excluded women, offered Jewish women a place in public life. Jewish women entered these sick care associations and even founded their own associations. In Frankfurt am Main, men founded mutual aid associations in 1738 and in 1756. Women followed suit and founded the *Israelite Women's Sick Fund*, their own mutual aid association, in 1761. This fund was basically a health insurance that offered its members a range of services including doctor's visits, care by hired attendants, medicine, and financial support. Between 1745 and 1870, Jewish women in the German lands established more than 160 charitable associations and women directed these associations for decades.[52]

These women's associations in German-Jewish communities were founded, as Benjamin Baader showed for the case of the Jewish community in Grünstadt (Rhineland), following the model of and alongside similar male associations. A female charity association, which offered its members financial benefits and support during sickness, was founded in Grünstadt in May 1860. In case of the death of one of the members, all members participated in sewing the shrouds and ten women were charged with accompanying the coffin to the cemetery. The main difference between this female association and its male model was the involvement of its members in religious practices. The men's association did not only provide sick benefits to its members, it also provided financial support for its members for the period of *shiva* (morning period), and it covered burial costs. The members, further, performed the religious rites for the deceased.[53]

The major difference between these women's and men's Jewish voluntary associations rested with participation in religious rites; however, both male and female voluntary associations understood themselves to be sick-benefit societies, both disbursed charity to other Jews, and both formed the core of associational life within Jewish communities. The Jewish female sick-benefit associations, further, predated by several decades Christian female voluntary associations, which emerged only in the course of the Napoleonic Wars in the shape of patriotic associations. Baader referred to the example of the Jewish and Christian communities of Cassel. The first Jewish men's sick care association of that city was founded in 1773. It was followed by the first Jewish women's sick care association in 1811. The first Christian women's association for the care of the sick was created in 1813.[54]

Christian women associations were created during the Napoleonic Wars to provide poor relief, to take care of wounded soldiers, and to provide support for widows. After the wars, they disbanded. Only in the 1830s did the formation of associations for German Christian women gain momentum again and resulted in the permanent establishment of female benevolent associations.[55] It seems that Jewish women spearheaded the creation of benevolent associations, which in the course of the nineteenth century were dominated by Jewish women from middle- and upper-class backgrounds who sought integration into Christian society. After 1815, benevolent associations spread across the German lands, where they represented about a third of the social welfare institutions. From Europe, the model of the association spread to the United States where benevolent associations and supporting associations began to dominate the provision of philanthropic support for poor relief and sick care.[56]

Contesting Philanthropy between Christian and Jewish Donors

Philanthropy in nineteenth-century Western societies became inextricably linked to exercising power in urban communities. Old and new elites competed for dominance in urban societies and employed philanthropy to achieve control over public institutions. In the case of New York City, it was the old elites of merchants and real estate owners—many of Dutch descent—that dominated public life. They faced a new elite of industrialists whose forefathers had arrived more recently in the United States. The competition for dominance in urban society played out in many fields, from associational life to the building of mansions. Philanthropy developed into a hotly contested field. Members of both factions competed for dominance through the creation of charitable trusts and the founding of museums that were mostly funded through supporting associations. The old elites of New York City were responsible for the founding of the Metropolitan Museum of Art while the new elites supported the founding of the American Museum of Natural History.[57]

The creation of modern urban infrastructures was the result of this competition, which also involved Jewish donors at the end of the nineteenth century; however, in many cities in North America and Western Europe, Jewish donors were not invited or even excluded from participation in urban projects such as hospitals, social housing projects, museums, and even opera houses. Christian donors wanted to remain among themselves and to secure the dominance of Christian (mostly Protestant) domination of society. Recognizing the significance of philanthropy for social recognition, Jewish donors sought to include into the philanthropic projects of their cities. A particularly telling example is the story of Sigmund Samuel (1867–1962) in Toronto. Samuel was one of the richest citizens of Toronto after 1900. He had made his money in the steel business, yet, he was largely excluded from the Protestant establishment of Toronto. Samuel was not invited to join his business partners in the city's exclusive social clubs, which was of course a big problem from a business point of view, and his money was initially not accepted for the big philanthropic projects of Christian Toronto.[58]

Both Jewish and Christian donors recognized the power that came with participation in philanthropy for public institutions. Philanthropic engagement for museums and hospitals provided donors with recognition and integration into the leading circles of society. It also gave donors an opportunity to participate in the shaping of urban society. Jewish donors in the last decades of the nineteenth century recognized the significance of embracing participation in philanthropic projects of the Christian society in which they lived. The concept of donating for urban institutions that were general and open to all (including anti-Semitic donors) was embraced by Jewish donors who strove for social recognition beyond their religious community.

Samuel offered his riches to support the funding of big projects such as the Royal Ontario Museum. For decades, his offers were outright rejected until the Christian "philanthropic establishment" in Toronto run out of money. In 1920, Samuel's offer was finally accepted by a group of Christian philanthropists who had exhausted their financial resources and for whom Samuel's riches offered a guarantee for the success of the museum project. Using this opening, Samuel slowly but continuously expanded the scope of his philanthropic activities from the support of museums and hospitals to the funding of the University of Toronto. Samuel gave during his lifetime more than CAD$ 2 million for the support of various institutions including the Royal Ontario Museum, the University of Toronto, and the Western Hospital of Toronto. For this generosity, he received much criticism from within the Jewish community. The general accusation was that Samuel wasted resources on Christian projects in a city that was deeply anti-Semitic. His money could have been much better spent for purposes within the Jewish community.[59]

This represents the fundamental problem that every Jewish donor in contrast to Christian donors faced: for Christian donors' philanthropic activities occurred always within their religious space, while Jewish donors often went beyond their religious space if they donated money for the construction of a city museum. Jewish donors had to decide whether they wanted to limit their philanthropy to sustain their religious community and, thus, strengthen the isolation of the Jewish community or whether they wanted to donate toward projects of the larger and Christian-dominated society, thus, contributing to the integration of Jewish donors into Christian society.

Giving for central projects of Christian society had its rewards. In 1933, Samuel received for his support for institutions of learning in Toronto an honorary doctoral degree. Such honors highlighted the nature of philanthropy as an exchange of gifts. Donors expected something in return: public recognition not by the institution they supported but by their peers or their prospective peers. While Samuel appreciated the awarding of the doctoral degree by the University of Toronto, it was not the university from which he expected recognition, but rather it was his colleagues, neighbors, friends, and family from whom Samuel hoped to receive gratitude for his philanthropic behavior. After having received the honorary doctoral degree, the businessman Samuel expected, for instance, that everyone, including his family members, address him as Dr. Samuel, and he even felt compelled to produce a monograph—actually a collection of sources—about Canada in the Seven Years War in lieu of a doctoral dissertation. In his public appearances, he made sure to be recognized "as donor and as a holder" of a doctoral degree rather than an industrialist.[60]

The awarding of honorary doctoral degrees to donors was not rare. Christian and Jewish donors received such titles quite frequently. Rudolf Mosse was a prominent German donor who was also awarded a doctoral degree in 1918. The famous publisher and millionaire had made, beginning in 1891, significant donations that included the donation of 120,000 marks in 1891 for the creation of the *Dr. Markus Mosse Hospital in Graetz* (Posen), the donation of 2.5 million marks for the establishment of the *Mosse-Stift* in Berlin-Wilmersdorf, which provided a home for 50 Christian and 50 Jewish children aged 6 to 16, in 1895, and the donation of 1 million mark in 1913 for the creation of the *Pension Fund for the City of Berlin*, which offered pensions of 500 to 1,000 marks annually to individuals who were at least 50 years old and were unable to work. Mosse also provided two endowments to the University of Heidelberg. In 1917, Mosse gave 100,000 marks for an exchange program for law students between the University of Heidelberg and the University of Berlin, and one year later, he donated 400,000 marks for an endowment in the history of law. It was these donations that brought Mosse's philanthropic activities into the spotlight of public attention. After the University of Heidelberg awarded Mosse in 1917 for his extensive career in philanthropy an honorary doctoral degree, anti-Semites such as the professor of medieval studies at Heidelberg University Karl Hampe publicly criticized what he called "the selling of titles to Jews for donations."[61] It is symptomatic of nineteenth-century antisemitism that such accusations were raised only and exclusively when Jewish donors were honored with such titles. The practice of awarding honorary degrees to Christian donors never caused a public backlash. This incident also tells us about the significance that was ascribed to philanthropy in the eyes of Conservative and anti-Semitic critiques. Anti-Semites seemed to have realized the integrative power of such activities and honors.[62]

Conclusion

Traditions of philanthropy are not just universal, they also seem to be interconnected over time, cultures, and religions. Philanthropic institutions such as the *waqf* and the foundation developed through cross-cultural contacts and the integration of traditions from various regions and backgrounds that were transferred between cultures by agents of intercultural transfer who moved between the cultures and religions which produced the *waqf* and the foundation. The same seems to hold true for voluntary associations. Developed within the Jewish communities across Europe for the provision of social welfare service, these associations seemed to have been appropriated by members—and women in particular—of the surrounding Christian culture after 1800. These transfers might have been the result of a direct attempt to transfer an idea from one culture to another, but it could also have been a byproduct of cultural contact and thus unconscious and unintended borrowing. In both cases, the transfers have either not been documented by the individuals involved or such documents have disappeared in the course of history. It might, therefore, be impossible to find conclusive written evidence.

Yet, while scholars require conclusive evidence that would prove that transfers between Islam and Christianity in the creation of the *waqf* and the foundation occurred, the same historians are content with accepting that in spite of so many similarities these institutions could not be related. Most scholars are not even aware of the similarities between these two institutional forms of philanthropy since most scholars are trained to study only one cultural, religious or national space. If scholars look beyond their narrow space of scholarly inquiry, they are unable to see the similarities which are often obscured by language and terminology.

The approaches of transnational history and intercultural transfer studies do not offer us ways to unearth more and better evidence to prove the relatedness between forms and traditions of philanthropy in different religions; they force us, however, to reconsider our perspective. Transnational history is founded upon the belief that human experience and history is interconnected across geographic and political borders. Frequent transfers created networks in which information and ideas flowed freely but not unopposed from one community to another. These communities could be separated by oceans and continents, and yet phenomena in these distant communities could be the result of transfers that have been obscured by the people involved in the transfer and by historians who tended to write transfers out of history since they wrongly assumed that such transfers created relationships of dependency. Yet, transfers of objects did not take away from the significance of an institution or a tradition created within one religious system. The trust, to take just one example, was not a copy of the *waqf* but an institution that was probably inspired by the *waqf* and which subsequently developed into an institution in its own right. Intercultural transfers have always served to enrich cultures and religions instead of impoverishing them.

Notes

1 Warren F. Ilchman, Stanley N. Katz, and Edward L. Queen II, "Introduction," in: Warren F. Ilchman, Stanley N. Katz, and Edward L. Queen II (eds.), *Philanthropy in the World's Traditions*, Bloomington: Indiana University Press, 1998, ix–xv.
2 Ilchman/Katz/Queen, *Philanthropy in the World's Traditions*. See also: Michael Borgolte, *Weltgeschichte als Stiftungsgeschichte von 3000 v. u. Z. bis 1500 u. Z.*, Darmstadt: Wissenschaftliche Buchgesellschaft 2017; Michael Borgolte (ed.), *Enzyklopädie des Stiftungswesens in mittelalterlichen Gesellschaften* 3 volumes, Berlin and Boston: De Gruyter, 2014–2017; Michael Borgolte, *Stiftungen in Christentum, Judentum und Islam vor der Moderne: Auf der Suche nach ihren Gemeinsamkeiten und Unterschieden in religiösen Grundlagen, praktischen Zwecken und historischen Transformationen*, Berlin: Akademie Verlag, 2005; Rainer Liedtke and Klaus Weber (eds.), *Religion und Philanthropie in den europäischen Zivilgesellschaften: Entwicklungen im 19. und 20. Jahrhundert*, Paderborn: Ferdinand Schöningh, 2009; Sitta von Reden (ed.), *Stiftungen zwischen Politik und Wirtschaft: Geschichte und Gegenwart im Dialog (Historische Zeitschrift* Beiheft 66), Oldenbourg: De Gruyter, 2015.
3 Recent examples include David C. Hammack and Helmut K. Anheier, *A Versatile American Institution: The Changing Ideals and Realities of Philanthropic Foundations*, Washington D.C.: Brookings Institution Press, 2013; Lawrence J. Friedman and Mark D. McGarvie (eds.), *Charity, Philanthropy, and Civility in American History*, Cambridge: Cambridge University Press, 2003. See also, Thomas Adam (ed.), *Philanthropy, Patronage, and Civil Society: Experiences from Germany, Great Britain, and North America*, Bloomington: Indiana University Press, 2004.
4 Robert D. Putnam, *Bowling Alone: The Collapse and Revival of American Community*, New York: Simon and Schuster, 2000; Friedman/McGarvie, *Charity, Philanthropy, and Civility in American History*.
5 Thomas Adam, *Philanthropy, Civil, Society, and the State in German History, 1815–1989*, Rochester: Camden House, 2016; Thomas Adam, "Stiften und Stiftungen im deutsch-amerikanischen Vergleich von 1815 bis 1945," in: Reden, *Stiftungen zwischen Politik und Wirtschaft*, 23–50.
6 Jerry H. Bentley, *Old Worlds Encounters: Cross-Cultural Contacts and Exchanges in Pre-Modern Times*, New York: Oxford University Press, 1993.
7 Benedict Anderson, *Imagined Communities: Reflections on the Origins and Spread of Nationalism*, London: Verso, 2006, 5–7; Eric J. Hobsbawn, *Nations and Nationalism Since 1780: Programme, Myth, Reality*, Second Edition, Cambridge: Cambridge University Press, 1992, 14–45.

8   Stefan Berger, "The German Tradition of Historiography, 1800–1995," in: Mary Fulbrook (ed.), *German History since 1800*, London: Arnold, 1997, 477–92.
9   Clifford Geertz, *The Interpretation of Cultures*, New York: Basic Books, 1973, 3–30; Daniel T. Rodgers, *Atlantic Crossings: Social Politics in a Progressive Age*, Cambridge and London: The Belknap Press of Harvard University Press, 1998, 1–7; Thomas Adam, *Intercultural Transfers and the Making of the Modern World, 1800–2000: Sources and Context*, New York: Palgrave Macmillan, 2012.
10 Thomas Adam "New Ways to Write the History of Western Europe and the United States: The Concept of Intercultural Transfer," in: *History Compass* 11, 10 (2013): 880–92; Pierre-Yves Saunier, *Transnational History*, New York: Palgrave Macmillan, 2013.
11 Adam, *Intercultural Transfers*, 1–7; Rodgers, *Atlantic Crossings*, 5.
12 For the concept of diffusion see for instance: Everett M. Rogers, *Diffusion of Innovations*, New York: The Free Press, 1995.
13 Rob Kroes, "American Empire and Cultural Imperialism: A View from the Receiving End," in: Thomas Bender (ed.), *Rethinking American History in a Global Age*, Berkeley: University of California Press, 2002, 310.
14 The following discussion about the relationship between *waqf*, *heqdesh*, and foundation is inspired by Peter C. Hennigan, *The Birth of a Legal Institution: The Formation of the Waqf in Third-Century A.H. Hanafī Legal Discourse*, Leiden: Brill, 2004, 51–70.
15 Hennigan, *The Birth of a Legal Institution*, 55–56; Gabriel Baer, "The Muslim *Waqf* and Similar Institutions in Other Civilizations," in: Borgolte, *Stiftungen in Christentum, Judentum und Islam vor der Moderne*, 264. See also, Amy Singer, *Charity in Islamic Societies*, Cambridge: Cambridge University, 2008; Engin Isin and Ebru Üstündağ, "Wills, Deeds, Acts: Women's Civic Gift-Giving in Ottoman Istanbul," in: *Gender, Place & Culture: A Journal of Feminist Geography* 15, 5 (2008): 519–32.
16 Timur Kuran, "The Provision of Public Goods under Islamic Law: Origins, Impact, and Limitations of the Waqf System," in: *Law & Society Review* 35 (2001): 848.
17 John Robert Barnes, *An Introduction to Religious Foundations in the Ottoman Empire*, Leiden: Brill, 1986, 16.
18 Alfred Söllner, "Zur Rechtsgeschichte des Familienfideikommisses," in: Dieter Medicus and Hans Hermann Seiler (eds.), *Festschrift für Max Kaser zum 70. Geburtstag*, Munich: C. H. Becksche Verlagsbuchhandlung, 1976, 657–69; Jörn Eckert, *Der Kampf um die Familienfideikommisse in Deutschland: Studie zum Absterben eines Rechtsinstitutues*, Frankfurt am Main: Peter Lang, 1992.
19 Barnes, *An Introduction to Religious Foundations*, 16.
20 Hennigan, *The Birth of a Legal Institution*, 53.
21 Baer, "The Muslim Waqf and Similar Institutions in Other Civilizations," 261; Hennigan, *The Birth of a Legal Institution*, 55, 63–64.
22 Hennigan, *The Birth of a Legal Institution*, 57–58. See also, Mark R. Cohen, "Foundations and Charity in the Jewish Community of Medieval Egypt," in Borgolte, *Stiftungen in Christentum, Judentum und Islam*, 179–89; Yom Tov Assis, "Welfare And Mutual Aid in the Spanish Jewish Communities," in: Haim Beinart (ed.), *Moreshet Sepharad: The Sephardi Legacy* vol. 1, Jerusalem: The Magnes Press/The Hebrew University, 1992, 318–23.
23 Hennigan, *The Birth of a Legal Institution*, 59–61; Murat Çizakça, *A History of Philanthropic Foundations: The Islamic World from the Seventh Century to the Present*, Istanbul: Boğaziçi University Press, 2000, 5; Said Amir Arjomand, "Philanthropy, the Law, and Public Policy in the Islamic World before the Modern Era," in Ilchman/Katz/Queen,

Philanthropy in the World's Traditions, 110–12; Maria Macuch, "Die sasanidische Stiftung 'für die Seele'—Vorbild für den islamischen waqf?" in: Petr Vavroušk (ed.), *Iranian and Indo-European Studies: Memorial Volume of Otakar Klíma*, Praha: Enigma Corporation, 1994, 163–80.

24 Hennigan, *The Birth of a Legal Institution*, 60.
25 Ann Van Wynen Thomas, "Note on the Origin of Uses and Trusts—Waqfs," in: *Southwestern Law Journal* 3, 2 (1949): 166.
26 Baer, "The Muslim *Waqf* and Similar Institutions in Other Civilizations," 265.
27 Baer, "The Muslim *Waqf* and Similar Institutions in Other Civilizations," 266; Henry Cattan, "The Law of Waqf," in: Majid Khadduri and Herbert J. Liebesny (eds.), *Law in the Middle East: Origin and Development of Islamic Law* volume 1, Washington D.C.: The Middle East Institute, 1955, 213. See also: William F. Fratcher, "Trust," in: *International Encyclopedia of Comparative Law* vol. 6: *Property and Trust*, Tübingen: J.C.B. Mohr (Paul Siebeck), 1973, 1–120.
28 George Makdisi, *The Rise of Colleges: Institutions of Learning in Islam and the West*, Edinburgh: Edinburgh University Press, 1981, 227.
29 Monica M. Gaudiosi, "The Influence of the Islamic Law of Waqf on the Development of the Trust in England," in: *University of Pennsylvania Law Review* 136 (1988): 1254–55.
30 Çizakça, *A History of Philanthropic Foundations*, 8; Gaudiosi, "The Influence of the Islamic Law of Waqf on the Development of the Trust in England," 1231–61.
31 Hennigan, *The Birth of a Legal Institution*, 62.
32 Baer, "The Muslim Waqf and Similar Institutions in Other Civilizations," 267.
33 Kuran, "The Provision of Public Goods under Islamic Law," 848.
34 Hennigan, *The Birth of a Legal Institution*, 66–70; Barnes, *An Introduction to Religious Foundations in the Ottoman Empire*, 5–20.
35 Michael Borgolte, "Planen für die Ewigkeit—Stiftungen im Mittelalter," in: *Geschichte in Wissenschaft und Unterricht* 63, 1–2 (2012): 37–49; Michael Borgolte, "Die Stiftungen des Mittelalters in rechts- und sozialhistorischer Sicht," in: *Zeitschrift der Savigny-Stiftung für Rechtsgeschichte* Kanonistische Abteilung 74 (1988): 71–94.
36 Baer, "The Muslim Waqf and Similar Institutions in Other Civilizations," 262.
37 See for instance for the University of Tübingen and the City of Leipzig as administrator of endowments: Volker Schäfer, "'Zur Beförderung der Ehre Gottes und Fortpflanzung der Studien': Bürgerliche Studienstiftungen an der Universität Tübingen zwischen 1477 und 1750," in: Erich Maschke and Jürgen Sydow (eds.), *Stadt und Universität im Mittelalter und in der früheren Neuzeit*, Sigmaringen: Jan Thorbecke Verlag, 1977, 99–111; Heinrich Geffcken and Hayim Tykocinski, *Stiftungsbuch der Stadt Leipzig*, Leipzig: Bär und Hermann, 1905, 3–60.
38 Rupert Graf Strachwitz, *Die Stiftung—ein Paradox? Zur Legitimität von Stiftungen in einer politischen Ordnung*, Stuttgart: Lucius & Lucius, 2010, 48–50.
39 Bernhard Ebneth, *Stipendienstiftungen in Nürnberg: Eine historische Studie zum Funktionszusammenhang der Ausbildungsförderung für Studenten am Beispiel einer Großstadt (15. – 20. Jahrhundert)*, Nuremberg: Stadtarchiv Nürnberg, 1994, 48–49; Arno Seifert, "Das höhere Schulwesen: Universitäten und Gymnasien," in: Notker Hammerstein and August Buck (eds.), *Handbuch der deutschen Bildungsgeschichte* vol. 1: *15. bis 17. Jahrhundert: Von der Renaissance und der Reformation bs zum Ende der Glaubenskämpfe*, Munich: Beck, 1996, 256–58.
40 Ebneth, *Stipendienstiftungen in Nürnberg*, 49.

41 Walter Heinemeyer (ed.), *Studium und Stipendium: Untersuchungen zur Geschichte des hessischen Stipendiatenwesens*, Marburg: Elwert, 1977; Thomas Adam, *Stipendienstiftungen und der Zugang zu höherer Bildung in Deutschland von 1800 bis 1960*, Stuttgart: Franz Steiner Verlag, 2008, 49–51.
42 Ebneth, *Stipendienstiftungen in Nürnberg*, 49–52.
43 Strachwitz, *Die Stiftung—ein Paradox?* 48.
44 Thomas Adam, "Der unverzichtbare Beitrag von Stiftungen zur Finanzierung des höheren Schulwesens in Preußen im 19. Jahrhundert," in: *Paedagogica Historica* 48, 3 (2012): 456–57.
45 Adam, "Der unverzichtbare Beitrag," 459–61.
46 The article is translated and printed in: *The Life and Writings of Turgot Comptroller-General of France 1774–6* edited for English Readers by W. Walker Stephens, London: Longmans, Green, and Co., 1895, 219–28.
47 Strachwitz, *Die Stiftung—ein Paradox?* 54–65; Kathleen D. McCarthy, "Frauen im Spannungsfeld von Religion, Philanthropie und Öffentlichkeit, 1790–1860," in: Thomas Adam, Simone Lässig, and Gabriele Lingelbach (eds.), *Stifter, Spender und Mäzene: USA und Deutschand im historischen Vergleich*, Stuttgart: Franz Steiner Verlag, 2009, 30–33.
48 Strachwitz, *Die Stiftung—ein Paradox?* 59, 62.
49 Stefan-Ludwig Hoffmann, *Civil Society, 1750–1914*, New York: Palgrave MacMillan, 2006.
50 Assis, "Welfare And Mutual Aid in the Spanish Jewish Communities," 323–38.
51 See for instance: Tirtsah Levie Bernfeld, *Poverty and Welfare Among the Portuguese Jews in Early Modern Amsterdam*, Oxford: The Littman Library of Jewish Civilization, 2012; Julia R. Lieberman, "Adolescence and the Period of Apprenticeship among the Western Sephardim in the Seventeenth Century," in: *El Prezente: Studies in Sephardic Culture* 4 (2010): 11–23; David B. Ruderman, "The Founding of a Gemilut Hasadim Society in Ferrara in 1515," in: *AJS Review* 1 (1976): 233–67; Maria Benjamin Baader, "Rabbinic Study, Self-Improvement, and Philanthropy: Gender and the Refashioning of Jewish Voluntary Associations in Germany, 1750–1870," in: Adam, *Philanthropy, Patronage, and Civil Society*, 163–67; Benjamin Maria Baader, *Gender, Judaism, and Bourgeois Culture in Germany, 1800–1870*, Bloomington: Indiana University Press, 2006, 161–67.
52 Baader, *Gender, Judaism, and Bourgeois Culture in Germany*, 160, 167; Baader, "Rabbinic Study, Self-Improvement, and Philanthropy," 168.
53 Baader, *Gender, Judaism, and Bourgeois Culture in Germany*, 168–69; Baader, "Rabbinic Study, Self-Improvement, and Philanthropy," 168.
54 Baader, *Gender, Judaism, and Bourgeois Culture in Germany*, 171.
55 Jean H. Quataert, *Staging Philanthropy: Patriotic Women and the National Imagination in Dynastic Germany, 1813–1916*, Ann Arbor: The University of Michigan Press, 2001.
56 Quataert, *Staging Philanthropy*, 21–53; McCarthy, "Frauen im Spannungsfeld von Religion, Philanthropie und Öffentlichkeit"; Thomas Adam, *Buying Respectability: Philanthropy and Urban Society in Transnational Perspective, 1840s to 1930s*, Bloomington: Indiana University Press, 2009, 126–52.
57 Adam, *Buying Respectability*, 102–7.
58 Adam, *Buying Respectability*, 164–79.
59 Adam, *Buying Respectability*, 171–77.
60 Adam, *Buying Respectability*, 177–78. Sigmund Samuel, *The Seven Year's War in Canada, 1756–1763: Being a Volume of Records and Illustrations Together with a Pictorial Travelogue*

Showing the Stage of Development Which America Had Reached Seventy Years after the Seven Years' War, Toronto: Ryerson Press, 1934.
61 Karl Hampe, *Kriegstagebuch 1914–1919*, edited by Folker Reichert and Eike Wolgast, Munich: Oldenbourg Verlag, 2004, 631–32.
62 Elisabeth Kraus, *Die Familie Mosse: Deutsch-jüdisches Bürgertum im 19. und 20. Jahrhundert*, Munich: C. H. Beck, 1999, 400–52; Karl Hampe, *Kriegstagebuch*, 631–32.

Bibliography

Adam, Thomas. *Philanthropy, Civil, Society, and the State in German History, 1815–1989*. Rochester: Camden House, 2016.
Adam, Thomas. *Intercultural Transfers and the Making of the Modern World, 1800–2000*. New York: Palgrave Macmillan, 2011.
Adam, Thomas. *Buying Respectability: Philanthropy and Urban Society in Transnational Perspective, 1840s to 1930s*. Bloomington and Indianapolis: Indiana University Press, 2009.
Adam, Thomas. *Stipendienstiftungen und der Zugang zu höherer Bildung in Deutschland von 1800 bis 1960*. Stuttgart: Franz Steiner Verlag, 2008.
Adam, Thomas, ed. *Philanthropy, Patronage, and Civil Society: Experiences from Germany, Great Britain, and North America*. Bloomington: Indiana University Press, 2004.
Adam, Thomas. "Stiften und Stiftungen im deutsch-amerikanischen Vergleich von 1815 bis 1945." In: *Stiftungen zwischen Politik und Wirtschaft: Geschichte und Gegenwart im Dialog (Historische Zeitschrift Beiheft 66)*, edited by Sitta von Reden. Oldenbourg: De Gruyter, 2015, 23–50.
Adam, Thomas. "New Ways to Write the History of Western Europe and the United States: The Concept of Intercultural Transfer." *History Compass* 11, 10 (2013): 880–92.
Adam, Thomas. "Der unverzichtbare Beitrag von Stiftungen zur Finanzierung des höheren Schulwesens in Preußen im 19. Jahrhundert." *Paedagogica Historica* 48, 3 (2012): 451–68.
Anderson, Benedict. *Imagined Communities: Reflections on the Origins and Spread of Nationalism*. London: Verso, 2006.
Arjomand, Said Amir. "Philanthropy, the Law, and Public Policy in the Islamic World before the Modern Era." In: *Philanthropy in the World's Traditions*, edited by Warren F. Ilchman, Stanley N. Katz, and Edward L. Queen II. Bloomington: Indiana University Press, 1998, 109–32.
Assis, Yom Tov. "Welfare and Mutual Aid in the Spanish Jewish Communities." In: *Moreshet Sepharad: The Sephardi Legacy* volume 1, edited by Haim Beinart. Jerusalem: The Magnes Press/The Hebrew University, 1992, 318–23.
Baader, Benjamin Maria. *Gender, Judaism, and Bourgeois Culture in Germany, 1800–1870*. Bloomington: Indiana University Press, 2006.
Baader, Maria Benjamin. "Rabbinic Study, Self-Improvement, and Philanthropy: Gender and the Refashioning of Jewish Voluntary Associations in Germany, 1750–1870." In: *Philanthropy, Patronage, and Civil Society: Experiences from Germany, Great Britain, and North America*, edited by Thomas Adam. Bloomington: Indiana University Press, 2004, 163–78.
Baer, Gabriel. "The Muslim *Waqf* and Similar Institutions in Other Civilizations." In: *Stiftungen in Christentum, Judentum und Islam vor der Moderne: Auf der Suche nach ihren Gemeinsamkeiten und Unterschieden in religiösen Grundlagen, praktischen Zwecken und historischen Transformationen*, edited by Michael Borgolte. Berlin: Akademie Verlag, 2005, 257–80.

Barnes, John Robert. *An Introduction to Religious Foundations in the Ottoman Empire*. Leiden: Brill, 1986.
Bentley, Jerry H. *Old Worlds Encounters: Cross-Cultural Contacts and Exchanges in Pre-Modern Times*. New York: Oxford University Press, 1993.
Berger, Stefan. "The German Tradition of Historiography, 1800–1995." In: *German History since 1800*, edited by Mary Fulbrook. London: Arnold, 1997, 477–92.
Bernfeld, Tirtsah Levie. *Poverty and Welfare Among the Portuguese Jews in Early Modern Amsterdam*. Oxford: The Littman Library of Jewish Civilization, 2012.
Borgolte, Michael. *Weltgeschichte als Stiftungsgeschichte von 3000 v. u. Z. bis 1500 u. Z*. Darmstadt: Wissenschaftliche Buchgesellschaft, 2017.
Borgolte, Michael, ed. *Enzyklopädie des Stiftungswesens in mittelalterlichen Gesellschaften* 3 volumes. Berlin and Boston: De Gruyter, 2014–2017.
Borgolte, Michael. *Stiftungen in Christentum, Judentum und Islam vor der Moderne: Auf der Suche nach ihren Gemeinsamkeiten und Unterschieden in religiösen Grundlagen, praktischen Zwecken und historischen Transformationen*. Berlin: Akademie Verlag, 2005.
Borgolte, Michael. "Planen für die Ewigkeit—Stiftungen im Mittelalter." *Geschichte in Wissenschaft und Unterricht* 63, 1–2 (2012): 37–49.
Borgolte, Michael. "Die Stiftungen des Mittelalters in rechts- und sozialhistorischer Sicht." *Zeitschrift der Savigny-Stiftung für Rechtsgeschichte* Kanonistische Abteilung Abt. 74 (1988): 71–94.
Cattan, Henry. "The Law of Waqf." In: *Law in the Middle East: Origin and Development of Islamic Law* volume 1, edited by Majid Khadduri and Herbert J. Liebesny. Washington D.C.: The Middle East Institute, 1955, 203–22.
Çizakça, Murat. *A History of Philanthropic Foundations: The Islamic World from the Seventh Century to the Present*. Istanbul: Boğaziçi University Press, 2000.
Cohen, Mark R. "Foundations and Charity in the Jewish Community of Medieval Egypt." In: *Stiftungen in Christentum, Judentum und Islam vor der Moderne: Auf der Suche nach ihren Gemeinsamkeiten und Unterschieden in religiösen Grundlagen, praktischen Zwecken und historischen Transformationen*, edited by Michael Borgolte. Berlin: Akademie Verlag, 2005, 179–89.
Ebneth, Bernhard. *Stipendienstiftungen in Nürnberg: Eine historische Studie zum Funktionszusammenhang der Ausbildungsförderung für Studenten am Beispiel einer Großstadt (15. – 20. Jahrhundert)*. Nuremberg: Stadtarchiv Nürnberg, 1994.
Eckert, Jörn. *Der Kampf um die Familienfideikommisse in Deutschland: Studie zum Absterben eines Rechtsinstitutues*. Frankfurt am Main: Peter Lang, 1992.
Fratcher, William F. "Trust." In: *International Encyclopedia of Comparative Law* volume vi: *Property and Trust*. Tübingen: J.C.B. Mohr (Paul Siebeck), 1973, 1–120.
Friedman, Lawrence J. and Mark D. McGarvie, eds. *Charity, Philanthropy, and Civility in American History*. Cambridge: Cambridge University Press, 2003.
Gaudiosi, Monica M. "The Influence of the Islamic Law of Waqf on the Development of the Trust in England." *University of Pennsylvania Law Review* 136 (1988): 1231–61.
Geertz, Clifford. *The Interpretation of Cultures*. New York: Basic Books, 1973.
Geffcken, Heinrich and Hayim Tykocinski. *Stiftungsbuch der Stadt Leipzig*. Leipzig: Bär und Hermann, 1905.
Hammack, David C. and Helmut K. Anheier. *A Versatile American Institution: The Changing Ideals and Realities of Philanthropic Foundations*. Washington D.C.: Brookings Institution Press, 2013.
Hampe, Karl. *Kriegstagebuch 1914–1919*, edited by Folker Reichert and Eike Wolgast. Munich: Oldenbourg Verlag, 2004.

Heinemeyer, Walter, ed. *Studium und Stipendium: Untersuchungen zur Geschichte des hessischen Stipendiatenwesens.* Marburg: Elwert, 1977.

Hennigan, Peter C. *The Birth of a Legal Institution: The Formation of the Waqf in Third-Century A.H. Hanafī Legal Discourse.* Leiden: Brill, 2004.

Hobsbawm, Eric J. *Nations and Nationalism Since 1780: Programme, Myth, Reality*, Second Edition. Cambridge: Cambridge University Press, 1992.

Hoffmann, Stefan-Ludwig. *Civil Society, 1750–1914.* New York: Palgrave MacMillan, 2006.

Ilchman, Warren F., Stanley N. Katz, and Edward L. Queen II. "Introduction." In: *Philanthropy in the World's Traditions*, edited by Warren F. Ilchman, Stanley N. Katz, and Edward L. Queen II. Bloomington: Indiana University Press, 1998, ix–xv.

Isin, Engin and Ebru Üstündağ. "Wills, Deeds, Acts: Women's Civic Gift-giving in Ottoman Istanbul." *Gender, Place & Culture: A Journal of Feminist Geography* 15, 5 (2008): 519–32.

Kraus, Elisabeth. *Die Familie Mosse: Deutsch-jüdisches Bürgertum im 19. und 20. Jahrhundert.* Munich: C. H. Beck, 1999.

Kroes, Rob. "American Empire and Cultural Imperialism: A View from the Receiving End." In: *Rethinking American History in a Global Age*, edited by Thomas Bender. Berkeley/Los Angeles/London: University of California Press, 2002, 295–313.

Kuran, Timur. "The Provision of Public Goods under Islamic Law: Origins, Impact, and Limitations of the Waqf System." *Law & Society Review* 35, 4 (2001): 841–98.

Lieberman, Julia R. "Adolescence and the Period of Apprenticeship among the Western Sephardim in the Seventeenth Century." *El Prezente: Studies in Sephardic Culture* 4 (2010): 11–23.

Liedtke, Rainer and Klaus Weber, eds. *Religion und Philanthropie in den europäischen Zivilgesellsc haften: Entwicklungen im 19. und 20. Jahrhundert.* Paderborn: Ferdinand Schöningh, 2009.

The Life and Writings of Turgot Comptroller-General of France 1774–6 edited for English Readers by W. Walker Stephens. London: Longmans, Green, and Co., 1895.

Macuch, Maria. "Die sasanidische Stiftung 'für die Seele'—Vorbild für den islamischen waqf?" In: *Iranian and Indo-European Studies: Memorial Volume of Otakar Klíma*, edited by Petr Vavroušk. Praha: Enigma Corporation, 1994, 163–80.

Makdisi, George. *The Rise of Colleges: Institutions of Learning in Islam and the West.* Edinburgh: Edinburgh University Press, 1981.

McCarthy, Kathleen D. "Frauen im Spannungsfeld von Religion, Philanthropie und Öffentlichkeit, 1790–1860." In: *Stifter, Spender und Mäzene: USA und Deutschand im historischen Vergleich*, edited by Thomas Adam, Simone Lässig, and Gabriele Lingelbach. Stuttgart: Franz Steiner Verlag, 2009, 17–40.

Putnam, Robert D. *Bowling Alone: The Collapse and Revival of American Community.* New York: Simon and Schuster, 2000.

Quataert, Jean H. *Staging Philanthropy: Patriotic Women and the National Imagination in Dynastic Germany, 1813–1916.* Ann Arbor: The University of Michigan Press, 2001.

Reden, Sitta von, ed. *Stiftungen zwischen Politik und Wirtschaft: Geschichte und Gegenwart im Dialog* (*Historische Zeitschrift* Beiheft 66). Oldenbourg: De Gruyter, 2015.

Rodgers, Daniel T. *Atlantic Crossings: Social Politics in a Progressive Age.* Cambridge and London: The Belknap Press of Harvard University Press, 1998.

Rogers, Everett M. *Diffusion of Innovations.* New York: The Free Press, 1995.

Ruderman, David B. "The Founding of a Gemilut Hasadim Society in Ferrara in 1515." *AJS Review* 1 (1976): 233–67.

Samuel, Sigmund. *The Seven Year's War in Canada, 1756–1763: Being a Volume of Records and Illustrations Together with a Pictorial Travelogue Showing the Stage of Development Which America Had Reached Seventy Years after the Seven Years' War*. Toronto: Ryerson Press, 1934.

Saunier, Pierre-Yves. *Transnational History*. New York: Palgrave Macmillan, 2013.

Schäfer, Volker. "'Zur Beförderung der Ehre Gottes und Fortpflanzung der Studien': Bürgerliche Studienstiftungen an der Universität Tübingen zwischen 1477 und 1750." In: *Stadt und Universität im Mittelalter und in der früheren Neuzeit*, edited by Erich Maschke and Jürgen Sydow. Sigmaringen: Jan Thorbecke Verlag, 1977, 99–111.

Seifert, Arno. "Das höhere Schulwesen: Universitäten und Gymnasien." In: *Handbuch der deutschen Bildungsgeschichte* volume 1: *15. bis 17. Jahrhundert: Von der Renaissance und der Reformation bs zum Ende der Glaubenskämpfe*, edited by Notker Hammerstein and August Buck. Munich: Beck, 1996, 197–345.

Singer, Amy. *Charity in Islamic Societies*. Cambridge: Cambridge University, 2008.

Söllner, Alfred. "Zur Rechtsgeschichte des Familienfideikommisses." In: *Festschrift für Max Kaser zum 70. Geburtstag*, edited by Dieter Medicus and Hans Hermann Seiler. Munich: C. H. Becksche Verlagsbuchhandlung, 1976, 657–69.

Strachwitz, Rupert Graf. *Die Stiftung—ein Paradox? Zur Legitimität von Stiftungen in einer politischen Ordnung*. Stuttgart: Lucius & Lucius, 2010.

Thomas, Ann Van Wynen. "Note on the Origin of Uses and Trusts—Waqfs." *Southwestern Law Journal* 3, 2 (1949): 162–66.

Chapter 6

CHANGE THROUGH NON-VIOLENCE: THE RATIONALIZATION OF CONFLICT SOLUTION

Abstract: This chapter explores the development of Gandhi's concept of non-violent resistance first against racial discrimination in South Africa and then against the British oppression of Indians' desire for self-government in India. This idea did not evolve in a vacuum, rather Gandhi was influenced by several thinkers including Leo Tolstoy and John Ruskin. From India, this idea spread across the globe and influenced movements in Europe, North and South America, and Asia. The experience of World War I provided for an opening in European societies for the concept of non-violent resistance in the 1920s and 1930s. The experience of trench warfare had called into doubt claims about European superiority and the notion of progress in general. In this context, Gandhi's non-violent resistance captivated European and North American audiences. The German theologian Dietrich Bonhoeffer actively sought an invitation from Gandhi and hoped to find ideas for the renewal of Christianity in Gandhi's teachings. After World War II and in the context of the Cold War, Gandhi's non-violent strategy attracted attention on a global scale. Faced with the possibility of nuclear war, social and political change in individual countries required non-violent rather than violent strategies. Both the civil rights fight of African-Americans and of Mexican-American farm workers for a fair and humane treatment in the United States was infused with the ideas of Gandhism. Martin Luther King, Jr. and César Chávez embraced Gandhi's strategy in the pursuit of gaining equality. In the last two decades of the twentieth century, non-violent movements across the globe challenged and toppled authoritarian governments and systems including the Communist dictatorships of Eastern Europe.

This chapter was first published in Thomas Adam, *Intercultural Transfers and the Making of the Modern World, 1800–2000: Sources and Context*, Palgrave Macmillan, 2012, 111–35. This text has been modified by the addition of endnotes.

The Birth of Satyagraha

Mohandas Karamchand Gandhi's exposure to racial discrimination in South Africa marked a turning point in his life and set him on his path to develop non-violent means of resistance to European domination. After he had completed his training as a lawyer in London, Gandhi accepted in 1893 out of financial necessity a position as a legal counsel to Indian Muslim traders and merchants in South Africa. Just one week after his arrival, Gandhi took a train ride from Durban to Pretoria on legal business. He bought a ticket for the first-class car and, dressed in his European suit, he entered the appropriate train compartment. When, during the trip, a white passenger took offense at the presence of a colored passenger in first class, Gandhi was thrown of the train and left at an unpleasant train station for the night. This encounter made Gandhi realize that in the British Empire racial discrimination affected even the well-off and well-trained members of the colonial elite. The outrage he felt during this cold night at the empty train station in the middle of nowhere was the starting point for his resolution to find means and ways to fight racial discrimination.[1]

In his search for ideas and concepts Gandhi was deeply influenced by two European writers: Leo Tolstoy and John Ruskin. Gandhi was in particular intrigued by Tolstoy's book *The Kingdom of God Is Within You* (1894) and Ruskin's *Unto This Last*.[2] While the first book introduced Gandhi to the supposition that there is never justification for violence, the second book's call for a simpler life of labor caused Gandhi to found an ashram (a self-sufficient communal settlement). Gandhi further received inspiration from Henry David Thoreau's essay *Civil Disobedience* (1849) and Thoreau's refusal to pay taxes to a government that engaged in policies he fundamentally opposed.[3] Through the readings of these texts, his Hindu beliefs, Christian influences, and the experience of racism in South Africa, Gandhi developed his concepts of ahimsa and Satyagraha. The Sanskrit "ahimsa" refers to non-harm, non-injury, or non-violence. It symbolizes an approach to solving conflicts peacefully and renouncing violence in favor of love and justice. "Satyagraha" is Gandhi's way of resisting an oppressive force not by destroying the enemy but by attempting to win him over. The goal is not to destroy the enemy but to solve the conflict.[4] It reflects a desire to overcome existing rifts and fault lines in society by creating a harmonious community that provides for the integration of both sides. Satyagraha is grounded in the complete rejection of physical force even in the face of brutal oppression. In practice, Satyagraha calls for non-participation in the institutions and practices of the opponent. Boycotts, strikes, marches, sit-ins are prominent means of non-violent resistance. It would be wrong to see Gandhi's strategy as "passive resistance" since it includes active acts such as marching and protesting as well as passive acts such as non-participation and refusal to obey. Non-violent resistance clearly challenges the established order by ignoring that order.[5] In his book *Satyagraha in South Africa* Gandhi distinguished Satyagraha from passive resistance and elaborated upon the differences. He wrote:

> I have no idea as to when the phrase "passive resistance" was first used in English and by whom. But among the English people, whenever a small minority did not approve of some obnoxious piece of legislation, instead of rising in rebellion they took the passive or milder step of not submitting to the law and inviting the penalties of such non-submission upon their heads. When the British Parliament passed the Education Act some years ago, the Non-conformists offered passive resistance under the leadership of Dr. Clifford. The greatest movement of the English women for the vote was also known as passive resistance. It was in view of these two cases that Mr. Hosken described passive resistance as a weapon of the weak or the voteless. Dr. Clifford and his friends had the vote, but as they were in a minority in the Parliament they could not help the passage of the Education Act. That is to say, they were weak in numbers. Not that they were averse to the use of arms for the attainment of their aims, but they had no hope of succeeding by force of arms. And in a well-regulated state, recourse to arms every now and then in order to secure popular rights would defeat its own purpose. Again some of the Non-conformists would generally object to taking up arms even if it was a practical proposition. The suffragists had no franchise rights. They were also weak in numbers as well as in physical force. Thus their case too lent colour to Mr. Hosken's observations. The suffragist movement did not eschew the use of physical force. Some suffragists fired buildings and even assaulted men. I do not think they ever intended to kill any one. But they did intend to thrash people when an opportunity occurred, and even thus to make things hot for them.
>
> But brute force had absolutely no place in the Indian movement in any circumstance, and the reader will see, as we proceed, that no matter how badly they suffered, the Satyagrahis never used physical force, and that too although there were occasions when they were in a position to use it effectively. Again, although the Indians had no franchise and were weak, these considerations had nothing to do with the organisation of Satyagraha. This is not to say, that the Indians would have taken to Satyagraha even if they had possessed arms or the franchise. Probably there would not have been any scope for Satyagraha if they had the franchise. If they had arms, the opposite party would have thought twice before antagonising them. One can therefore, understand, that people

who possess arms would have fewer occasions for offering Satyagraha. My point is that I can definitely assert that in planning the Indian movement there never was the slightest thought given to the possibility or otherwise of offering armed resistance. Satyagraha is soul force pure and simple, and whenever and to whatever extent there is room for the use of arms or physical force or brute force, there and to that extent is there so much less possibility for soul force. These are purely antagonistic forces in my view, and I had full realisation of this antagonism even at the time of the advent of Satyagraha.

We will not stop here to consider whether these views are right or wrong. We are only concerned to note the distinction between passive resistance and Satyagraha, and we have seen that there is a great and fundamental difference between the two. If without understanding this, those who call themselves either passive resisters or Satyagrahis believe both to be one and the same thing, there would be injustice to both leading to untoward consequences. The result of our using the phrase "passive resistance" in South Africa was, not that people admired us by ascribing to us the bravery and the self-sacrifice of the suffragists but we were mistaken to be a danger to person and property which the suffragists were, and even a generous friend like Mr. Hosken imagined us to be weak. The power of suggestion is such, that a man at last becomes what he believes him self to be. If we continue to believe ourselves and let others believe, that we are weak and helpless and therefore offer passive resistance, our resistance would never make us strong, and at the earliest opportunity we would give up passive resistance as a weapon of the weak. On the other hand if we are Satyagrahis and offer Satyagraha believing ourselves to be strong, two clear consequences result from it. Fostering the idea of strength, we grow stronger and stronger every day. With the increase in our strength, our Satyagraha too becomes more effective and we would never be casting about for an opportunity to give it up. Again, while there is no scope for love in passive resistance, on the other hand not only has hatred no place in Satyagraha but is a positive breach of its ruling principle. While in passive resistance there is a scope for the use of arms when a suitable occasion arrives, in Satyagraha physical force is forbidden even in the most favourable circumstances. Passive resistance is often looked upon as a preparation for the use of force while Satyagraha can never be utilized as such. Passive resistance may be offered side by side with the use of arms. Satyagraha and brute force, being each a negation of the other, can never go together. Satyagraha may be offered to one's nearest and dearest; passive resistance can never be thus offered unless of course they have ceased to be dear and become an object of hatred to us. In passive resistance there is always present an idea of harassing the other party and there is a simultaneous readiness to undergo any hard ships entailed upon us by such activity; while in Satyagraha there is not the remotest idea of injuring the opponent. Satyagraha postulates the conquest of the adversary by suffering in one's own person.[6]

The discussion of the Black Act in summer 1906 provided the context for the development of Gandhi's concept of non-violent resistance and its very first test. The South African government was concerned with the increase in African immigration to its territory. In his desire to keep South Africa a "white man's country," General Jan Christiaan Smuts, the leading minister of the government, called for the registration of all Indians, Arabs, and Turks (Asiatics) who were older than eight years. The law further required the fingerprinting of all Asiatics and involved personal inspections to identify specific body marks. At that time there were about 13,000 Indians living in Transvaal. Failure to submit to registration would have resulted in expelling that person from South Africa. Gandhi took center stage in the Indian's refusal to comply with these new policies. At a meeting of Indian community representatives in September 1906, the assembled men discussed the new laws and the best ways to respond to them. They firmly supported a resolution that called on all Indians not to submit to this new regulation if it should become law. To prevent the South African government from implementing this new law, Gandhi went to London, where he won the support of the British government and the promise that the law would not be enacted. However, when the South African government was granted extended autonomy in 1907 it went ahead and enacted the law. The ensuring campaign of civil disobedience against the law ended with a compromise between Gandhi and Smuts according to which the Black Act was rescinded in exchange for voluntary registration of all Indians. Although the opposition against registration remained strong among Indians, Gandhi was among the first to register. The conflict continued and went beyond the question of registration. New laws declared non-Christian marriages illegal and caused an even stronger response from the Indian population and outrage in Britain and India. Pressure grew on the South African government to find a solution to the conflict. A commission was convened to investigate the grievances of the Indian population and to make suggestions for a solution to this crisis. The Indians' Relief Bill of 1914 alleviated many of the grievances and thus ended the need for public protest.[7]

Coming Home: Gandhi's Salt March

After Gandhi's return to India in 1915, he traveled around the country to reacquaint himself with his home country and abstained from politics for some time. In 1917, he plunged back into politics by visiting Champaran at the request of local tenant farmers who complained about their brutal exploitation by British planters. Gandhi spoke with many tenants and recorded the information he gathered from these encounters. While this was not, at least initially, an act of non-violent protest, it increased Gandhi's standing in Indian society since no other politician showed such a concern for the situation of the poor tenant farmers. With the end of World War I and the plans of the British rulers to continue legislation passed during the war that limited freedoms of speech, association, and the press, Gandhi launched his first mass Satyagraha in India. He asked his fellow subjects to defy the new laws by engaging in a nationwide hartal—a daylong strike that included fasting and prayer. Although many of his countrymen joined in the hartal, it proved premature and unsuccessful. The strike erupted into spontaneous violence and defied Gandhi's calls for non-violent resistance and in the end did not achieve the repealing of the laws. However, Gandhi learned from his "Himalayan miscalculation" that he needed to prepare his fellow countrymen better for non-violent resistance.[8]

Among the many campaigns Gandhi instigated, the Salt March of 1930 became his greatest success and attracted the attention of European and North American intellectuals and civil rights activists. Salt played an important role for food conservation in Indian civilization with its subtropical climate. It also had become a disputed issue between the indigenous population and the British rulers since the introduction of the colonial government's monopoly on the production, sale, and taxation of salt in 1882. Salt was thus seen as a cultural necessity and an instance of colonial exploitation. The 61-year-old Gandhi called in 1930 on his fellow countrymen to make their own salt. To this end, he embarked on a 240-mile walk to the village of Dandi (Gujarat) on the Arabian Sea. When he arrived at the coastline in early April he purposefully broke the law by picking up a muddy salt clump and producing his own salt.[9]

Although the colonial authorities responded by arresting many opponents, they proved incapable of stopping the movement to violate the salt monopoly of the state. The British had to give in and allowed salt production for home use. Gandhi's careful selection of those followers who joined him in his arduous march assured an effective display of non-violent resistance. The brutal force employed by colonial authorities in response to the non-violent resistance of Indians produced moral outrage and galvanized opposition to colonial rule. It further called into question the supposedly higher civilized stage of Europeans in contrast to non-Europeans.

The Appeal of Satyagraha beyond India

Beginning in the 1930s, Gandhi's insistence on non-violent resistance attracted and inspired people around the world. Two books introduced Gandhi to a European and North American audience: Romain Rolland's *Mahatma Gandhi* (1924) and Fredrick B. Fisher's *That Strange Little Brown Man Gandhi* (1932).[10] While Rolland's book was among the earliest—and certainly among the most influential—biographies of Gandhi, it relied exclusively on printed publications. Rolland did not travel to India or met with Gandhi in person. His first meeting with Gandhi occurred seven years after the book's publication, in 1931, at Rolland's home in Switzerland.[11] Fisher, by contrast, considered India his home. He settled in Agra, the city of the Taj Mahal, in 1904 and met with Gandhi for the first time in 1917. From 1920 to 1930, Fisher resided in Calcutta. He described himself as "pro-Indian but not anti-British" and wanted to present in his book the Indian-British conflict through Gandhi's eyes. Even though Fisher did not grasp Gandhi's distinction between non-violent and passive resistance, his attempt at an explanation for the success of Satyagraha is remarkable. In his biography of Gandhi, Fisher wrote:

> The terrible silence of India! I have experienced it. Thousands of soft feet slipping through the warm dust, pliant sandals and slippers making no sound on the pavement. No sound; no voice. You were alone on a street corner of Bombay; then, suddenly you turned your head, and all of India was there at your shoulder. All day long on June 21st, 1930, the crowds of Indians had been gathering against the strict orders of the constabulary that there must be no national meetings or parades. The people had begun coming in the early morning, yet so silent was their approach that before the government knew it, every square yard of the main avenue of Bombay was covered by a vast human sea of bodies.
>
> Silence, absolute, menacing, more terrible than trumpets. It was only when the police put up machine guns on the street corner and threatened the mob if they did not disperse, that India began its march.
>
> "If you come as far as the corner, we will shoot!"
>
> The message was brought to the man heading the parade, by an armed soldier, the clatter of his horse's feet beating defiantly against the menacing quiet.
>
> "We will fire to kill!"
>
> "Very well, fire."

With a sigh of released patience, the crowd began to move slowly, relentlessly, proudly, towards the deadly corner. The leaders held their heads high ... till the rat tat tat of machine guns sent them bowing awkwardly into the dust. The English had fired as they promised.

Still there was little confusion; only the gasps of the wounded and dying, their clumsy twitching in the street. The leaders were gone. Would the crowd march on? Silently, slowly, yet as certainly as an incoming tide that cannot be stemmed, the next in rank stepped over the dead and came towards the guns. Once more the stutter of guns, and the gleam of metal under a blazing sun. More men whirled, fell, coughing blood, clutched helplessly at their bursting stomachs, and

then fell dead. But still the steady stream came on, more and more men, more and more women; stern, implacable, ready to die. It could not be true! but it was. It was a scene out of Dante's hell, imagined, not to be believed.

"I say. This is terrible. We can't do this, Captain!"

It was the young English lieutenant speaking. "Can't we move the guns up to the next corner?"

There was sweat on the Captain's forehead.

"Yes. Move them up. And warn the Indians that if they stop now we will not shoot. But they must not come to the next corner.

The crowd was told ... but it still marched on. Guns were hurried to another corner. Still the crowd swept silently forward. What was to be done? All Bombay could not be slaughtered. "What can we do to get you stop?" the English officer called.

The low voice of the Indian leader stirred the thick layer of Indian silence for the first time.

"So long as you point your guns at us, we will march. Rescind your order against our meeting, take away your guns ... and we will disperse."

"But that would be to surrender!"

"Very well then. We will march till every one of these thousands is dead."

It was India demanding a chance to be heard. The guns were removed, the crowd melted away like magic, lifting up the wounded and burying their dead. But the voice of silent India had been heard on her own street of Bombay.

Such passive resistance methods would not have been successful in the days of Attila the Hun, or even of Jaime, the Spanish conquistador, who only 700 years ago burned his Majorcan heathen captives in Christian oil. The effectiveness of these methods of the Indian passive resisters today depends upon enlightened public opinion, upon the verdict of a modern world which labels wholesale slaughter of unarmed men as belonging to the days of barbarism, rather than to 1932.

Moreover, a new international will to peace had been born from the womb of the World War. In 1919 the whole white world was weary of guns. Hardly a home in England, France, Belgium, Germany, but had its crape upon the door; even America had not escaped unscathed. The years from 1917 to 1919 had been rather a war of muddy endurance than of enthusiastic combat. The gilt edge of battle had been rubbed off and the world was clutching at the safety of peace. At this psychological moment came Gandhi with the first practical plan of gaining national ends through non-violent effort that the world had ever seen.

Fifty years ago such a passive resistance movement would not have created a stir. A year before the World War it would probably not have succeeded. Certainly it would not have attracted such international interest. But now a world which had crawled home to lick its scars, was interested in a constructive method for peace. Almost any plan of peace, for the moment. The will to peace was for the most part planless, diaphanous, oratorical, as polite and aimless as a lecture at a Friday morning women's club. But it was there. Gandhi took this will to peace and shaped it into a practical political weapon.[12]

The experience of trench warfare in World War I, with its devastation of men and nature, provided the context for left-leaning and pacifist European intellectuals to develop enthusiasm for Gandhi's movement. The German theologian Dietrich Bonhoeffer was deeply impressed by Gandhi's teachings and hoped that one day he would be able to visit and study with him.[13] He hoped to find inspiration for a renewal of Christianity and the Christian Church in Germany from a visit with Gandhi. The Nazi takeover of Germany in 1933 and the lack of resistance from the Protestant churches against Nazi intrusion into society and religion caused Bonhoeffer to believe that Western Christianity was in deep trouble. Gandhi and his emphasis on social justice and non-violent resistance attracted Bonhoeffer, who was actively seeking an invitation from Gandhi to live with him in his ashram for some time. While it is not clear when Bonhoeffer first learned about Gandhi, his attraction to Gandhi's ideas was obvious in the early 1930s. In his lecture on the right of self-assertion, which he gave in February 1932 at the Technical University at Berlin, Bonhoeffer contrasted two modes of civilization: (1) the Indian civilization, which was based on self-sufficiency, respect for nature, a reverence for the sacredness of life, and the suppression of violent urges; and (2) the European-American civilization, which was founded on the belief of human superiority over nature, war, and violence. He celebrated Gandhi and his followers for rejecting violence in their struggle for independence from Great Britain and embraced the notion that it is better to suffer than to live in violence. The self-sacrifice of Indians, who marched in the face of British soldiers who shot at them, represented, for Bonhoeffer, the highest form of self-assertion since humans become human only when they are ready to die.[14]

Bonhoeffer convinced his mentor and ecumenical friend Bishop George Bell of Chichester to write a letter of introduction to Gandhi and to seek an official invitation for Bonhoeffer. Bell's letter was well received by Gandhi and resulted in an official invitation.[15] Unfortunately, circumstances did not allow Bonhoeffer to travel to India and fulfill his dream.[16] Friends and colleagues such as Karl Barth and Reinhold Niebuhr, however, felt it was somehow strange for Bonhoeffer to find enlightenment in pagan India and questioned the wisdom of such a desire. Niebuhr in particular remained very skeptical toward Gandhi's concept of non-violent resistance. In his book *Moral Man* (1932), Niebuhr contended that violent resistance is not so different from non-violent resistance:

> The chief distinction in the problem of coercion, usually made by moralists, is that between violent and non-violent coercion. The impossibility of making this distinction absolute has been previously considered. It is nevertheless important to make a more careful analysis of the issues involved in the choice of methods of coercion in the social process. The distinguishing marks of violent coercion and conflict are usually held to be its intent to destroy either life or property. This distinction is correct if consequences are not confused with intent. Non-violent conflict and coercion may also result in the destruction of life or property and they usually do. The difference is that destruction is not the intended but the inevitable consequence of non-violent coercion. The chief difference between violence and non-violence is not in the degree of destruction which they cause, though the difference is usually considerable, but in the aggressive character of the one and the negative character of the other. Non-violence is essentially noncooperation. It expresses itself in the refusal to participate in the ordinary process of society. It may mean the refusal to pay taxes to the government (civil disobedience), or to trade with the social group which is to be coerced (boycott), or to render customary services (strike). While it represents a passive and negative form of resistance, its consequences may be very positive. It certainly places restraints upon the freedom of the objects of its discipline and prevents them from doing what they desire to do. Furthermore it destroys property values, and it may destroy life; though it is not generally as destructive of life as violence. Yet a boycott may rob a whole community of

its livelihood and, if maintained long enough, it will certainly destroy life. A strike may destroy the property values inherent in the industrial process which it brings to a halt, and it may imperil the life of a whole community which depends upon some vital service with which the strike interferes. Nor can it be maintained that it isolates the guilty from the innocent more successfully than violent coercion. The innocent are involved with the guilty in conflicts between groups, not because of any particular type of coercion used in the conflict but by the very group character of the conflict. No community can be disciplined without affecting all its members who are dependent upon, even though they are not responsible for, its policies. The cotton spinners of Lancashire are impoverished by Gandhi's boycott of English cotton, though they can hardly be regarded as the authors of British imperialism. If the League of Nations should use economic sanctions against Japan, or any other nation, workmen who have the least to do with Japanese imperialism would be bound to suffer most from such a discipline.

Non-co-operation, in other words, results in social consequences not totally dissimilar from those of violence.[17]

Niebuhr confused Satyagraha with total passivity and could therefore not grasp the meaning of Gandhi's concept of non-violent resistance. In his *Moral Man*, Niebuhr took the inclusion of physical acts of coercion such as civil disobedience, boycotts, and strikes as evidence for what he called Gandhi's pragmatism and recognition of the limits of non-violent resistance. Based on this misinterpretation of non-violent resistance, Niebuhr concluded that non-violent resistance would not prevent the spread of totalitarianism and could only be successful if the authorities resisted possessed some degree of moral conscience as it was the case with the British colonial rulers in India. Nazi Germany was no such place since the Nazis were amoral.[18]

Bonhoeffer remained undeterred by such warnings and continued to embrace Gandhism for most of the 1930s. Niebuhr's argument that Nazi Germany was no place for non-violent resistance did not convince Bonhoeffer. Like Gandhi, Bonhoeffer expected that the ruling authorities would respond with physical punishment for those who resisted them. Suffering was anticipated and even sought, because only through suffering would it be possible to overcome evil. However, with time Bonhoeffer seemed to have realized that society and morality was contaminated by Nazi ideology and those who opposed Nazism remained a very small minority. His attempts at convincing his fellow citizens that Adolf Hitler's demands for the subordination of all Germans to his will as well as his antisemitism were incompatible with Christianity did not bring the results for which Bonhoeffer had hoped. In contrast to Gandhi's mass movement against colonialism, opposition and resistance against the Nazis remained limited to small groups within German society. By the early 1940s, Bonhoeffer gave up his hopes for non-violent resistance and entered the conspiracy to depose of Hitler.[19] Participation in the plotting of tyrannicide was, however, not an easy decision for Bonhoeffer who sought justification in his writings. The ethics of responsibility was the outcome of Bonhoeffer's internal struggle over this decision. Since murder remains murder, even if it is the killing of a monster such as Hitler, Bonhoeffer came to conclude that individuals have under extraordinary circumstances to accept the possibility that they incur guilt for their actions. Killing Hitler remained a sin, but not killing him might be the greater sin.[20] In his *Ethics*, Bonhoeffer wrote:

> As one who acts responsibly in the historical existence of men Jesus becomes guilty. It must be emphasized that it is solely His love which makes Him incur guilt. From His selfless love, from His freedom from sin, Jesus enters into the guilt of men and takes this guilt upon Himself. Freedom from sin and the question of guilt are inseparable in Him. It is as the one who is without sin that Jesus takes upon Himself the guilt of His brothers, and it is under the burden of this guilt that He shows Himself to be without sin. In this Jesus Christ, who is guilty without sin, lies the origin of every action of responsible deputyship. If it is responsible action, if it is action which is concerned solely and entirely with the other man, if it arises from selfless love for the real man who is our brother, then, precisely because this is so, it cannot wish to shun the fellowship of human guilt. Jesus took upon Himself the guilt of all men, and for that reason every man who acts responsibly becomes guilty. If any man tries to escape guilt in responsibility he detaches himself from the ultimate reality of human existence, and what is more he cuts himself off from the redeeming mystery of Christ's bearing guilt without sin and he has no share in the divine justification which lies upon this event. He sets his own personal innocence above his responsibility for men, and he is blind to the more irredeemable guilt which he incurs precisely in this; he is blind also to the fact that real innocence shows itself precisely in a man's entering into the fellowship of guilt for the sake of other men. Through Jesus Christ it becomes an essential part of responsible action that the man who is without sin loves selflessly and for that reason incurs guilt.[21]

The discussion of guilt and responsible action reflects Bonhoeffer's uneasiness with his involvement in the attempt to kill Hitler. It might be too much to read into Bonhoeffer's decision to abandon nonviolent resistance his surrender to Niebuhr's argument that Nazi Germany was no place for Satyagraha. The problem was not or not only the lack of morality on the side of the Nazis but more importantly the lack of a mass movement to support non-violent resistance against oppression. It was the complacency of the German population that forced Bonhoeffer into violent resistance and into the theological justification of tyrannicide.

The Fate of Non-Violent Resistance in South Africa

Gandhi's non-violent resistance left a deep impression on the oppressed African community in South Africa. The ability to organize large groups of people and the willingness of those protesters to suffer and sacrifice set an example for the leaders of the African National Congress (ANC), who in 1949 embraced non-violence in their fight against the apartheid system. However, as Nelson Mandela pointed out in his autobiography, non-violence was a strategic and pragmatic choice but not a principled one. Manilal Gandhi, the third son of Mahatma Gandhi who was left in charge of Gandhi's work in South Africa after his father's departure for India in 1915, worked hard to convince the ANC leadership to accept non-violence as the only choice for resistance, a principle observed at all cost and in all situations. The ANC leaders, however, were not willing to go that far and considered non-violent action only because the apartheid regime responded with overwhelming force to any challenge of its supremacy. Violent resistance would have been futile. In this context, Gandhi's non-violent resistance became a sign of weakness and was not driven by a desire for reconciliation.[22]

The 1950s and 1960s saw non-violent resistance and some violent acts by the ANC. And although the official stand of the ANC was still non-violence, many of its leaders began to question this strategy. The apartheid system continued ruthlessly to suppress all forms of resistance, whether they were violent or non-violent, and imposed harsh prison sentences on any kind of behavior that could be interpreted as resistance. Nelson Mandela started to doubt that non-violent resistance would accomplish anything in the early 1950s. He saw a difference between the conflict of the indigenous population with a foreign power in India and the conflict of the African population with the European settlers (Afrikaners) in South Africa. For Mandela the British colonial elite in India appeared to be simply more realistic and far-sighted. Mandela raised an interesting point by suggesting that the difference between the Indian and the South African situation rested with the immorality of the opposed system: moral English colonial rulers versus immoral white racists. He suggested that for non-violence to succeed both sides have to respect each other and to consider the other an equal. This was, according to Mandela, obviously not the case in South Africa. However, it is doubtful that the English in India considered the native population their equal. Further, non-violent resistance led to the killing of numerous Indians too. Gandhi, further, did not see such sacrifices as a failure of his movement but accepted these human losses since he believed that they would embarrass those who were responsible for these brutal acts. The success of the perpetrators would be short-lived and immoral. Mandela did not share Gandhi's believe that such atrocities would force the apartheid proponents to reconsider their position.[23]

Mandela's interpretation of events points to another important distinction. The conflict in India occurred between a colonial elite with limited roots in India while the Afrikaners in South Africa had over generations settled in that country and made it their home. After the Sharpeville Massacre of 1960 in which the police killed 69 non-violent protestors, the ANC felt it necessary to change its strategy. Since non-violent resistance was a strategic and not a principled choice for the ANC such a change was not problematic. In the eyes of the ANC leaders, non-violence simply did not seem to accomplish anything. They abandoned Gandhi's non-violence and decided to create an underground violent resistance.[24]

The Reading of Gandhi and the African-American Civil Rights Struggle

The struggle of African-Americans against racism differed fundamentally from the situation encountered by Bonhoeffer in the forms of oppression and the degree of mass mobilization of the oppressed. Gandhism attracted many civil rights activists who, just as much as Bonhoeffer, desired to travel to India and to meet with Gandhi. Among the first to embark on this journey were Benjamin E. Mays and Howard Thurman. Thurman, professor at Howard University, met with Gandhi in 1936, his colleague Mays, who was accompanied by reverend and YMCA representative Channing H. Tobias arrived a year later. Mays and Tobias' interview with Gandhi has been recorded by Mahdev Desai who published Gandhi's answers to the questions of the two Americans in the newspaper *Harijan*.[25] The two Americans told Gandhi that they were deeply influenced by his call for non-violent resistance. They seemed to need, however, reassurance and advice for the continued struggle against racial discrimination in the United States.

In his autobiography, Benjamin E. Mays summarized the content of his 90-minute conversation with Gandhi.[26] From these reflections, it becomes clear that Mays embraced Gandhi's approach of non-violent protest and that he understood that non-violent resistance was not a sign of weakness. Non-violent forms of protest were born out of love and not out of hate. It acknowledged the strength of the opponent, the existing legal system and did not aim at the destruction of one's opponent. Non-violent protest included concern for the welfare of the opponent and rejected calls for revenge and hatred. While both Mays and Tobias were very impressed by Gandhi's belief in non-violent resistance, Mays sought advice for exercising non-violent protest on a large scale. He asked Gandhi about instructions for disciplining the masses so that they would not resort to violence if faced by an oppressive system. Gandhi responded that one could not preach nonviolence to people. The only way to train followers in non-violent behavior was to practice it and, for the leaders of the resistance, to live it as an example.[27] The principle of non-violence was not easy to comprehend by African-Americans who had faced violence repeatedly and were therefore skeptical that they would gain anything by using this tactic. Thurman's wife Sue Thurman, who accompanied her husband on his trip to India in 1936, listened patiently to Gandhi's conversation with her husband for some time. But when Gandhi proclaimed that non-violent resistance would be the only acceptable form of resistance, she asked Gandhi how an African-American was to respond to the lynching of African-Americans by white Americans. Gandhi calmly responded that the answer was to stop cooperating with white Americans. The livelihood even of white Americans depended on African-American participation in all aspects of communal life from production to consumption. The refusal to cooperate with white America provided, in Gandhi's eyes, the greatest weapon to African-Americans in their struggle for equality.[28]

Through Mays, Tobias, and Thurman Gandhism was introduced to the African-American civil rights struggle in the United States. It fell, however, to Mordecai Johnson, who had never met with Gandhi personally since he traveled to India only in late 1949 (Gandhi had been killed in January 1948), to introduce Gandhism to Martin Luther King Jr., In 1950, Johnson, at the time president of Howard University, a predominantly black college in Washington, D.C., spoke about his visit to India, his meetings with Gandhi's disciples, and the concept of non-violent resistance in Philadelphia.[29] In the audience was the 21-year-old Martin Luther King, Jr. This sermon left a lasting impression on King who set out to learn more about Gandhi and his legacy. King went out and bought several books on Gandhi to learn about his technique of Satyagraha. Among the books King bought was Fisher's *That Strange Little Brown Man Gandhi*. Fisher's description of the Salt March of 1930 caught King's eye and stayed in his mind for a long time.[30] However, King's road toward acceptance of non-violent resistance as appropriate for the African-American civil rights struggle was long. He had his doubts that Gandhi's strategies would work in the United States since the situation and circumstances were so different. The British in India were colonial rulers who represented a small minority in a country that did not belong to them. The whites in the United States were no colonial occupiers and represented a majority of the population. King remained skeptical that non-violent protest could transform the relations between the African-American minority and the white majority in his country. It was the continued conversations with non-violent activists such as Bayard Rustin and James Lawson as well as the Montgomery Bus Boycott that convinced King to embrace non-violence.[31]

The Montgomery Bus Boycott, which had been sparked by Rosa Parks' refusal to relinquish her seat to a white passenger on a segregated bus in Montgomery (Alabama) in December 1955, proved to King the power of non-violent means of opposition. Parks' refusal to give up her seat was not motivated by any far-reaching political motivations, but simply by her exhaustion from her work as a seamstress in a department store. Her simple answer "no" to the request to give up her seat, however, resulted in legal proceedings against her and a year-long boycott of the busses by the local African-American population. This simple act of defiance galvanized the African-American struggle for civil rights and showed the potential of non-cooperation with the opponent. Gandhi's demand that one does not cooperate with one's opponent and thereby proves that the opponent depends on the people who refuse to cooperate proved to be immensely successful. The boycott ended after the United States Supreme Court had declared unconstitutional all of Alabama's segregation laws with regard to busses.[32]

Since King had become pastor of the Dexter Avenue Baptist Church in Montgomery in September 1954, he was one of the central figures and organizers of the bus boycott. Driven by doubts and looking for adequate strategies, King engaged in long conversations with Rustin during this time. Rustin was a champion of non-violent action with a sparkling biography. Openly homosexual and at one point a member of the Communist Party, Rustin was a member of the Congress of Racial Equality (CORE) and a key organizer of the 1963 March on Washington, which brought more than 200,000 people together for a peaceful demonstration for equal rights for all American citizens. The march's crowning event was King's famous "I Have a Dream" speech.[33]

The Congress for Racial Equality was one of the earliest manifest influences of Gandhism in the African-American civil rights struggle. Founded by a few students at the University of Chicago in 1942, which included among others Bayard Rustin, it embraced the ideas of Henry David Thoreau and Mahatma Gandhi. These students were convinced that non-violent means of protest were the best way to achieve equal rights for African-Americans in the United States. They learned about Gandhi and non-violent protest through Krishnalal Shridharani, a student of Gandhi and participant in the Salt March who had immigrated to the United States in 1934. Here he worked on his book about Gandhi's techniques of non-violent resistance, which was published in 1939 under the title *War Without Violence*.[34] The members of CORE embraced Shridharani's book and made it their bible.[35] They organized the Journey of Reconciliation (1947), the Freedom Rides (1961), and helped in the organization of the March on Washington (1963). In the Journey of Reconciliation, CORE sent in 1947 eight white and eight black men into the Deep South to test the Supreme Court ruling of the previous year that had declared segregation in interstate travel in public transportation unconstitutional. The members of the team were arrested several times and Rustin was jailed for six months.[36]

Rustin discussed with King non-violent protest and is largely responsible for King's conversion to Gandhism. At the outset of the bus boycott King kept a gun under his pillow for the purpose of self-defense and he also permitted guards to carry guns. When Rustin became aware of these weapons, he argued with King and finally convinced him to get rid of all guns in his house. From this point onwards, King rejected guns and violence, even for purposes of self-defense.[37] He embraced Gandhi's ideas publicly and preached in his sermons about love and peace in all social relations. In his book *Stride towards Freedom* King remembered:

> The whole concept of *satyagraha* (*satya* as truth equals love, and *agraha* is force; *satyagraha* therefore means truth-force or love-force) was profoundly significant to me. As I delved deeper into the philosophy of Gandhi, my skepticism concerning the power of love gradually diminished, and I came to see for the first time its potency in the area of social reform. Prior to reading Gandhi, I had about concluded that the ethics of Jesus were only effective in individual relationship. The "turn the other cheek" philosophy and the "love your enemies" philosophy were only valid, I felt, when individuals were in conflict with other individuals; when racial groups and nations were in conflict, a more realistic approach seemed necessary. But after reading Gandhi, I saw how utterly mistaken I was.
>
> Gandhi was probably the first person in history to lift the love ethic of Jesus above mere interaction between individuals to a powerful and effective social force on a large scale. Love for Gandhi was a potent instrument for social and collective transformation. It was in this Gandhian emphasis on love and nonviolence that I discovered the method for social reform that I had been seeking for so many months. The intellectual and moral satisfaction that I failed to gain from the utilitarianism of Bentham and Mill, the revolutionary methods of Marx and Lenin,

the social-contract theory of Hobbes, the "back to nature" optimism of Rousseau, and the superman philosophy of Nietzsche, I found in the nonviolent resistance philosophy of Gandhi. I came to feel that this was the only morally and practically sound method open to oppressed people in their struggle for freedom.[38]

In February 1959 King traveled to India to experience the legacy of Gandhi and to search for new ideas for the civil rights struggle. He saw himself in India not as a tourist but as a pilgrim in search of the presence of the Mahatma. The India trip opened King's mind and strengthened his commitment to non-violence. He was impressed by what he learned about Gandhi's frugal lifestyle and his self-restraint. However, King struggled with Gandhi's vow of poverty and did not embrace Gandhi's demand that a man should rid himself of all worldly possessions. In public speeches, he praised Gandhi's work and showed admiration for the political changes accomplished by the movement for Indian independence. He further began to see the struggle of African-Americans for their civil liberties as part of the global movement of people of color for fundamental human rights. With the Cold War conflict in the background, King realized that the choices were not between violence and non-violence but between non-violence and non-existence. Non-violent protest thus became the inevitable choice for King.[39]

From Gandhi and King to the Struggle of Mexican-American Farm Workers for a Fair and Humane Treatment

The influence of Gandhi's ideas went beyond the African-American civil rights struggle and impacted campaigns and movements against American involvement from Vietnam to Iraq as well as labor fights such as the conflict between Mexican-American laborers and growers in California. Landowners in California had acquired enormous stretches of land, which they turned into large-scale farms. To operate these farms, the landowners depended on field workers who were paid a pitiful compensation for their hard work. The ethnicity of these farm workers changed quickly from Chinese during the 1870s to Japanese around 1900 and finally to Mexican by the 1920s. Mexican-Americans and Mexicans came to California in search of employment and escaping from the Mexican revolution. Among these migrants was the family of César Chávez, which relocated from Arizona to California during the Great Depression. His parents had operated a small grocery store in Yuma (Arizona) until the economic crisis forced them to close their store and join the farm laborers in California. Chávez grew up in poverty and excluded from a decent school education.[40]

In the 1950s César Chávez became involved in the attempts to organize Mexican-American farm laborers in unions and to encourage them to register for voting. Recognizing the limited education he was given, Chávez broadened his horizon by studying the lives of St. Francis of Assisi, Henry David Thoreau, and Mahatma Gandhi. His first encounter with Gandhi and his ideas stemmed from viewing a news reel when Chávez was still a boy. This little "half-naked" man had successfully stood up to the British and triumphed over the British Empire. Later in life, Chávez read Louis Fischer's *The Life of Mahatma Gandhi* (published in 1950).[41]

Gandhi's and Martin Luther King's non-violent campaigns deeply impressed Chávez and convinced him that social change could be accomplished by following the path of non-violence.[42] Since Chávez was deeply religious, he felt compelled to favor non-violent over violent conflict solution. His followers were required to take a vow of non-violence. Violence against people and damage to property were inacceptable for Chávez. In his Good Friday Letter addressed to E. L. Barr, Jr., the president of the California Grape and Tree Fruit League, Chávez insisted:

> Once again, I appeal to you as the representative of your industry and as a man. I ask you to recognize and bargain with our union before the economic pressure of the boycott and strike takes an irrevocable toll; but if not I ask you to at least sit down with us to discuss the safeguards necessary to keep our historical struggle free of violence. I make this appeal because as one of the leaders of our nonviolent movement, I know and accept my responsibility for preventing, if possible, the destruction of human life and property. For these reasons and knowing of Gandhi's admonition that fasting is the last resort in place of the sword, during a most critical time in our movement last February 1968 I undertook a 25-day fast. I repeat to you the principle enunciated to the membership at the start of the fast; if to build our union required the deliberate taking of life, either life of a grower or his child, or the life of a farm worker or his child, then I choose not to see the union built.
>
> Mr. Barr, let me be painfully honest with you. You must understand these things. We advocate militant nonviolence as our means for social revolution and to achieve justice for our people, but we are not blind or deaf to the desperate and moody winds of human frustration, impatience and rage that blow among us. Gandhi himself admitted that if his only choices were cowardice or violence, he would choose violence. Men are not angels and the time and tides wait for no man. Precisely because of these powerful human emotions, we have tried to involve masses of people in their own struggle. Participation and self-determination

remain the best experience of freedom; and free men instinctively prefer democratic change and even protect the rights guaranteed to seek it. Only the enslaved in despair have need of violent overthrow.[43]

His choosing of non-violence over violence was a principled as well as a pragmatic decision. Inspired by Gandhi's example and compelled by his Catholic faith, Chávez felt an ethical obligation and general conviction that non-violence was the only acceptable way to change society. But pragmatic deliberations also played a decisive role. Violence against growers and destruction of property would alienate potential allies, as well as supporters within the Catholic community, and enable the police to take drastic countermeasures. The spiral of violence would harden the resistance to change and the resolve of the growers and of society at large to confront those who embrace violent resistance. Non-violence was not, as Chávez pointed out, a sign of cowardice but a sign of strength and a symbol for the willingness of those who embrace non-violence to accept suffering and to potentially sacrifice their lives.[44]

César Chávez recognized the ethical-moral power of non-violent resistance, which rested with the perception of brutal mistreatment of non-violent resisters by their opponents. Such occurrences could cause the public opinion to shift in favor of the non-violent resisters and thus to shift the balance of power between the growers and the farm workers in favor of the latter. The acceptance of suffering, as well as the incapability of the authorities adequately to respond to this suffering, which led to a moral outcry among those who previously have not taken a stance, represents the great power of non-violent resistance.

Economic boycotts appeared to Chávez the most powerful practice of non-violent resistance. After several localized boycotts, the National Farmworkers Association (NFA), founded and organized by César Chávez,[45] carried the conflict between farm workers and growers to the national stage. In 1968, the NFA called for a national boycott of Californian grapes.[46] This consumer boycott quickly caught on and led to significant financial losses for Californian growers. The public support forced the growers to sign a settlement with the farm workers' union that brought its members higher wages, the provision of health care as well as the introduction of safety requirements with regards to the use of pesticides. The success of this boycott did not just rest with the economic gains but with the recognition of the farm workers' dignity and humanity.

Gandhi's Non-Violence and the Peaceful Revolutions of the 1980s

Gandhi's principles and tactics gave shape and inspiration to nonviolent protest movements around the world after World War II. His ideas found resonance among people resisting or confronting unresponsive and authoritarian governments in North and South America, Europe, and Asia. The success of these movements rested with their ability to mobilize masses, as well as the inability of the opposed systems to mount morally credible countermeasures. In the 1980s, non-violent movements and tactics led to the downfall of once powerful and oppressive systems in Asia and Eastern Europe. The moral superiority of the protesters who came out in millions to support change, the decay of these political systems, and the moral bankruptcy of these systems in the public eye were the preconditions for the success of these peaceful revolutions.

The Philippines were the first to witness political change through a non-violent uprising. When Ferdinand Marcos, the dictator of the Philippines for fourteen years, called a presidential election in early 1986, he unintentionally opened the door to a peaceful end to his dictatorship. This election pitted Marcos against his challenger Cory Aquino, who embraced non-violence as the guiding principle of her political campaign. Since Aquino expected the election to be manipulated, she prepared with her followers for actions against election fraud. It was the 1982 movie about Gandhi that apparently inspired Aquino and her advisors to follow his example. This movie contains a scene which depicts the famous raid of non-violent protesters on the Dharasana Salt Works in 1930. Waves after waves of Indians approached the salt works and were brutally beaten by the police. They suffered their beatings without even raising their arms in defense and continued to march toward the salt works. The reports about this event went around the world and caused moral outrage.[47]

Some of Aquino's advisors envisioned waves of non-violent protestors who would march to the Malacanang Palace, the official seat of the President in Manila, regardless of how many would be killed by the police forces. However, the opposition movement moved carefully and slowly before risking human lives. On February 16 1 million people attended a rally in Manila at which the Seven Point Program of the opposition was announced. This program proposed non-violent means of resistance on an escalating scale. It included the following steps:

1. A general work stoppage on February 26, the day after Marco's planned inauguration;
2. A withdrawal of funds from seven banks controlled by Marcos's cronies;
3. A boycott of media controlled by the government or by Marcos's cronies;
4. A delay in payments of electric and water bills;
5. A boycott of products of the San Miguel corporation and its subsidiaries, controlled by Marcos and his cronies;

6. Following a nightly broadcast by Cory [Aquino—insertion by the author], a 15-minute noise barrage (a tactic borrowed from Latin America); and
7. Whatever other forms of nonviolent resistance that people might find appropriate.[48]

Facing peaceful and unarmed protestors, soldiers called in by Marcos to confront the opposition began to defect and thus undermined Marcos' power base. Within 77 hours the regime was toppled and American interference avoided. It was the non-violent character of this movement that assured the neutrality of the American government, which in case of a violent challenge to Marcos would have intervened on Marcos' behalf. The worldwide public sympathy for the non-violent overthrow of Marcos, as well as the sympathetic media coverage assured Aquino of international support and American non-intervention.[49]

The events in the Philippines foreshadowed the peaceful revolutions that ended Communist rule in Eastern Europe in the course of 1989 and 1990. With the exception of Romania and Yugoslavia, the transition in the other Communist countries occurred through peaceful demonstrations and nonviolent resistance. In the case of East Germany, peaceful protest and demonstration originated from groups within the Nikolai Church in Leipzig. Throughout September and October 1989 the city of Leipzig emerged at the center of the confrontation between regime and opponents. Fueled by fear that the East German government would use brutal force if challenged by violent means, dissident activists and clergymen insisted on nonviolence as the only acceptable path for social change. The images of the Tiananmen Square massacre in summer 1989 still were in the minds of East German citizens. So was the fact that the East German government was among the few governments to congratulate their Chinese comrades on the successful suppression of the unrest in Beijing.[50]

In the case of East Germany, the opposition's decision to embrace nonviolence was, however, pragmatic and principled. One of the dominating slogans chanted at the Monday Demonstration on October 9, 1989, was "No Violence" and was intended to remind those protesting the regime as well as those protecting the regime to abstain from the use of force. On that night, the city of Leipzig was filled with tens of thousands of protestors on the one hand and thousands of policemen and soldiers on the other. A single violent attack—provoked or not—could have resulted in a massacre. The restraint of the protestors as well as the organizers of the protest, who formed human chains around buildings of the state authorities such as the building of the Secret Service, and the inability of the authorities to respond to a non-violent challenge resulted in the quick dissolution of the East German dictatorship.[51]

The non-violent character of the protests contributed to the swift dismantling of the regime, which was paralyzed by a structural crisis and unprepared for a non-violent challenge. However, the non-violent transition was as much a testament to the strength of the protest movement as it was to its limitations. The peaceful change resulted from the pressure that emerged from the streets and the millions of people who demanded change, but it also depended on the cooperation of the representatives of the old regime that engaged in dialogue and negotiations with their opponents. On the night of October 9 representatives of the civic movement and of the local ruling party authorities in Leipzig agreed to publish a call for a peaceful dialogue. Since the events of fall 1989, historians and political scientists struggle to define the events that ended the division of Germany and the Cold War. Was it a revolution? Or was it an implosion and dissolution of the system?[52]

Conclusion

Even though the twentieth century with its two world wars, genocides, and many more violent conflicts was undoubtedly a violent century, non-violent resistance has played an important role in the (1) anti-colonial struggle, (2) in civil rights struggles within various countries, and (3) the end of Communism and the end of the Cold War. In contrast to the other examples of intercultural transfer discussed in this book, non-violent resistance did not originate in Europe and traveled from here to the Americas, Africa, and Asia, but it originated in South Africa and traveled from here to various parts of the world. Non-violent resistance developed as a powerful strategy for the fight against injustice and against authoritarian systems. It does not, as has been suggested many times, depend on the morality of the enemy but on the strength of the opposition movement. The argument that non-violent resistance would not have worked against the Nazis since they were simply immoral is fundamentally flawed and hides the truth. It was not the immorality of the Nazis but the complete lack of a mass movement in Germany against the Nazis that made the use of non-violent resistance impossible. Resistance in Nazi Germany was the resistance of a few individuals without mass backing. The majority of the German population supported the Nazi system and were not willing to risk their lives for system change.

Non-violent resistance nevertheless poses a great moral and ethical dilemma for those in power since it takes away any morally acceptable justification for violent confrontation. A system challenged by a mass movement that embraces non-violent resistance can, in the long run, only lose. The success of non-violent movements is, however, as much a testament to the strength of the movement as it is a testament to the weakness of the system opposed.

Notes

1. *The Gandhi Reader: A Source Book of his Life and Writings*, edited by Homer A. Jack, Bloomington: Indiana University Press, 1956, 29–34; Mahatma K. Gandhi, *Satyagraha in South Africa* (translated from the Gujarati by Valji Govindji Desai), Madras: S. Ganesan, 1928.
2. Leo Tolstoy, *"The Kingdom of God Is Within You": Christianity not as a Mystic Religion but as a New Theory of Life*, New York: The Cassel Publishing Co., 1894; John Ruskin, *"Unto This Last": Four Essays on the First Principles of Political Economy*, London: Smith, Elder and Co., 1862; Peter Ackermann and Jack DuVall, *A Force More Powerful: A Century of Nonviolent Conflict*, New York: St. Martin's Press, 2000, 64–65; Martin Green, *The Origins of Nonviolence: Tolstoy and Gandhi in Their Historical Settings*, University Park and London: The Pennsylvania State University Press, 1986; *Mahatma Gandhi and Leo Tolstoy Letters*, edited by B. Sriivasa Murthy, Long Beach: Long Beach Publications, 1987.
3. Henry D. Thoreau, "Resistance to Civil Government; a lecture delivered in 1847," in: Elizabeth P. Peabody (ed.), *Aesthetic Papers*, Boston and New York: G. P. Putnam, 1849, 189–211; Frederick B. Fisher, *That Strange Little Brown Man Gandhi*, New York: Ray Long & Richard R. Smith, 1932, 72–84.
4. Thomas Weber, *Gandhi as Disciple and Mentor*, Cambridge: Cambridge University Press, 2004, 19–53.
5. M. K. Gandhi, *Non-Violent Resistance (Satyagraha)*, New York: Schocken Books, 1961; *Gandhi on Non-Violence: Selected Texts from Mohandas K. Gandhi's Non-Violence in Peace and War*, edited by Thomas Merton, New York: New Directions Publishing Corporation, 1964.
6. Gandhi, *Satyagraha in South Africa*, 175–79.
7. *The Gandhi Reader*, 96–97.
8. *The Gandhi Reader*, 182–209.
9. Jad Adams, *Gandhi: The True Man behind Modern India*, New York: Pegasus Books, 2011, 189–91; Judith M. Brown, *Gandhi and Civil Disobedience: The Mahatma in Indian Politics 1928–34*, Cambridge, London, New York, Melbourne: Cambridge University Press, 1977, 99–116; *The Gandhi Reader*, 235–42; Thomas Weber, *On the Salt March: The Historiography of Gandhi's March on Dandi*, New Delhi: HarperCollins Publishers India, 1997.
10. Romain Rolland, *Mahatma Gandhi; The Man Who Became One With the Universal Being*, New York and London: Century Co., 1924; Fisher, *That Strange Little Brown Man Gandhi*.
11. *The Gandhi Reader*, 381–88.
12. Fisher, *That Strange Little Brown Man Gandhi*, 52–55.
13. *Dietrich Bonhoeffer, Ökumene, Universität, Pfarramt 1931–1932*, edited by Eberhard Amelung and Christoph Strohm, Gütersloh: Chr. Kaiser Verlag, 1994, 215–26; Eberhard Bethge, *Dietrich Bonhoeffer: Man of Vision, Man of Courage*, New York and Evanston: Harper & Row, 1970, 74; Larry L. Rasmussen, *Dietrich Bonhoeffer: Reality and Resistance*, Nashville and New York: Abingdon Press, 1972, 213. See also: Charlie Cahill, "The Pragmatic Roots of Bonhoeffer's Ethics: A Reappraisal of Bonhoeffer's Time at Union Theological Seminary, 1930–1931," in: *German Studies Review* 36, 1 (2013): 21–39.
14. *Dietrich Bonhoeffer, Ökumene, Universität, Pfarramt 1931–1932*, 215–26; Rasmussen, *Dietrich Bonhoeffer*, 216.

15 Bethge, *Dietrich Bonhoeffer*, 74; Rasmussen, *Dietrich Bonhoeffer*, 213. See also: Cahill, "The Pragmatic Roots of Bonhoeffer's Ethics."
16 Bethge, *Dietrich Bonhoeffer*, 206–10, 329–36, 338–491; John A. Moses, *The Reluctant Revolutionary: Dietrich Bonhoeffer's Collision with Prusso-German History*, New York and Oxford: Berghahn Books, 2009, 103–29. See also: Richard Steigmann-Gall, *The Holy Reich: Nazi Conceptions of Christianity 1919–1945*, Cambridge: Cambridge University Press, 2003.
17 Reinhold Niebuhr, *Moral Man and Immoral Society: A Study in Ethics and Politics*, New York: Charles Scribner's Sons, 1932, 240–41.
18 Rasmussen, *Dietrich Bonhoeffer*, 213.
19 Ferdinand Schlingensiepen, *Dietrich Bonhoeffer 1906–1945: Martyr, Thinker, Man of Resistance*, London and New York: T & T Clark International, 2010, 234–313; Moses, *The Reluctant Revolutionary*.
20 Moses, *The Reluctant Revolutionary*, 141–45.
21 Dietrich Bonhoeffer, *Ethics*, edited by Eberhard Bethge, New York: The Macmillan Company, 1955, 210.
22 *Long Walk to Freedom: The Autobiography of Nelson Mandela*, Boston, New York, Toronto, London: Little, Brown and Company, 1994, 111; Martin Meredith, *Nelson Mandela: A Biography*, New York: St. Martin's Press, 1997, 93.
23 *Long Walk to Freedom*, 137.
24 Ackerman/DuVall, *A Force More Powerful*, 339–340; *Long Walk to Freedom*, 137, 206–8; David Hardiman, *Gandhi in his Time and Ours: The Global Legacy of his Ideas*, New York: Columbia University Press, 2003, 278–80; Meredith, *Nelson Mandela*, 173.
25 Mahadev Desai, "Non-Violence and the American Negro," in: *Harijan*, March 20, 1937. This interview was reprinted in: *The Gandhi Reader*, 308–13.
26 Benjamin E. Mays, *Born to Rebel: An Autobiography*, Athens and London: The University of Georgia Press, 2003, 156–57.
27 *The Gandhi Reader*, 308–13; J. Deotis Roberts, "Gandhi and King: On Conflict Resolution," in: *Shalom Papers* 2, 1 (2000): 34–35.
28 *The Gandhi Reader*, 325–16; Roberts, "Gandhi and King: On Conflict Resolution," 32–34.
29 J. Deotis Roberts, *Bonhoeffer and King: Speaking Truth to Power*, Louisville: Westminster John Knox Press, 2005, 71; J. Deotis Roberts, "Gandhi and King: On Conflict Resolution," 38–39; Martin Luther King, Jr., *Stride Toward Freedom: The Montgomery Story*, New York: Harper & Brothers, 1958, 96; *The Autobiography of Martin Luther King, Jr.*, edited by Clayborne Carson, New York: Warner Books, 1998, 23.
30 Fisher, *That Strange Little Brown Man Gandhi*, King, Jr., *Stride Toward Freedom*, 96–99.
31 King, Jr., *Stride Toward Freedom*, 101–4; *The Autobiography of Martin Luther King, Jr.*, 23–24.
32 King, Jr., *Stride Toward Freedom*, 43–49.
33 Ackerman/DuVall, *A Force More Powerful*, 310–11; Hardiman, *Gandhi in his Time and Ours*, 256–57.
34 Krishnalal Shridharani, *War Without Violence: A Study of Gandhi's Method and its Accomplishments*, New York: Harcourt, Brace and Company, 1939; David Cortright, *Gandhi and Beyond: Nonviolence for an Age of Terrorism*, Boulder and London: Paradigm Publishers, 2006, 41.
35 Hardiman, *Gandhi in his Time and Ours*, 256–57.
36 August Meier and Elliott Rudwick, *CORE: A Study in the Civil Rights Movement 1942–1968*, New York: Oxford University Press, 1973.

37 Hardiman, *Gandhi in his Time and Ours*, 259; Thomas F. Jackson, *From Civil Rights to Human Rights: Martin Luther King, Jr. and the Struggle for Economic Justice*, Philadelphia: University of Pennsylvania Press, 2007, 61–62.
38 King, Jr., *Stride toward Freedom*, 96–7.
39 *The Autobiography of Martin Luther King, Jr.*, 121–34; Jackson, *From Civil Rights to Human Rights*, 98–101.
40 Roger Bruns, *Cesar Chavez: A Biography*, Westport and London: Greenwood Press, 2005, 1–19.
41 Jacques E. Levy, *Cesar Chavez: Autobiography of La Causa*, New York: W. W. Norton & Company, 1975, 91–92; Luis D. León, "Mapping the New Global Spiritual Line," in: Ilan Stavans (ed.), *Cesar Chavez*, Santa Barbara, Denver, Oxford: Greenwood, 2010, 81; Jorge Mariscal, "Negotiating César," in: Stavans (ed.), *Cesar Chavez*, 35 (n 9); Bruns, Cesar Chavez, 17.
42 León, "Mapping the New Global Spiritual Line," 81–82.
43 Cesar E. Chavez, "Letter from Delano", in: *Christian Century* vol. 86, no. 17 (April 23, 1969): 540.
44 Levy, *Cesar Chavez*, 93, 269–71.
45 Bruns, *Cesar Chavez*, 34–39.
46 Bruns, *Cesar Chavez*, 41–54; *César Chávez: A Brief Biography with Documents*, edited by Richard W. Etulain, New York: Palgrave, 2002, 82–95; John Gregory Dunne, "From Delano: The Story of the California Grape Strike," in: Stavans, *Cesar Chavez*, 143–48.
47 Ackerman/DuVall, *A Force More Powerful*, 375; *The Gandhi Reader*, 248–53; Adams, *Gandhi*, 191.
48 Stephen Zunes, "The Origins of People Power in the Philippines", in: Stephen Zunes, Lester R. Kurtz, and Sarah Beth Asher (eds), *Nonviolent Social Movements: A Geographical Perspective*, Malden and Oxford: Blackwell Publishers, 2000, 144.
49 Ackerman/DuVall, *A Force More Powerful*, 381–93.
50 Charles S. Maier, *Dissolution: The Crisis of Communism and the End of East Germany*, Princeton: Princeton University Press, 1997; Steven Pfaff, *Exit-Voice Dynamics and the Collapse of East Germany: The Crisis of Leninism and the Revolution of 1989*, Durham and London: Duke University Press, 2006; Hartmut Zwahr, *Ende einer Selbstzerstörung: Leipzig und die Revolution in der DDR*, Göttingen: Vandenhoeck & Ruprecht, 1993.
51 Zwahr, *Ende einer Selbstzerstörung*, 96–102.
52 Corey Ross, *The East German Dictatorship: Problems and Perspectives in the Interpretation of the GDR*, New York: Oxford University Press, 2002, 126–48.

Bibliography

Primary Sources

Bonhoeffer, Dietrich. *Ethics* edited by Eberhard Bethge. New York: The Macmillan Company, 1955.

Chavez, Cesar E. "Letter from Delano." *Christian Century* vol. 86, no. 17 (April 23, 1969): 539–40.

Desai, Mahadev. "Non-Violence and the American Negro." *Harijan*, March 20, 1937.

Fisher, Frederick B. *That Strange Little Brown Man Gandhi*. New York: Ray Long & Richard R. Smith, 1932.

Gandhi, M. K. *Non-Violent Resistance (Satyagraha)*. New York: Schocken Books, 1961.

Gandhi, Mahatma K. *Satyagraha in South Africa* (translated from the Gujarati by Valji Govindji Desai). Madras: S. Ganesan, 1928.
Gandhi on Non-Violence: Selected Texts from Mohandas K. Gandhi's Non-Violence in Peace and War edited by Thomas Merton. New York: New Directions Publishing Corporation, 1964.
King, Jr., Martin Luther. *Stride Toward Freedom: The Montgomery Story*. New York: Harper & Brothers, 1958.
Levy, Jacques E. *Cesar Chavez: Autobiography of La Causa*. New York: W. W. Norton & Company, 1975.
Long Walk to Freedom: The Autobiography of Nelson Mandela. Boston, New York, Toronto, London: Little, Brown and Company, 1994.
Mahatma Gandhi and Leo Tolstoy Letters edited by B. Sriivasa Murthy. Long Beach: Long Beach Publications, 1987.
Mays, Benjamin E. *Born to Rebel: An Autobiography*. Athens and London: The University of Georgia Press, 2003.
Niebuhr, Reinhold. *Moral Man and Immoral Society: A Study in Ethics and Politics*. New York: Charles Scribner's Sons, 1932.
Rolland, Romain. *Mahatma Gandhi; The Man Who Became One With the Universal Being*. New York and London: Century Co., 1924.
Ruskin, John. *"Unto This Last": Four Essays on the First Principles of Political Economy*. London: Smith, Elder and Co., 1862.
Shridharani, Krishnalal. *War Without Violence: A Study of Gandhi's Method and its Accomplishments*. New York: Harcourt, Brace and Company, 1939.
The Autobiography of Martin Luther King, Jr. edited by Clayborne Carson. New York: Warner Books, 1998.
The Gandhi Reader: A Source Book of his Life and Writings edited by Homer A. Jack. Bloomington: Indiana University Press, 1956.
Thoreau, Henry D. "Resistance to Civil Government; a lecture delivered in 1847." In: *Aesthetic Papers*, edited by Elizabeth P. Peabody. Boston and New York: G. P. Putnam, 1849, 189–211.
Tolstoy, Leo. *"The Kingdom of God Is Within You": Christianity not as a Mystic Religion but as a New Theory of Life*. New York: The Cassel Publishing Co., 1894.
Zwahr, Hartmut. *Ende einer Selbstzerstörung: Leipzig und die Revolution in der DDR*. Göttingen: Vandenhoeck & Ruprecht, 1993.

Secondary Sources

Ackermann, Peter and Jack DuVall. *A Force More Powerful: A Century of Nonviolent Conflict*. New York: St. Martin's Press, 2000.
Adams, Jad. *Gandhi: The True Man behind Modern India*. New York: Pegasus Books, 2011.
Bethge, Eberhard. *Dietrich Bonhoeffer: Man of Vision, Man of Courage*. New York and Evanston: Harper & Row, 1970.
Brown, Judith M. *Gandhi and Civil Disobedience: The Mahatma in Indian Politics 1928–34*. Cambridge, London, New York, Melbourne: Cambridge University Press, 1977.
Bruns, Roger. *Cesar Chavez: A Biography*. Westport and London: Greenwood Press, 2005.
Cahill, Charlie. "The Pragmatic Roots of Bonhoeffer's Ethics: A Reappraisal of Bonhoeffer's Time at Union Theological Seminary, 1930–1931." *German Studies Review* 36, 1 (2013): 21–39.

César Chávez: A Brief Biography with Documents, edited by Richard W. Etulain. New York: Palgrave, 2002.

Cortright, David. *Gandhi and Beyond: Nonviolence for an Age of Terrorism.* Boulder and London: Paradigm Publishers, 2006.

Dietrich Bonhoeffer, Ökumene, Universität, Pfarramt 1931–1932, edited by Eberhard Amelung and Christoph Strohm. Gütersloh: Chr. Kaiser Verlag, 1994.

Dunne, John Gregory. "From Delano: The Story of the California Grape Strike." In: *Cesar Chavez,* edited by Ilan Stavans. Santa Barbara, Denver, Oxford: Greenwood, 2010, 143–48.

Green, Martin. *The Origins of Nonviolence: Tolstoy and Gandhi in Their Historical Settings.* University Park and London: The Pennsylvania State University Press, 1986.

Hardiman, David. *Gandhi in his time and ours: the global legacy of his ideas.* New York: Columbia University Press, 2003.

Jackson, Thomas F. *From Civil Rights to Human Rights: Martin Luther King, Jr. and the Struggle for Economic Justice.* Philadelphia: University of Pennsylvania Press, 2007.

León, Luis D. "Mapping the New Global Spiritual Line." In: *Cesar Chavez,* edited by Ilan Stavans. Santa Barbara, Denver, Oxford: Greenwood, 2010, 70–91.

Maier, Charles S. *Dissolution: The Crisis of Communism and the End of East Germany.* Princeton: Princeton University Press, 1997.

Mariscal, Jorge. "Negotiating César." In: *Cesar Chavez,* edited by Ilan Stavans. Santa Barbara, Denver, Oxford: Greenwood, 2010, 12–41.

Meier, August and Elliott Rudwick. *CORE: A Study in the Civil Rights Movement 1942–1968.* New York: Oxford University Press, 1973.

Meredith, Martin. *Nelson Mandela: A Biography.* New York: St. Martin's Press, 1997.

Moses, John A. *The Reluctant Revolutionary: Dietrich Bonhoeffer's Collision with Prusso-German History.* New York and Oxford: Berghahn Books, 2009.

Pfaff, Steven. *Exit-Voice Dynamics and the Collapse of East Germany: The Crisis of Leninism and the Revolution of 1989.* Durham and London: Duke University Press, 2006.

Rasmussen, Larry L. *Dietrich Bonhoeffer: Reality and Resistance.* Nashville and New York: Abingdon Press, 1972.

Roberts, J. Deotis. "Gandhi and King: On Conflict Resolution." *Shalom Papers* 2, 1 (2000): 29–42.

Roberts, J. Deotis. *Bonhoeffer and King: Speaking Truth to Power.* Louisville: Westminster John Knox Press, 2005.

Ross, Corey. *The East German Dictatorship: Problems and Perspectives in the Interpretation of the GDR.* New York: Oxford University Press, 2002.

Schlingensiepen, Ferdinand. *Dietrich Bonhoeffer 1906–1945: Martyr, Thinker, Man of Resistance.* London and New York: T & T Clark International, 2010.

Steigmann-Gall, Richard. *The Holy Reich: Nazi Conceptions of Christianity 1919–1945.* Cambridge: Cambridge University Press, 2003.

Weber, Thomas. *Gandhi as Disciple and Mentor.* Cambridge: Cambridge University Press, 2004.

Weber, Thomas. *On the Salt March: The Historiography of Gandhi's March on Dandi.* New Delhi: HarperCollins Publishers India, 1997.

Zunes, Stephen. "The Origins of People Power in the Philippines." In: *Nonviolent Social Movements: A Geographical Perspective,* edited by Stephen Zunes, Lester R. Kurtz, and Sarah Beth Asher. Malden and Oxford: Blackwell Publishers, 2000, 129–57.

Chapter 7

FROM *WEIHNACHTEN* TO CHRISTMAS: THE INVENTION OF A MODERN HOLIDAY RITUAL AND ITS TRANSFER FROM GERMANY TO ENGLAND AND THE UNITED STATES

Abstract: The celebration of Christmas with Christmas trees and gift giving emerged from Pagan traditions as a holiday ritual in the early nineteenth century in Northern German homes. It was part of the creation of a bourgeois culture of celebration and the invention of a national (German) identity. From the time of its invention, American observers followed with fascination and envy the development of this new custom and arranged for its intercultural transfer across the Atlantic. Americans such as Charles Loring Brace and George Ticknor described this festival as a truly German custom that could be found in every German home. They recognized in this ritual the potential for providing the glue that could hold together the society and culture of new countries such as Germany and the United States. Therefore, they advocated the appropriation of this custom by Anglo-American families in the 1840s and 1850s.

This marked the second introduction of the tradition of Christmas into American society. Years before Ticknor began to advocate the celebration of this festival, German-American families had already brought this custom to the United States. However, the first introduction of this custom into American society had not resulted in the wide acceptance of this alien custom. It remained confined to the German-American subculture. The intercultural transfer of Christmas between German and American societies provides important insights into the role of agents of intercultural transfer and points to the necessity for the belonging of those agents to the receiving society if such a transfer is to succeed.

This chapter has not been previously published but emerged from several presentations and lectures.

The Origin of *Weihnachten* and of the *Weihnachtsbaum*

The celebration of Christmas with the exchange of gifts that children and adults find under the Christmas tree has become a ritual with a clearly established sequence of events and clearly defined roles for everyone involved. In the United States, this holiday has come to be seen as a celebration of Christ's birth. Yet, the modern Christmas ritual in the nineteenth century emerged not from Christian tradition but rather from Pagan tradition. American observers, furthermore, identified this ritual with the project of nation building and the invention of national identity, the German national identity in particular. In fact, American observers such as George Ticknor contended that *Weihnachten* was a ritual specific to the German nation and that it was celebrated wherever one could find a German home.[1] Weihnachten was, thus, in its beginnings recognized as a national (German) holiday rather than a religious celebration. This is confirmed by the complete absence of religious practices from the descriptions of *Weihnachts* celebrations in the travelogues produced by Americans and Englishmen who participated in and observed this ritual in German homes in the first half of the nineteenth century. None of these texts mentions church services or religious practices of any kind in their extremely detailed accounts of these celebrations, which often extended for many pages and in some cases even provided the topic for entire book chapters.[2]

Both the Pagan origins of the ritual of Weihnachten as well as its contribution to creating national identities in Germany and the United States have received little attention in the existing literature. The transfer of this holiday ritual from Germany to the United States has, further, been ascribed to the actions of German migrants who brought this custom with them across the Atlantic. While it is true that German-Americans such as Charles Follen were the first to put up Christmas trees in their American homes, the custom of trimming trees for Christmas did not spread from the homes of German-Americans to the American society at large. It was the second introduction of the trimming of Christmas trees by Anglo-American travelers such as George Ticknor, who observed this custom in German homes in places such as Dresden, that provided for the successful transfer and the inclusion of this custom into Anglo-American culture and society.[3]

In their accounts of the celebration of Weihnachten, American and English observers initially used the German term "Weihnachten" in its correct spelling or in some misspelled ways such as *Weighnacht*.[4] The term "Weihnachten," which could and which has been misunderstood and mistranslated by English-speakers as Holy Night or Christmas, had, however, no Christian meaning. The *German Dictionary* of the Brothers Grimm provides an etymology of the word "Weihnachten" that has no connection to Christian tradition. The ritual of Weihnachten referred to a Pagan midwinter celebration and not to the misdated Holy Night of Christ's birth. The Grimm Brothers further noted that the term "Weihnachten" was used rarely in German publications before 1800.[5] The closest and most appropriate English term to translate the German term "Weihnachten" would have been Yule, which represented a Pagan and Germanic midwinter festival. Yet, English and American observers began to translate Weihnachten as Christmas early in the nineteenth century as part of the process of transferring this ritual to English and American societies and, thereby, Christianized this holiday ritual.

The custom of trimming Christmas trees with wax candles and other decorations emerged in the context of Romanticism and nationalism. Romanticism sought, in contrast to the Enlightenment that saw Greek and Roman Antiquity as inspiration, to recover traditions of Germanic Antiquity. It was the time when the Brothers Grimm collected and codified fairy tales in the pursuit of identifying and preserving the essence of Germanness.[6] Romanticism provided inspiration to nationalists who sought to define the distinctive features of the German nation as well as its composition and location. Many contrasting concepts about Germanness and the German nation emerged. Some defined the German nation by the German language and suggested that the German nation extended into all areas where the German tongue was spoken. However, much disagreement existed as to the definition of the German language. Other concepts took a much narrower approach and considered German identity to be identical with Protestantism and thereby limited the German nation to Northern Germany. The concept of the German nation was still an open one and allowed for competing models to evolve. The celebration of certain rituals and festivals that derived from pre-Christian times provided another way of identifying the German nation. In this context Pagan traditions such as the winter solstice received new prominence. Winter solstice was an old Germanic and Pagan ritual that had survived the Christianization of Central European people. On December 21, when Germans experienced the longest night of the year, they came together on fields and forests to start large bonfires. These fires were intended to recall the sun and to show her the way so that she could return. Putting wax candles onto Christmas trees was reminiscent of these bonfires and represented a domesticated version of these Pagan bonfires. Embracing the celebration of such rituals provided one of many ways in determining who belonged to the German nation and who did not.

The invention of Christmas as a family affair that involved all members of the family and ascribed active roles to children and adults reflected the emergence of a non-aristocratic upper class and a new social order. This upper class sought to create holidays and rituals that differed from the holiday culture of the nobility. Instead of public festivals that focused on individual rulers, celebrations such as Weihnachten introduced a new culture of celebrations and festivals that appealed to urban middle and upper classes because of its egalitarian principles of mutual gift giving and communal celebration. Weihnachten put the Christmas tree and not an individual ruler in the center of the celebration. It was, furthermore, a private celebration that was centered on the bourgeois family. Weihnachten was, thus, a two-pronged attempt to create a bourgeois culture.[7]

This new cultural ritual attracted from the beginning the attention of English and American travelers who observed with fascination and wrote extensively about the formation of Weihnachten in German cities. We have in fact more English sources that document the emergence of the German ritual of Weihnachten than we have German sources. These observations found their way into published and unpublished travelogues, travel journals, and letters, which offer a fascinating picture of how this German ritual emerged. They, further, provided a site for the intercultural transfer of this new custom from German homes to English and American homes since these English texts were written for an English and American audience.[8]

The Introduction of the Christmas Tree into English Society

Bringing evergreen trees into the homes of upper-class families and decorating them with wax candles began at the end of the eighteenth century in the Northern and Protestant parts of the Holy Roman Empire. Stories that ascribed the invention of the Christmas tree to the sixteenth-century Protestant Reformer Martin Luther have been rightfully dismissed as legends.[9] There is no historical evidence for the tradition of trimming trees from the time before the second half of the eighteenth century. The very first German literary record of a Christmas tree decorated with apples, sweets, and lights was found in E. T. A. Hoffmann's famous *Nutcracker and Mouse King* of 1816.[10] And the English poet Samuel Taylor Coleridge provided the first known observation of this custom by an Englishman. When in 1798 Coleridge traveled to Ratzeburg, which was part of the Duchy of Mecklenburg-Strelitz, he observed "a great yew bow ... fastened on the table" with "a multitude of little tapers ... fixed in the bough ... and coloured paper etc. hangs and flutters from the twigs." He also saw presents put underneath the bough.[11]

Coleridge's description of a Christmas tree has relevance not only as an early document about this emerging tradition but also for its early transfer to England. When in 1761 Duchess Sophie Charlotte of Mecklenburg-Strelitz became the wife of George III of England, she brought with her the new Northern German custom of celebrating Weihnachten. The first documented celebration of Christmas at Windsor Castle with a Christmas tree occurred in December of 1800. John Watkins wrote in his *Memoirs of Queen Sophia Charlotte* about this celebration:

> At the beginning of October the royal family left the coast for Windsor, where Her Majesty kept the Christmas-day following in a very pleasing manner. Sixty poor families had a substantial dinner given them; and in the evening the children of the principal families in the neighbourhood were invited to an entertainment at the Lodge. Here, among other amusing objects for the gratification of the juvenile visitors, in the middle of the room stood an immense tub with a yew-tree placed in it, from the branches of which hung bunches of sweetmeats, almonds, and raisins, in papers, fruits, toys, most tastefully arranged, and the whole illuminated by small wax candles. After the company had walked round and admired the tree, each child obtained a portion of the sweets which it bore, together with a toy, and then all returned home quite delighted.[12]

The description of the ritual of Weihnachten included two important elements of this new custom: the decorated Christmas tree and the giving of gifts. From the outset, the Christmas tree came with the new tradition of exchanging gifts between all family members. After the trees were decorated, gifts were laid underneath them. While in this public Christmas celebration the royal couple provided gifts for the children of poor families without expecting them to reciprocate, the family-centered form of Weihnachten was based on the mutual exchange of gifts between adults and children. Everyone was expected to participate in the making/buying of gifts and in their exchanging. This tradition of gift giving on December 24 was as new as the decorating of the Christmas tree. Beforehand, gifts were exchanged on New Year's Eve. Both the trees and the gifts were hidden in a secret room that was closed to the children until the evening of December 24. The opening of this room to all family members on that night was awaited with great anticipation.

From Windsor, this custom slowly spread across the British Isles through the agency of Northern German noblemen and noblewomen such as the Countess Katharina Alexandra Dorothea von Lieven. Born in Riga into the Baltic-German family of Christoph von Benckendorff, she married Prince Christoph Heinrich von Lieven who served as Russian ambassador in London from 1812 to 1834. Princess Lieven organized in December 1829 a Christmas party at the estate of Panshanger that was the home of the Earl of Cowper. Most of the guests in attendance such as Frederick Lamb who had served as ambassador to Vienna had a direct connection to the German states and were acquainted with the German tradition of Weihnachten. The clerk of the Privy Council Charles Greville wrote in his *Memoirs* about this Christmas party:

> On Christmas Day the Princess [Lieven] got up a little *fête* such as is customary all over Germany. Three trees in great pots were put upon a long table covered with pink linen; each tree was illuminated with three circular tiers of coloured wax candles—blue, green, red, and white. Before each tree was displayed a quantity of toys, gloves, pocket-handkerchiefs, workboxes, books, and various articles—presents made to the owner of the tree. It was very pretty. Here it was only for the children; in Germany the custom extends to persons of all ages.[13]

It took decades for this German custom to be accepted among the British nobility and much longer for this custom to also trickle down into the culture of the lower and middle classes. William Howitt wrote in the second volume of his *The Rural Life of England* (1838) about the ways in which his countrymen celebrated Christmas. In his book, Howitt wrote that this holiday was largely "the festival of the fireside."[14] It involved "the Yule block on the fire, the plum-porridge and mince-pies on the table, with mighty rounds of beef, plum-pudding, turkeys, capons, geese, goose-pies, herons, and sundry other game and good things."[15] Women also bought holly, ivy, and mistletoe to decorate windows and doors.[16] Nowhere in his book did Howitt mention a Christmas tree as part of the English holiday custom.

Howitt suggested in his book that the transition from Catholicism to Protestantism was the reason for the lack of proper Christmas traditions in nineteenth-century England. "In Rome," Howitt wrote, "all the splendor of the church is called forth. On Christmas eve, the pipes of the Pifferari, or Calabrian minstrels, are heard in the streets. The decorators are busy in draping the churches, clothing altars, and festooning façades."[17] It was, however, not the turn from Catholicism to Protestantism that had robbed England of a proper holiday culture surrounding Christmas but rather the establishment of Puritanism that dominated in both England and later also in the United States and prevented the creation of elaborate holiday celebrations such as Weihnachten. Puritan tradition did not support the enjoyment of festivities that were not mentioned in the New Testament and had roots in non-Christian traditions. Puritans also objected to engaging in any activities that violated the keeping of the Sabbath. In 1632 the fanatical Puritan lawyer William Prynne wrote in *Histriomastix*, in which he condemned almost any kind of amusement (including theatre performances) as a sin, that the celebration of Christmas was a particularly sinful act. Puritans rightly recognized that Christmas celebrations had no basis in biblical tradition and that they were of pre-Christian origin. Therefore, they advocated the banning of such activities.[18]

The Introduction of the Christmas Tree into American Society

Such Puritan positions carried over from England into the English colonies in North America and created a culture that was deeply hostile to rituals such as Weihnachten. Colonial authorities went so far as to ban the celebration of Christmas. The General Court of the Massachusetts Bay Colony passed in 1659 a law that prohibited Christmas celebrations altogether and imposed a fine for those who violated the rule. Such attitudes survived the American Revolution and thrived among Anglo-Americans.[19]

However, since the creation of the first German settlement in Germantown, Pennsylvania, in 1683 the English colonies offered a home to more and more German-speakers who came to North America mostly from Western and Central Germany.[20] And these German migrants brought with them the custom of trimming trees for Weihnachten. The Christmas trees put up by these German-Americans attracted the curiosity and even fascination among children and adults from Anglo-American families who had been raised in the Puritan tradition. The engineer and chronicler of everyday life in New York City Charles Haswell remembered in his *Reminiscences of an Octogenarian* that in the 1830s the number of German families living in Brooklyn had significantly increased. And these families introduced to this city the custom of dressing up Christmas trees. "So novel was the exhibition," Haswell wrote, "that it evoked much comment. I have a vivid remembrance of my going over to Brooklyn of a very stormy and wet night to witness the novelty."[21]

Authors such as Penne L. Restad suggested in his *Christmas in America* that it was the German-Americans who introduced American society to the Christmas tree and gift giving and established it in this country. It was certainly true that with German migrants, the custom of decorating evergreen trees for Weihnachten and the exchange of gifts first came to the United States. Several famous German-Americans put up Christmas trees in their homes in the 1830s. Among them were Charles Minnegerode who taught classics at the College of William and Mary and Charles Follen who was the first professor of German Literature at Harvard College.[22]

Follen's Christmas tree of 1835 was documented by the English author Harriet Martineau in the second volume of her *Western Travel*. Martineau wrote that she "was present at the introduction into the new country of the spectacle of the German Christmas-tree." Follen's son "Charley and three companions had been long preparing for this pretty show." They had used eggshells to make gilded and colored cups—a custom typical in Germany at Easter and not at Weihnachten—that were used for decorating the tree. The use of eggshells for decorative purposes points to the lack of proper decorations in the United States that one could easily find at a Christmas market back in Germany. But such markets did not transfer to North America and American society did not provide for a Christmas economy yet that could have offered decorations for Christmas trees. German-Americans were left to their own ingenuity in creating decorations that could fit onto a Christmas tree. Eggshells colored and gilded were known to Germans from the custom of Pagan Easter celebrations. In Pagan tradition, they symbolized new life and fertility. Germans would hang such eggs on birch branches during the Easter period. In Follen's house in Boston, the children filled these cups with comfits, lozenges, and barley-sugar before they were put onto the tree. "The tree was the top of a young fir, planted in a tub, which was ornamented with moss. Smart dolls and other whimsies glittered in the evergreen, and there was not a twig which had not something sparkling upon it."[23]

However, the custom of dressing Christmas trees during the 1820s and 1830s remained confined to German-American families and the German subculture within American society.[24] As much as Christmas trees fascinated Anglo-Americans of all ages, the practice appeared too alien to many to adopt this foreign custom. This changed only in the 1840s after several prominent Anglo-Americans such as George Ticknor who had served as the first professor of Romance Languages at Harvard College had traveled to Germany, observed Christmas celebrations together with their children, and upon their return to the United States—and most likely under great pressure from their impressionable children—advocated the introduction of Christmas trees and gift giving into mainstream American society. This second introduction of this German and Pagan ritual into American society might be one of the rare instances in which children played a significant role in history.[25]

In the course of the nineteenth century, Germans had developed an elaborate and extensive ritual of Weihnachten. This ritual extended far beyond the narrow confines of Christmas Day (December 24) and included the Advent period. The Advent period of the four weeks that led up to December 24 was attributed a specific function—a countdown to Christmas Day—in the context of social reform in the vicinity of Hamburg. One of the most prominent projects of social reform in Hamburg was Johann Hinrich Wichern's *Rauhes Haus* (Rough House). Wichern had founded the *Rauhes Haus* in 1833 as an institution for orphans and children of poor families. This home was to provide children from destitute backgrounds with opportunities to learn, work, and pray. However, Wichern insisted that this home was to offer children the atmosphere of a family. Children should be raised with love. When the home was opened in 1833 it admitted twelve children between the ages of five and eighteen. By 1845 it had become home to ninety-three children.[26]

These children, who had not much joy in their lives, bothered Wichern repeatedly in the months of November and December with questions about how much longer they would have to wait for Weihnachten. This constant questioning inspired Wichern to construct in 1839 an *Adventskranz* (a wreath) with 24 candles (4 big ones and 20 small ones). Each small candle represented a weekday and each big candle a Sunday. Each day, one candle was lightened. This way, children received a visual countdown to December 24. Wichern created two important traditions that became part of the ritual of Weihnachten: the Adventskranz and the *Adventskalender* (a calendar with 24 windows that hide sweets, which children could obtain after opening one window each morning beginning on December 1).[27] These traditions became part of the Northern German tradition of Weihnachten from the 1840s onward. Yet, English and American observers, for whatever reason, did not mention them and, thereby, excluded them from transfer to England and the United States. German Weihnachten, in the eyes of English and American observers, was limited to the decorated Christmas tree and the exchange of gifts.

George Ticknor was among the first Americans who traveled across the German states and who provided a detailed description of German Weihnachten for a larger American audience. Ticknor went to Germany first in 1815 to study at the University of Göttingen. He stayed in Germany from late summer 1815 to late spring 1817. His extensive and detailed travel journals, however, did not contain a single word about Weihnachten, decorated Christmas trees, or gift giving. When he returned together with his wife and his two little children in November 1835 to spend a few months in Dresden, Ticknor wrote about his experiences with Weihnachten during his second and his first stay. During this second stay, Ticknor and his daughter Anna were invited to a lavish *Weihnachtsparty* in the home of Wilhelm Hartwig August von Ungern-Sternberg. In his travel journal, Ticknor provided an extensive description of this party. From the outset, Ticknor described this Christmas Eve party not in terms of religious significance but in terms of a "very peculiar national feeling and custom." When Ticknor and his daughter arrived, they joined the family of Ungern-Sternberg who were waiting for the ring of a bell. This bell signaled that the doors were thrown open to the secret room, in which the Christmas tree "filled with little wax lights, which is peculiar to these occasions" had been standing. Underneath the Christmas tree were the presents. Children had made presents for the adults. And adults had bought presents for the children at the Christmas market in downtown Dresden. Ticknor judged: "The whole was indeed quite brilliant—for, I should think, five or six hundred thalers worth of presents were distributed—and the delight of the children was in proportion." And he went on to characterize the festivity as "a fine national celebration, which works very deeply into the hearts and characters of the whole population." And in this context, Ticknor also wrote that he had already encountered this custom twenty years earlier during his student years at the University of Göttingen. "I witnessed its effect twice in Göttingen in 1815 and 1816, and I have no doubt it is the same everywhere—everywhere, I mean, where the German nation is found."[28]

There is no word about the religious connotations of this festivity in Ticknor's journal. For Ticknor, Weihnachten was a celebration of family and German nation, which in his mind was essentially a Northern and Central German nation. The celebration of Weihnachten was not limited to a specific social class but involved all families from the richest to the poorest. Weihnachten was, in Ticknor's observation, a universal celebration that offered the glue that could bring German society together. And Ticknor was not alone in his assessment. J. Bayard Taylor asked readers of his travelogue not to dismiss the emotional and social value of such festivals. "We may laugh at such simple festivals at home," Taylor wrote, "but we would certainly be happier if some of these beautiful old customs were better honored. They renew the bond of feeling between families and friends, and strengthen their kindly sympathy; even life-long friends require occasions of this kind to freshen the wreath that binds them together."[29] And the social reformer Charles Loring Brace judged about the Weihnachten he experienced in Berlin:

> There is something about this German Festival, which one would seldom see in our home enjoyments. People do not seem to be enjoying them selves, because it is a "duty to be cheerful;" and because a family-gathering is a very beautiful and desirable thing. They are cheerful, because they cannot help it, and because they all love one another. ... They were all so happy, because they had been making one another happy. As I recall our hollow home-life in many parts of America—the selfishness and coldness in families—the little hold HOME has on any one, and the tendency of children to get rid of it as early as possible, I am conscious how much after all we have to learn from these easy Germans.[30]

And Brace continued to complain about Americans who "are not a happy people." For him, the introduction of German rituals such as birthday parties and Christmas trees would significantly improve American society.[31]

Ticknor, Taylor, and Brace were convinced that the introduction into American society of this peculiar German festival could provide the social glue that would give the family as the cornerstone of society greater coherence and, thereby, also enhance the coherence of American society at large. And they were not alone with this assessment. The Philadelphia theologian William Henry Furness complained in 1849: "We obviously suffer much in this country, from the fact that our population, out of New England, and some of the Southern states, is not indigenous." Anglo-Americans lacked, according to Furness, "strong local attachments and venerable customs." American society had not yet taken root in American soil and the political body of this state somehow hovered aboveground—"it has not struck its roots down deep into the soil." The German Christmas tree and Christmas ritual offered to Furness an opportunity to develop what Americans missed most: a venerable custom that would connect the American people with their soil.[32]

In the eyes of American observers, Weihnachten worked very well as a glue for the German society. This German holiday celebration proved, further, attractive to Anglo-Americans who sought to distinguish American society from English society. The introduction of cultural practices that set American society apart from English society contributed to the formation of an independent American identity. It also could become a motor for the integration into American society of those people who had come to North America from the European continent (not the British Isles) before and after the American Revolution and who had belonged to various ethnic, religious, and linguistic backgrounds.[33]

It was travel logs such as the ones produced by George Ticknor rather than the practice of Weihnachten by German-Americans such as Charles Follen that induced Anglo-Americans to adopt some of the German traditions of celebrating Weihnachten. It is curious that Ticknor learned about Weihnachten in faraway Göttingen and Dresden and not once mentioned that his colleague at Harvard—Charles Follen—played any role in introducing this custom to Boston. Given that Follen is credited with introducing the Christmas tree to the United States, one wonders whether Ticknor was actually aware of it or whether he willfully ignored it in order to claim this introduction for himself.

Ticknor's travelogues proved influential in Boston's High Society since he regularly sent his travelogues from Europe back to family and friends in Boston. These travelogues, as we learn from a letter by Elizabeth Peabody, were circulated for public reading among Boston's Brahmin families.[34] They served as a source of vicarious entertainment for those who did not travel to the European continent. They also induced others to follow in Ticknor's footsteps and travel to Europe on their own. And they finally served as a treasure trove of information about German culture and traditions that provided inspiration not only for the intercultural transfer of holiday customs such as Weihnachten but also for the reform of Harvard College along the lines of German high schools and the creation of the public lending library in Boston.[35]

The Ticknors went a step further when they held a Christmas party in 1843 to which they invited prominent friends such as Henry Longfellow and his wife Frances Appleton Longfellow. This party resembled exactly the ritual of Weihnachten as George Ticknor had encountered it in Dresden in 1835. Frances Appleton Longfellow wrote about the "beautiful Christmas tree decorated with presents" and the excitement of the children "when the folding doors opened and the pyramid of lights sparkled from the dark boughs of a lofty pine."[36]

Two years later, in 1845, the poet and travel writer J. Bayard Taylor observed "the most beautiful and interesting of all German festivals" in Frankfurt am Main.[37] Like Ticknor ten years earlier in Dresden he did not just observe the Christmas tree and the gift giving but also observed the Christmas market where one could buy presents and decorations. Such markets offered toys, wax candles, "gingerbread with printed mottos in poetry, beautiful little earthenware, basket-work, and a wilderness of playthings."[38]

Taylor was the first American to also report on the custom of St. Nicholas Day (December 5). That night St. Nicholas visits children and punishes those who had behaved badly while rewarding those who had behaved well with nuts and apples. The Christmas market in Frankfurt also offered, among other things, rods with gilded bands for parents. These rods were used by those men who dressed up as St. Nicholas to punish children with beatings. While the tradition of St. Nicholas Day did not find inroads into American society, the figure of St. Nicholas "with a mask, fur rob, and long tapering cap" was later absorbed into the figure of Santa Claus.[39]

St. Nicholas was an advance messenger for Christmas Day. He put children on notice if they had a track record of bad behavior and signaled to them that they might not receive any presents on December 24. The exchange of gifts on Christmas Eve was based, as some observers such as the German-American legal scholar and editor of the *Encyclopaedia Americana* Francis Lieber noted, on wishes made by children in the circle of their family about six weeks before Weihnachten. Lieber introduced Americans to this German custom in a letter written and published in *The New-York Mirror* in 1834:

> Six weeks before Christmas, children, and grown people too, begin to "wish," i.e. to intimate or openly to tell what presents they particularly desire. They consist, with children, mostly of toys. The nearer the times draws, the more mystery is there among families; packages come in, whose size and form are scrutinized by the children; yet none dare to open them, because every thing of the kind is considered *taboo* in this season.[40]

The Regional Diversity of Christmas Traditions in Germany

Based on a geographically limited experience—in Dresden and Berlin—American observers such as Ticknor and Brace presented to their American audience the ritual of Weihnachten as a truly national (German) celebration. Both observers overlooked the regional diversity of this emerging cultural practice. The English author William Howitt observed, by contrast, some important regional differences with regard to the St. Nicholas tradition. In his *The Rural and Domestic Life of Germany* (1842), Howitt wrote that "about a fortnight before Christmas" children received a visit from Pelznichel or Knecht Ruprecht who represents "no other than St. Nicholas."[41] Pelznichel was, according to Howitt, "a man disguised in a fur cap, and otherwise made awful to children by his singular habiliments, being armed with a rod, having a capacious bag or pouch hanging before him, and a large chain thrown around him, whose end being dropped on the ground as he walks."[42] Howitt introduced Pelznichel as a mediator in the gift-giving process. St. Nicholas, Pelznichel, or Knecht Ruprecht did not bring large gifts on December 5. But they assessed the worthiness of children: the good ones received nuts and apples, and the bad ones beatings. And these actions provided hints to the children with regard to the presents they could expect on December 24. Those who received nuts and apples on December 5 could be sure to also receive presents and those who received beatings with the rod or threats thereof were at least put on notice. If they did not behave well, they would not receive presents. Pelznichel appeared as omniscient. He walked around the homes at night and listened into conversations between children and parents.[43]

However, Pelznichel was a figure that threatened but rarely engaged in the punishment of children. Howitt wrote,

> Pelznichel talks sternly, and with menacing agitations of his rod, to those who have been stubborn, lazy, or disobedient, and commends those who have been otherwise. He hands the rod to the father, and commands him to use it when necessary, or he vows to come and use it himself. He seldom, however, proceeds on this occasion to any actual chastisement, as it is intended rather as a means of reformation, by instilling a salutary fear.[44]

Pelznichel and Knecht Ruprecht did not populate the narratives provided by Ticknor, Taylor, and Brace. These American descriptions of Weihnachten centered on the tree and the presents that were prepared in a separate and closed room to which children received access only after the ring of a bell. This bell signaled the beginning of the festivities. Since presents were exchanged directly between children and adults, no mediating figure was needed in this process. However, William Howitt observed in some regions customs that included the Christ-child (Southern Germany) and Knecht Ruprecht (Northern Germany) as bringer of gifts. The Christ-child existed in many forms and Germans had a wide range of notions about the nature of this figure. This child was imagined in some regions as male and in others as female. He or she was "dressed in white, with a gilt crown and wings, and with a long white veil ornamented with gold." Whatever its gender, the Christ-child was always a child. He or she guarded the room with the Christmas tree and the presents and had the power to prevent a misbehaved child from entering the room.[45]

Pelznichel was said to work together with the Christ-child in some regions. Pelznichel was expected to report to the Christ-child whether children behaved or misbehaved and, thereby, help make decisions for the giving of gifts on December 24. In some regions, the Christ-child worked together with Knecht Ruprecht. Both appeared on December 24 and distributed presents to children. Knecht Ruprecht was, however, active only in Germany's northeastern parts. Here presents were not laid out underneath Christmas trees but rather sent to a family friend who came to the homes on Christmas Eve. Knecht Ruprecht dressed in "high buskins, a white robe, a mask, and an enormous flax wig" went on Christmas Eve from house to house to distribute the presents in accordance with the instructions provided by the parents. Before he gave out the presents, he inquired with children and parents whether the children had been well-behaved and deserved the presents designated for them.[46]

Neither of these figures—Pelznichel, the male or female Christ-child, and Knecht Ruprecht—were included in the second transfer of Christmas customs from German homes to American homes that was facilitated by Anglo-Americans such as Ticknor and that occurred from the 1830s to the 1850s. The most popular and widely influential stories that presented the ritual of Weihnachten to an American audience—the travel journals of George Ticknor and the travelogues of J. Bayard Taylor and Charles Loring Brace—did not mention any of these figures. Customs such as the *Adventswreath* and the *Adventskalender* were equally absent from the American descriptions of Weihnachten. Interestingly, Charles Loring Brace's first stop on his German journey in 1850 was Wichern's Rough House in Hamburg. Brace arrived there in October and moved on to Berlin before he could encounter the tradition of the Advent period that was started at Wichern's Rough House. No mention is made in Brace's *Home-Life in Germany* (1853) of the Adventswreath and the Adventskalender. Brace missed by chance these two iconic elements of the Northwestern German tradition of the pre-Weihnachts period. His elaborate and detailed description of Weihnachten in Berlin mirrored the description Ticknor provided for the Christmas party he experienced in Dresden in 1835. However, while Ticknor confined his description to just two pages, Brace's description occupied an entire chapter of his travelogue.[47]

By the 1850s, American travelers and journalists could barely avoid Christmas trees in Germany since this custom had moved from private homes to the public sphere. The correspondent for the New York *Christian Advocate and Journal* observed in December 1854 that Christmas trees were put up in public institutions such as hospitals for the sick and disabled soldiers in Berlin. And these trees came with gifts provided by benefactors for the individuals confined to such institutions. Each individual in this institution received a book that presented a history of the Christmas ceremony and a store of tobacco and pipes.[48]

Translating Weihnachten into Christmas

The example set by Anglo-Americans such as George Ticknor inspired more and more Anglo-American families to appropriate this new and alien holiday ritual. They, however, did not appropriate all traditions developed in Germany in the first half of the nineteenth century. The Ticknors embraced only the Christmas tree and gift giving but not the gift bringer in the form of Knecht Ruprecht and not the tradition of the Adventskranz or Adventskalender. In that, they closely followed the ritual they had encountered in Dresden with the hiding away of the tree in a room closed off until the evening of December 24. And they used a bell to signal the opening of that room. Christmas markets that provided the toys and decorations for the Christmas trees did not make it across the Atlantic since the market for this kind of products was too narrow. American families, thus, had to make their own Christmas tree decorations. And as the example of the Christmas tree decoration in the home of Charles Follen shows, American children had to use much imagination in making the things they wanted to put onto the Christmas tree. Only the wax candles were universal with regard to the tree.

The figures of the Christ-child, Pelznichel, and Knecht Ruprecht did not make the voyage across the Atlantic. In the beginning, American Christmas existed without a figure who brought presents. This lack of transfer of these figures was due to the regions to which American travelers went and the places in which they observed the ritual of Weihnachten. Weihnachten in Berlin, Dresden, and Frankfurt am Main, which were the three main places in which Americans observed this ritual, did not include these figures at this time. The Christ-child occupied the Southern region of Germany, Pelznichel the central Western region, and Knecht Ruprecht the Northeastern German region.

Most American travelers did not encounter these figures or ignored them. The only English description of these figures and their role in the ritual of Weihnachten was provided by Howitt in his *Rural and Domestic Life of Germany* (1842).[49]

Howitt also linked both Pelznichel and Knecht Ruprecht to the figure of St. Nicholas.[50] They appeared to Howitt as incarnations of St. Nicholas and were moved from the ritual of December 5 to the ritual of December 24. Since neither of these figures was adopted by American audiences in the first half of the nineteenth century, the American version of Weihnachten initially relied on a gift exchange between adults and children without a mediator who was bringing the gifts.

The translation of Weihnachten and *Weihnachtsbaum* with Christmas and Christmas tree, respectively, contributed to the acceptance of this holiday custom into American society. The term "Weihnachten" was simply too alien to English-speakers to be integrated into American English. An English equivalent was needed. The English term of "Yule" was probably not considered for its Pagan and British-English background. Applying the term of Christmas to this German ritual, however, did not give Christian religion a greater role in its celebration. The early descriptions of American Christmas celebrations did not include church services or other religious practices.

Many Anglo-Americans were at first hesitant about replacing older customs such as the hanging of stockings with the new custom of presenting gifts under a decorated Christmas tree. They clang to the stockings that were hung up on the fireplace. The *New York Evangelist* from 1852 sheds some light on the slow appropriation of this German holiday practice. The author recounted the story of a family that decided to give the new custom a try. The unnamed author wrote,

> For the first time, a Christmas-tree was to be substituted for the immemorial custom of "having up stockings." Uncle Charles had recently returned from Germany, with glowing recollections of its happy and friendly homes. With some difficulty, the children were won over to the new project. Mary thought that "Christmas would not be Christmas," if she did not hang up her stocking; ... Philly had been its warm advocate from the first. He had read, and Uncle Charles had told him, too, of the German children, dancing, in delight around the brilliant, decorated tree, and it was a bright vision to his young imagination.[51]

This family decorated their Christmas tree in ways that emulated the German custom as close as possible. The tree was set up in a separate room to which the children had no access before Christmas Eve. On that night folding doors opened and gave free sight to a large box with a Christmas tree that had "its dark green boughs illuminated with a profusion of wax tapers. It was ornamented with fancy papers of different colors, curiously cut, and hung in tasteful festoons. Apples, covered with gilding in various devices, oranges, grapes, frosted cakes, and tempting confectionary hung from its branches."[52]

Christmas trees were not only introduced into the private homes of Anglo-Americans but also integrated into public events and places. The *Liberator* from 1843 reports about the placing of a *Christkindleinbaum* as a central attraction at the Ninth Massachusetts Anti-Slavery Fair. The use of the German term "Christkindleinbaum" seems to suggest that the author of the article was still struggling with finding an appropriate English term for this German custom that was slowly finding its way into Anglo-American culture. This tree was, after all, put on public display in the same year in which George Ticknor invited friends and family to celebrate Christmas with a trimmed Christmas tree in his private home for the first time. The Christkindleinbaum at the fair was "loaded with its Christmas gifts, brilliant with sparkling cones and gilded butterflies, so arranged by invisible supporters as to seem about to light among its treasures, and every branch bristling with wax candles, while the trunk was thickly studded with colored lamps."[53] This Christmas tree attracted thousands of visitors and many were sent away since the exhibition hall provided space for only 800 people. And the report from the *Liberator* went on:

> But to those who did obtain entrance, the blaze of the Christmas Tree was a spectacle even beyond the bright expectations they had formed. The crush was so great as to prevent the culling of the numbered fruitage from the tree, and its distribution to the holders of the tickets, to the great chagrin of the managers, who did not bear the disappointment so well as the children seemed disposed to do. When it was explained to them that the unexpected crowd would prevent the execution of the plan at that moment, but that it would be completed during the week, they all cried "good," yielding like good children to the necessity which could not be overcome, and came on Monday morning in successive crowds to receive their prizes.[54]

In the context of increasing acceptance of the German Weihnachten ritual in American society, the poem "A Visit from St. Nicholas" (commonly known as "Twas the Night Before Christmas") was published in 1844 by Clement Clark Moore. This poem had already been anonymously published almost twenty years earlier, but its republication in 1844 contributed to the public Christmas craze. However, the poem was the only American document that referred to St. Nicholas of the German tradition but credited him with bringing presents on Christmas Eve. It does not mention a Christmas tree but rather stockings as the central place for placing gifts. The reindeers of this poem were not part of the German tradition of Christmas and were not mentioned in any other description of the emerging Christmas ritual in the United States in the 1840s and 1850s.

In the context of the American Civil War, American Christmas was significantly transformed by the addition of the figure of Santa Claus. The inspiration for this addition originated again within the German culture of Weihnachten. In the first few decades of Christmas celebrations in the United States, no mediator in the gift-giving process was needed. Even though Weihnachten in some German regions already included a mediating figure for the distribution of gifts, such a figure was not appropriated by American observers. Giving gifts was, thus, a direct exchange between children and adults.

In the time of the American Civil War, the German-American cartoonist Thomas Nast who began working for *Harper's Weekly* in 1862 created in his drawings the figure of Santa Claus.[55] This figure was inspired and built upon the various German figures of St. Nicholas, Knecht Ruprecht, and Pelznichel. The January 3, 1863 edition of *Harper's Weekly* presented on its front page the very first image of Santa Claus who in this drawing visited the Union troops for Christmas of 1862. In the following years, Nast continued to create and modify the image of Santa Claus. In the first image, he was shown as an old man with a long white beard and dressed in a jacket and a pair of trousers in the colors of the American flag. A few years later, Nast turned Santa Claus into the jolly old man with a big belly and long white beard who was also smoking a pipe. And in the December 29, 1866 edition of *Harper's Weekly*, Nast provided an elaborate pictorial description of Santa Claus and his activities. The centerpiece of this sketch showed Santa Claus standing on a chair and filling stockings with presents. The Christmas tree was included in this picture but relegated to an image in the lower left corner. Santa Claus was shown to decorate the tree but the tree was not at the center of the sketch and the presents were not laid out underneath the tree. The other smaller inset drawings showed Santa Claus's many activities throughout the year. He looked out through his telescope for good children and entered the names of well-behaved and misbehaved children into an accounting book. He made dolls and sewed clothing for these dolls and from time to time took some leisure time in front of the fireplace. This sketch also introduced the notion that Santa Claus traveled by a sledge that was drawn by reindeers on Christmas Eve to bring presents. Nast, thereby, incorporated the narrative provided in the poem "A Visit from St. Nicholas" and mixed older traditions such as the giving of small gifts in stockings with newer traditions such as the trimming of the Christmas tree.

The drawings also suggest that even in the 1860s, the Christmas tree was not yet the center of the Christmas celebration. The center of the drawing was occupied by stockings hanging on a fireplace and not by the Christmas tree. Nast, thus, integrated various traditions and various narratives that subsequently formed the modern American Christmas ritual. He created a distinctive American holiday ritual that provided a place for both stockings and Christmas trees.

Notes

1. Thomas Adam and Gisela Mettele (eds.), *Two Boston Brahmins in Goethe's Germany: The Travel Journals of Anna and George Ticknor*, Lanham, Boulder, New York, Toronto, Oxford: Lexington Books, 2009, 110; Benedict Anderson, *Imagined Communities*, London and New York: Verso, 2006, 1–7.
2. See for instance: Charles Loring Brace, *Home-Life in Germany*, New York: Charles Scribner, 1853, 221–26 (chapter XXXIII).
3. Joe Perry, *Christmas in Germany: A Cultural History*, Chapel Hill: University of North Carolina Press, 2010; Penne L. Restad, *Christmas in America: A History*, New York and Oxford: Oxford University Press, 1995.
4. William Howitt, *The Rural and Domestic Life of Germany: With Characteristic Sketches of its Cities and Scenery, Collected in a General Tour, and during a Residence in the Country in the Years 1840, 41 and 42*, London: Longman, Brown, Green, and Longmans, 1842, 152.
5. See the entry on Weihnachten in: Jacob and Wilhelm Grimm's *Deutsches Wörterbuch* (online version) available at: http://woerterbuchnetz.de/cgi-bin/WBNetz/wbgui_py?sigle=DWB&mode=Vernetzung&lemid=GW13964#XGW13964 (accessed April 14, 2019).
6. Steffen Martus, *Die Brüder Grimm: Eine Biografie*, Berlin: Rowohlt, 2009.
7. Perry, *Christmas in Germany*.
8. Thomas Adam, "New Ways to Write the History of Western Europe and the United States: The Concept of Intercultural Transfer," in: *History Compass* 11, 10 (2013): 880–92.
9. Restad, *Christmas in America*, 57–58.
10. E. T. A. Hoffmann and Alexandre Dumas, *Nutcracker and Mouse King and the Tale of the Nutcracker*, translated by Joachim Neugroschel, New York: Penguin Random House, 2007.
11. Samuel T. Coleridge, "The Christmas Tree" (Ratzeburg, Germany, 1799). Available at: http://www.knoxvilletennessee.com/christmas/stories/ch_tree.html (accessed April 14, 2019).
12. *Memoirs of Her Most Excellent Majesty Sophia-Charlotte, Queen of Great Britain, from Authentic Documents*, by John Watkins, London: Henry Colburn, 1819, 462–63. The memoirs of George III contain an identical description of this Christmas celebration. See: *The Public and Domestic Life of His late Most Gracious Majesty, George the Third; Comprising the Most Eventful and Important Period in the Annals of British History: Compiled from Authentic Sources, and Interspersed with Numerous Anecdotes*, by Edward Holt, volume I, London: Sherwood, Neely, and Jones, 1820, 417.
13. *The Greville Memoirs: A Journal of the Reigns of King George IV. King William IV. and Queen Victoria by the late Charles C. F. Greville*, edited by Henry Reeve volume I, London, New York. Bombay: Longmans, Green and Co., 1896, 265–66.

14 William Howitt, *The Rural Life of England* volume II, London: Longman, Orme, Brown, Green & Longmans, 1838, 207.
15 Howitt, *The Rural Life of England* volume II, 193.
16 Howitt, *The Rural Life of England* volume II, 207.
17 Howitt, *The Rural Life of England* volume II, 199–200.
18 Restad, *Christmas in America*, 7; Stephen W. Nissenbaum *Christmas in Early New England, 1620–1820: Puritanism, Popular Culture, and the Printed Word* (*Proceedings of the American Antiquarian Society* January 1, 1996): 85–89; T. G. Crippen, *Christmas and Christmas Lore*, Detroit: Gale Research Company, 1971, 87–93.
19 Nissenbaum *Christmas in Early New England*, 81–82.
20 See, for instance, the contribution in: Frank Trommler and Joseph McVeigh (eds.), *America and the Germans: An Assessment of a Three-Hundred-Year History* volume I: *Immigration, Language, Ethnicity*, Philadelphia: University of Pennsylvania Press, 1985.
21 Charles H. Haswell, *Reminiscences of an Octogenarian of the City of New York (1816 to 1860)*, New York: Harper & Brothers, 1896, 330.
22 Restad, *Christmas in America*, 59–60.
23 Harriet Martineau, *Retrospect of Western Travel* volume II, London: Saunders and Otley, 1838, 178.
24 Heike Bungert, *Festkultur und Gedächtnis: Die Konstruktion einer deutschamerikanischen Ethnizität, 1848–1914*, Paderborn: Schöningh, 2016.
25 Restad, *Christmas in America*, 61–62.
26 Stephen Pielhoff, *Paternalismus und Stadtarmut: Armutswahrnehmung und Privatwohltätigkeit im Hamburger Bürgertum 1830–1914*, Hamburg: Verein für Hamburgische Geschichte, 1999, 292–323.
27 "Johann Heinrich Wichern und der Anfang des Adventskranzes" available at: https://derweg.org/feste/weihnachten/wichernadventskranz/ (accessed April 19, 2019).
28 Adam/Mettele, *Two Boston Brahmins in Goethe's Germany*, 109–10.
29 J. Bayard Taylor, *Views A-Foot; or Europe seen with Knapsack and Staff Part*, New York: Wiley and Putnam, 1846, 92.
30 Brace, *Home-Life in Germany*, 224–25.
31 Brace, *Home-Life in Germany*, 225–26.
32 W. H. Furness, "The Christmas Tree and Luther," in: *Sartain's Union Magazine of Literature and Art* vol. 5, No. 6 (December 1849): 18.
33 Furness, "The Christmas Tree and Luther," 18; Elise Lynn Prentis, "A Retrospect of 'Western' Travel: 1834–1836," in: *The Courier* 11, 4 and 12, 1 (1975): 6; Sam Haynes, *Unfinished Revolution: The Early American Republic in a British World*, Charlottesville: University of Virginia Press, 2010.
34 Letter of Elizabeth Peabody to Mary (Peabody), dated June 12, 1822, Peabody Family Papers, Sophia Smith Collection, Smith College, Northampton, Massachusetts.
35 Adam/Mettele, *Two Boston Brahmins in Goethe's Germany*; Thomas Adam, *Buying Respectability: Philanthropy and Urban Society in Transnational Perspective, 1840s to 1930s*, Bloomington and Indianapolis: Indiana University Press, 2009, 31–38.
36 Cited after Restad, *Christmas in America*, 60–61.
37 Taylor, *Views A-Foot*, 189.
38 Taylor, *Views A-Foot*, 90.
39 Taylor, *Views A-Foot*, 90.
40 Francis Lieber, "Letters to a Gentleman in Germany," in: *The New-York Mirror: A Weekly Gazette of Literature and the Fine Arts*, December 20, 1834, 194. For Lieber

see: Tibor Baukal, "Lieber, Francis (Franz)," in: Thomas Adam (ed.), *Germany and the Americas: Culture, Politics, and History* volume 2, Santa Barbara, Denver, Oxford: ABC CLIO, 2005, 666–68.
41 Howitt, *The Rural and Domestic Life of Germany*, 159.
42 Howitt, *The Rural and Domestic Life of Germany*, 160.
43 Howitt, *The Rural and Domestic Life of Germany*, 161.
44 Howitt, *The Rural and Domestic Life of Germany*, 162.
45 Howitt, *The Rural and Domestic Life of Germany*, 168.
46 S. T. Coleridge, *The Friend: A Series of Essays*, London: Gale and Curtis, 1812, 301; Howitt, *The Rural Life of England* volume II, 202–3.
47 Brace, *Home-Life in Germany*, 221–26.
48 *German Reformed Messenger* April 25, 1855, 34.
49 Howitt, *The Rural and Domestic Life of Germany*, 159–64.
50 Howitt, *The Rural and Domestic Life of Germany*, 159–60.
51 *New York Evangelist*, December 30, 1852, 1.
52 *New York Evangelist*, December 30, 1852, 1.
53 M. W. C., "Sketches of the Fair—No. 11: The Christmas Tree," in: *Liberator*, January 27, 1843: 15.
54 M. W. C., "Sketches of the Fair," 15.
55 Tobias Brinkmann, "Nast, Thomas," in: *Germany and the Americas* volume 2, 803–5.

Bibliography

Primary Sources

Brace, Charles Loring. *Home-Life in Germany*. New York: Charles Scribner, 1953.
Coleridge, Samuel T. *The Friend: A Series of Essays*. London: Gale and Curtis, 1812.
Coleridge, Samuel T. "The Christmas Tree" (Ratzeburg, Germany, 1799). Available at: http://www.knoxvilletennessee.com/christmas/stories/ch_tree.html (accessed April 14, 2019).
Furness, W. H. "The Christmas Tree and Luther." *Sartain's Union Magazine of Literature and Art*. 5, 6 (December 1849): 18–21.
German Reformed Messenger. April 25, 1855.
Haswell, Charles H. *Reminiscences of an Octogenarian of the City of New York (1816 to 1860)*. New York: Harper & Brothers, 1896.
Hoffmann, E. T. A. and Alexandre Dumas. *Nutcracker and Mouse King and the Tale of the Nutcracker*, translated by Joachim Neugroschel. New York: Penguin Random House, 2007.
Howitt, William. *The Rural and Domestic Life of Germany: With Characteristic Sketches of its Cities and Scenery, Collected in a General Tour, and during a Residence in the Country in the Years 1840, 41 and 42*. London: Longman, Brown, Green, and Longmans, 1842.
Howitt, William. *The Rural Life of England* volume II. London: Longman, Orme, Brown, Green & Longmans, 1838.
"Johann Heinrich Wichern und der Anfang des Adventskranzes." available at: https://derweg.org/feste/weihnachten/wichernadventskranz/ (accessed April 19, 2019).
Letter of Elizabeth Peabody to Mary (Peabody), dated June 12, 1822, Peabody Family Papers, Sophia Smith Collection, Smith College, Northampton, Massachusetts.
Lieber, Francis. "Letters to a Gentleman in Germany." *The New-York Mirror: A Weekly Gazette of Literature and the Fine Arts*. December 20, 1834: 194.

Martineau, Harriet. *Retrospect of Western Travel* volume II. London: Saunders and Otley, 1838.

Memoirs of Her Most Excellent Majesty Sophia-Charlotte, Queen of Great Britain, from Authentic Documents, by John Watkins. London: Henry Colburn, 1819.

M. W. C. "Sketches of the Fair – No. 11: The Christmas Tree." *Liberator*, January 27, 1843: 15.

New York Evangelist. December 30, 1852.

Taylor, J. Bayard. *Views A-Foot; or Europe seen with Knapsack and Staff Part.* New York: Wiley and Putnam, 1846.

The Greville Memoirs: A Journal of the Reigns of King George IV. King William IV. and Queen Victoria by the late Charles C. F. Greville, edited by Henry Reeve volume I. London, New York. Bombay: Longmans, Green and Co., 1896.

The Public and Domestic Life of His late Most Gracious Majesty, George the Third; Comprising the Most Eventful and Important Period in the Annals of British History: Compiled from Authentic Sources, and Interspersed with Numerous Anecdotes, by Edward Holt, volume I. London: Sherwood, Neely, and Jones, 1820.

Secondary Sources

Adam, Thomas. *Buying Respectability: Philanthropy and Urban Society in Transnational Perspective, 1840s to 1930s.* Bloomington and Indianapolis: Indiana University Press, 2009.

Adam, Thomas "New Ways to Write the History of Western Europe and the United States: The Concept of Intercultural Transfer." *History Compass* 11, 10 (2013): 880–92.

Adam, Thomas and Gisela Mettele, eds. *Two Boston Brahmins in Goethe's Germany: The Travel Journals of Anna and George Ticknor.* Lanham, Boulder, New York, Toronto, Oxford: Lexington Books, 2009.

Anderson, Benedict. *Imagined Communities.* London and New York: Verso, 2006.

Baukal, Tibor. "Lieber, Francis (Franz)." In: *Germany and the Americas: Culture, Politics, and History* volume 2, edited by Thomas Adam. Santa Barbara, Denver, Oxford: ABC CLIO 2005, 666–68.

Brinkmann, Tobias. "Nast, Thomas." In: *Germany and the Americas: Culture, Politics, and History* volume 2, edited by Thomas Adam. Santa Barbara, Denver, Oxford: ABC CLIO, 2005, 803–5.

Bungert, Heike. *Festkultur und Gedächtnis: Die Konstruktion einer deutschamerikanischen Ethnizität, 1848–1914.* Paderborn: Schöningh, 2016.

Crippen, T. G. *Christmas and Christmas Lore.* Detroit: Gale Research Company, 1971.

Grimm, Jacob and Wilhelm. *Deutsches Wörterbuch* (online version) available at: http://woerterbuchnetz.de/cgi-bin/WBNetz/wbgui_py?sigle=DWB&mode=Vernetzung&lemid=GW13964#XGW13964 (accessed April 14, 2019).

Haynes, Sam. *Unfinished Revolution: The Early American Republic in a British World.* Charlottesville: University of Virginia Press, 2010.

Martus, Steffen. *Die Brüder Grimm: Eine Biografie.* Berlin: Rowohlt, 2009.

Nissenbaum, Stephen W. *Christmas in Early New England, 1620–1820: Puritanism, Popular Culture, and the Printed Word* (*Proceedings of the American Antiquarian Society* January 1, 1996).

Perry, Joe. *Christmas in Germany: A Cultural History.* Chapel Hill: University of North Carolina Press, 2010.

Pielhoff, Stephen. *Paternalismus und Stadtarmut: Armutswahrnehmung und Privatwohltätigkeit im Hamburger Bürgertum 1830–1914.* Hamburg: Verein für Hamburgische Geschichte, 1999.

Prentis, Elise Lynn. "A Retrospect of 'Western' Travel: 1834–1836." *The Courier* 11, 4 and 12, 1 (1975): 3–21.

Restad, Penne L. *Christmas in America: A History*. New York and Oxford: Oxford University Press, 1995.

Trommler, Frank and Joseph McVeigh, eds. *America and the Germans: An Assessment of a Three-Hundred-Year History* volume I: *Immigration, Language, Ethnicity*. Philadelphia: University of Pennsylvania Press, 1985.

INDEX

A Patriot's History of the United States 10
A Visit From St. Nicholas 171–72
Abseits rule 83
academies of art 61
Academy of Fine Arts Berlin 61, 64
Adams, Herbert Baxter 15
Address before the Syracuse Chamber of Commerce regarding a Museum of Fine Arts 62
adult education societies 91
Advent period 162, 168
Adventskalender 163, 168–69
Adventskranz 163, 169
Adventswreath. *See* Adventskranz
Africa 76, 149
African National Congress (ANC) 139–40
Agent(s) of intercultural transfer 2–5, 9, 21, 23, 31–32, 45–46, 57, 78, 81, 83, 104, 155
Agra 133
Alabama 142
Albany 65
Albrecht, Rudolf 37
Allegheny College 60
Allen, Michael 10
Allgemeiner Turnverein zu Leipzig 92
amateurism 91
America 10, 20, 62, 135, 141
American Civil War 172
American museum associations 22
American Museum of Natural History 65, 114
American Revolution 15, 161, 165
American War of Independence. *See* American Revolution
Americanization 22, 78, 105
Amsterdam 36, 68

anti-colonial struggle 149
Antiquity, Germanic 157
Antiquity, Greek and Roman 157
antisemitism 115–17, 137
apartheid 139–40
applied arts museums 64
approach
    comparative 14
Aquino, Cory 4, 147, 148
Arabian Sea 132
Arbeiterturnerbund 92, 93
Argentina 76–80, 82, 89–91, 93
Argentina Football League 86, 90
Arizona 144
Arnold, Thomas 79, 88
Art Museum Berlin 64
art museums 22, 57, 59, 60–61, 63, 64
    American 57
    German 63
Aschrott, Paul Felix 41
Ashley, Lord 33
ashram 128
Asia 76, 127, 147, 149
Association for Improving the Condition of the Poor 45
associations 3, 113, 114
    art 57, 61, 63, 68
    American 63
    Dresden 63
    German 57, 62, 63
    Leipzig 61–63
    benevolent 114
    Christian 112
    Christian female 113–14
    female benevolent 114
    Jewish female 113
    Jewish male 113–14

Atlantic Ocean 9, 13, 17, 31, 40, 44–46, 58, 61, 155–56, 169
Atlantic Crossings 11, 30
Atlantic World 13, 45, 89, 103
Attila the Hun 134
Aufforderung zur Gründung einer gemeinnützigen Baugesellschaft in Frankfurt am Main 35
Austria 42, 60

Baader, Benjamin 113
Baden-Baden 84
Baer, Gabriel 109
Balanchine, George 16
Bancroft, George 58
Barnes, John Robert 106–7
Barr Jr., E. L. 145
Barth, Karl 136
Basel 36
Battle in the Teutoburg Forrest 104
Battle of Sedan 92
Bavaria 89
Beekman family 58
Beijing 148
Belgium 36, 42, 59, 60, 66, 135
Bell, George 136
Benckendorff, Christoph von 159
Bender, Thomas 11
Bentham, Jeremy 143
bequest 111
Berlin 5, 6, 30, 32–38, 40, 42, 44, 58, 60–62, 64, 68, 79, 91, 111, 164, 167–69
Berliner gemeinnützige Baugesellschaft 34, 35, 37, 38, 41, 42, 44
Berlin-Wilmersdorf 116
Bikur Holim 113
Black Act 131
Bombay 133, 134
Bonhoeffer, Dietrich 127, 135–40
Boston 3–6, 18, 20, 22, 29, 30, 32, 38, 39–40, 42, 43–44, 46, 65, 66, 67, 162, 165
Boston Cooperative Building Company 39, 40, 42
Boston Public Library 18, 19, 22
Bowditch, Henry I. 4, 29–30, 38–40, 42, 46
Brace, Charles Loring 20, 155, 164, 167–69

Braunschweig 76, 79, 82, 83, 85–87, 89–90, 93
Braunschweig, Duchy of 85
Brazil 79–80
Bremen 36, 61–62, 91
Bremer Kunsthalle 15
Breslau 68
Brimmer, Martin 39
British Channel 9, 31, 45
British Empire 128, 145
British imperialism 137
British Isles 159, 165
Brooklyn 161
Brothers Grimm 156–57
Brown, Diego 82
Brussels 35
Bryant, William Cullen 5, 59
Buddhism 102
Buenos Aires 76, 79–82, 84, 86, 90, 94
Buffalo 65
Byzantine Empire 106

Cahen, Claude 107
Cail, William 84
Cairo 107
Calcutta 133
Calder, Norman 108
California 144
California Grape and Tree Fruit League 145
Calvin, John 110
Cambridge 65
Canada 64, 116
Cannstatt 84
Cassel 113
Catholic Church 109, 110
Catholicism 103, 105, 109, 111, 160
Cattan, Henry 108
Celle 68
Century Club 59
Champaran 132
change, demographic 13
charitable institutions 109
charitable trusts 103, 108–12, 114, 118
charities, Jewish 112
charity 103, 105, 109, 112–13
Charles Miller, Charles William 79
Chávez, César 4, 11, 127, 144–46

Chicago 17, 65
Chichester 136
Christ-child 168, 169
Christian Advocate and Journal 169
Christian Church 135
Christianity 3, 101, 103, 105, 108–9, 117, 127, 135, 137
Christkindleinbaum 171
Christmas 2, 19, 20, 44, 155–73
Christmas Day 159–60, 162, 166
Christmas economy 162
Christmas Eve 166, 168, 170, 172
Christmas in America 161
Christmas market 162–63, 166, 169
Christmas party 4, 159, 160, 163, 166, 169
Christmas ritual 4, 5, 156–59, 162–63, 165–73
Christmas traditions 167–68
Christmas tree 5, 19–20, 155–73
Christoph Heinrich, Prince von Lieven 159
citizenship 11
City & Suburban Homes Company 45
city parks 9
Civil Disobedience 128
civil rights fight of African-Americans 127, 140–42, 144
civil rights struggles 149
civil society 9, 103
civil society, agents of 9
Çizakça, Murat 108
Clavin, Patricia 13
Clifford, Dr. 129
closed apartment 43
Cold War 10, 21, 127, 144, 149
Coledridge, Samuel Taylor 158
College of William and Mary 161
Cologne 111
colonialism 138
Comfort, George Fisk 57, 60–62, 64
communism 127, 148
   end of 149
Communist Party of the United States 142
Congress of Racial Equality (CORE) 142–43
connectivity 14
conquest 12
Conrad, Sebastian 13
Cooper, James Fenimore 58

cooperative(s) 33, 36–37, 39
   consumer 34, 91
   housing 32, 36–37, 91
      German 37
   savings and building 35, 37
cooperative movement, German 37
Copenhagen 36
Cox, Oscar 79–80
credit union 37
Crusades 108
cultural contact zones 16
cultural transfer concepts 3
Cutting, Robert Fulton 45

Dallas 11
Dandi 132
Darmstadt 67
democracy 103
democratization 37
Denmark 42
departmentalization of museums 67
Der Ganz Grosse Traum 81–82
Desai, Mahdev 140
Deutsche Turnerschaft 91–93
Dexter Avenue Baptist Church (Montgomery) 142
Dharasana Salt Works 147
diaspora, English 79, 81, 84, 86, 90
diasporas 62
Die Geschichte des Fußballs im Altertum und in der Neuzeit 82
diffusion 78, 105
Dolffs & Helle 85
Dr. Markus Mosse Hospital in Graetz 116
Dresden 3, 4, 18, 37, 58, 61–62, 68, 79, 84, 156, 163, 165–67, 169
Dresden art gallery 62
Dunning, Eric 87
Durban 128
Durham, William of 108

East Germany 148
Easter 162
education 9, 13, 17
   American 21
   German 79
   elementary 45
   higher 15, 45, 64

educational system, English 81
Egypt 61, 107
Elias, Norbert 87
Elizabeth Peabody 18
Elvers, Rudolf 33
Encyclopaedia Americana 166
Encyclopedia 112
endowment 3, 109–12, 116
   Protestant 111
England. See Great Britain
English colonies in North America 161
Enlightenment 3, 9, 112, 157
Escuela de Campeones 81
Espagne, Michel 13
Ethics 138
ethics of responsibility 138
Europe 2, 10, 17, 19, 22, 29–30, 32, 41, 46, 57, 59, 60, 62, 65, 66, 76, 80, 82, 88, 101, 103, 112–14, 117, 127, 147, 149, 165
   Eastern 127, 147–48
   Central 109, 110
   continental 38
   Northern 110
   Western 35, 38, 41, 43, 107–10, 113–14
European-American civilization 135

Facebook 11
factory villages 34, 38
fagging system 88
fairy tales 157
fidei commissum 106–7, 110
fine arts museum 62
First International Congress on Public Hygiene 35
Fischer, Louis 145
Fisher, Fredrick B. 133, 141
Flensburger Arbeiterbauverein 36
Follen, Charles 156, 161–62, 165, 169
Follen, Charley 161
football 1, 2, 4, 75–94
   nationalization of 76, 78
foundation 3, 101–2, 105–10, 112, 117
France 9, 35–36, 42, 59–60, 68, 85, 92, 112, 135
Franciscan Friars 108
Frankfurt am Main 5, 30, 32, 35, 36, 40, 68, 113, 166, 169

free lending library 18–19, 22
Freedom Rides 143
French Revolution 3, 9, 104, 112
Frey, Manuel 61
Froebel, Friedrich 17
Furness, William Henry 165

Gandhi, Manilal 139
Gandhi, Mohandas Karamchand (Mahatma) 4, 6, 127, 128–29, 131–33, 135–137, 139–47
Gandhism 127, 137, 140–43
Gaudiosi, Monica 108
gemeinnützige Baugesellschaft in Frankfurt am Main 36
General Court of the Massachusetts Bay Colony 161
George III, King of England 158
George the Pious, Great Elector of Saxony 110
German Dictionary 156
German subculture 162
German-American subculture 155
Germantown, Pennsylvania 161
Germany 9, 16, 17, 19, 22, 32, 36, 42, 44, 57–58, 60, 62, 64–66, 68, 76–77, 79, 82, 84–86, 89–93, 111, 135, 137, 139, 149, 155–56, 160, 162–63, 167, 169, 170
   Central 79, 161, 169
   Northern 85, 89, 157, 168–69
   Southern 79, 168–69
   Western 85, 89, 161
Geschichte des Fußballs im Altertum und in der Neuzeit 86
gift giving 5, 19–20, 155–56, 158–59, 161–63, 166–72
giving society 3–5, 9, 16, 20–23, 32, 78, 81, 104
Glasgow 79
globalization 2
Gotha 62
Göttingen 4, 20, 37, 79, 164–65
Gould, Elgin R. L. 29, 41–46
Graham, Martha 16
Grävell, A. 37
Great Britain 9, 32–33, 35–36, 38, 42, 44, 59, 60, 62, 66, 68–80, 82, 85,

88–89, 107–8, 131, 135–36, 155, 158, 160–63
Great Depression 144
Greece 60, 61
Green Vault in Dresden 66
Grever, Maria 11
Greville, Charles 160
Groningen 36
Grosse, Ernst 67
Grünstadt 113
Gujarat 132
Gymansium zum Grauen Kloster 111
Gymnasial- und Stiftungsfonds zu Köln 111
Gymnasium Martino-Katharineum at Braunschweig 3, 4, 79, 82–83, 85, 90
gymnastics 80, 84–87, 89, 92, 93
 free 86

Halle 68
Hamburg 17, 62, 162, 168
Hampe, Karl 116
Hanover 36, 37, 42–44
Harijan 140
Harper's Weekly 172
Harvard College 161–62, 165
Haswell, Charles 161
health care and hygiene movement 35
Hennigan, Peter C. 107, 109
heqdesh 101, 105, 107–8
Hermann, August 83, 85–86
high school(s) 2, 18, 76, 89, 111
 Argentine 75
 English 2, 80–82, 86, 90
 German 75, 80, 82
High Society 58
 Boston 18, 165
 New York 58
Hill, Octavia 38–40, 44
Hillebrand, Karl 79
history 104
 American 9, 11
 comparative 3, 14
 cultural 12, 104
 diplomatic 12
 German 9
 national 10–12, 13, 77, 94, 104
 social 12

transatlantic 11
transfer 31
transnational 11–13, 31, 77, 94, 104, 117
transnationalization of 11
Histriomastix 160
Hitler, Adolf 77, 137, 138
Hobbes, Thomas 144
Hoffmann, Carl Wilhelm 34, 37
Hoffmann, E. T. A. 158
Hoffmeister, Kurt 79
Holland 42, 59, 60, 66
Holy Roman Empire 110, 158
Home-Life in Germany 20, 168
Hosken, Mr. 129–30
hospitals 114–15
housing reform 35, 38, 42, 44
housing trusts 38, 39, 42, 43
Howard University 140–41
Howitt, William 160, 167–68, 170
Huber, Victor Aimé 30, 32–41
Hughes, Thomas 80
Hutton, Alexander Watson 79–82, 84, 86, 88
hygiene movement 35

identity 11
 American 165
 Argentine 76
 German 76, 86, 155–56
 national 13, 75–76, 81, 94, 103, 156
Ilchman, Warren 102
immigration 11
Improved Dwellings Company of New York 42
Improved Industrial Dwelling Company 39
India 4, 127, 131–37, 139–44
Indian civilization 135
Indians' Relief Bill 131
Industrial Revolution 103
industrialization 32, 41, 45, 84
innere Colonisation 33
insane asylum 35
institute for the blind and deaf 35
Introduction to Religious Foundations in the Ottoman Empire 106
Iraq 144

Iriye, Akira 12
Irving, Washington 58
Islam 3, 101, 103, 105–6, 108–9, 117
Islamic colleges 108
Islamic Empire 106, 109
Israelite Women's Sick Fund 113
Italy 21, 23, 60, 66

Jahn, Friedrich Ludwig 86, 92
Jaime 134
Jarrow Building Company 39
Jay, John 59
jeans 22
Johann Friedrich, Duke of Saxony 110
Johnson, Mordecai 141
Journey of Reconciliation 143
Judaism 3, 101, 102, 103, 105

Karlsruhe 84
Katharina Alexandra Dorothea, Countess von Lieven 159
Katz, Stanley 102
Kensington Museum 60, 64
kindergarten 9, 17, 19, 35
King Jr., Martin Luther 4, 127, 141–45
Knecht Ruprecht 167, 168–70, 172
Knickerbocker families 59, 63
Koch, Konrad 4, 79–86, 88
Kopenhagen Arbeiterverein 36
Krefeld 68
Kroes, Rob 22, 105
Krupp, Alfred 38
Kunsthalle in Hamburg 67
Kuran, Timur 106

La Pietra Report 11
Lamb, Frederick 159
Lancashire 137
Latin America 148
Lausanne 79, 80
Lawson, James 142
League of Nations 137
Leipzig 5, 6, 29, 30, 32, 37, 42, 44, 46, 61, 63, 68, 79, 91, 92–93, 148, 149
  art museum 62
Lenin, Vladimir 143
Letter from the Chairman of the State Board of Health 39

Leutze, Emanuel 15
Liagre, Gustav de 30
Liberator 171
library 18
  Dresden 3, 17–19, 22
  Göttingen 3, 17–19, 22
Lichtwark, Alfred 67
Lieber, Francis 166
lifestyle reform movement 90
limited dividend housing companies 5, 32–37, 40–42, 45, 46
limited liability 36–37
Lingelbach, Gabriele 15
London 5, 6, 29–30, 32–36, 38, 40–43, 46, 68, 85, 92, 128, 131, 159
Longfellow, Frances Appleton 166
Longfellow, Henry 20, 166
Louis XVI, King of France 112
Lübeck 68
Luther, Martin 110–11, 158

Magdeburg 92
Mahatma Gandhi 133
Makan, John 60–61
Makdisi, George 108
Malacanang Palace 147
Mandela, Nelson 139–40
Manhattan Club 59
Manila 147
March on Washington 142–43
Marcos, Ferdinand 147–48
Martineau, Harriet 161
Marx, Karl 143
Massachusetts 59
Mays, Benjamin E. 4, 140–41
McCarthy, Kathleen D. 112
Mecklenburg-Strelitz, Duchy of 158
Mediterranean World 103
Memoirs of Queen Sophia Charlotte 159
Merton College at Oxford 108
Merton, Walter de 108
Metropolitan Art Museum Association 63, 68
Metropolitan Association for Improving the Dwellings of the Industrious Classes 32, 34
Metropolitan Museum of Art 6, 15, 57–60, 62–64, 66, 114

INDEX

Mexican Revolution 144
Meyer, Adolf Bernhard 57, 65–66
Meyer, Herrmann Julius 42–45
Meyer's Housing Trust 42, 44
migration 12–13, 16, 45
Mill, John Stuart 143
Miller, Charles William 79–80
Milwaukee 17
Minnegerode, Charles 161
Monday Demonstration 148
monopoly on the production, sale, and taxation of salt 132
Montessori Method 21
Montessori schools 21
Montessori, Maria 21, 23
Montgomery 142
Montgomery Bus Boycott 142–43
Moore, Clement Clark 171
Moral Man 136–37
Mosse, Rudolf 116
Mosse-Stift 116
Motley, John Lothrop 58
Munich 61, 62, 68, 92
museum education 65
museum models 65
Museum of Fine Arts
   Boston 66–67
   Dresden 59
   German 67
   Madrid 59
museum reform 57
museum(s) 2, 9, 13, 57, 60–62, 64–68, 114–15
   American 6, 57, 65–67
   associations 5, 6, 22, 57, 68
   Belgian 66
   British 66
   European 66
   French 66
   German 6, 66
Museumskunde 68
mutual aid associations 113
mutual health insurance systems 91

Napoleonic Wars 17, 101, 103, 113–14
Nast, Thomas 172
nation states, agents of 9

National Academy of Design 59
National Farmworkers Association (NFA) 146
nationalism 1, 157
Nazism 137
Near East 109
Neckar, valley of the 84
New England 19, 20, 165
New Grand Ducal Museum in Darmstadt 67
New Museum Berlin 60
New Testament 160
New Year's Eve 159
New York 5–6, 15–19, 29–30, 38, 42–46, 57–59, 63–65, 68, 114, 161, 169
New York Evangelist 170
New York Historical Society 59
Niebuhr, Reinhold 136, 137, 139
Nietzsche, Friedrich 144
Nikolai Church in Leipzig 148
Ninth Massachusetts Anti-Slavery Fair 171
non-governmental organizations 12
non-violent resistance 2, 4, 127–29, 131–33, 135–44, 146–49
Nörrenberg, Constantin 21
North Africa 109
North America 57, 66, 68, 101, 103, 114, 127, 147, 149, 161–62, 165
North Atlantic 29–30
nuclear family 43, 45
Nuremberg 61–62
Nutcracker and Mouse King 158

Octavia Hill's house management system 38–40, 44
Old Museum Berlin 60
open apartment 43
opera houses 114
Orion 92
Owen, Robert 33
Oxford 108

Palestine 108
Panshanger, estate of 159
paradox of intercultural transfer 22
Paris 30, 59, 68, 85, 108
Parks, Rosa 142
passive resistance 6, 128–31, 133–36

patriotism 10
Peabody Trust 39, 43
Peabody, Elizabeth 17, 165
Peabody, George 39
Pelznichel 167–70, 172
Pennsylvania 19
Pennsylvania system of solitary imprisonment 35
Pension Fund for the City of Berlin 116
Perpignan 113
Peters, Rudolph 108
Philadelphia 17, 18, 30, 65, 141, 165
philanthropic housing companies 33, 38
philanthropy 2, 3, 31, 35–36, 39, 43, 45, 61, 101–3, 105–6, 110–12, 114–17
　American 103
　Catholic 111
　Protestant 111
　pure 31, 38
Philanthropy and Five Percent 30–32, 34, 36, 38–42
Philipp I, Count of Hesse 110
Philippines 147–48
piae causae 105–7
Pilates 16
Pilates Elders 16
Pilates exercise movement 16
Pilates, Joseph 16
Posen 61, 116
Pratt, Mary Louise 16
Pretoria 128
prison reform 35
private social welfare 30
Protestant Reformation 101, 103, 110, 112
Protestantism 103, 105, 109, 160
Prynne, William 160
public lending libraries 3, 18, 165
public library 18
public schools 79, 84, 86, 88
　Argentine 82
　English 2, 75–76, 88
　Eton 2, 76, 83, 89
　Marlborough 4, 83
　Rugby 2–3, 80, 83, 88
Puritanism 160–61
Putnam, George P. 59, 62

Queen, Edward L. 102

racial discrimination 127, 128, 140
racism 140
Raphael 58, 62
Ratzeburg 158
Rauhes Haus 162
receiving society 3–6, 9, 15, 17, 19–21, 23, 31, 32, 46, 75, 78, 81, 104, 155
Reck, Friedrich 85–87, 89
relational approaches 15
Reminiscences of an Octogenarian 161
Restad, Penne L. 161
Rhineland 113
Rhinelander family 58
Rhode Island 21
Riga 159
Rio de Janeiro 76, 79, 80
ritual 155–58, 161–62, 164, 169–70
　holiday 2, 155–57, 169, 173
Robbins, Jerome 16
Robinson, Edward 66
Rodgers, Daniel T. 10, 11, 13, 15, 16, 29–30
Rolland, Romain 133
Romania 148
Romantic period 19
Romanticism 157
Rome 21, 160
Rough House. *See* Rauhes Haus
Royal Art Museum in Dresden 6, 68
Royal Library Berlin 61
Royal Ontario Museum 115
Royal Saxon Collections of Art and Science 65
Royal Zoological, Anthropological, and Ethnographical Museum in Dresden 65
Rugby Football Union 84
Ruprecht, Wilhelm 41
Rural and Domestic Life of Germany 170
Ruskin, John 127–28
Russia 62
Rustin, Bayard 142–43

sadaqa 101, 105
salt 132
Salt March 132, 141–42
salt monopoly 132
salvation, Catholic conception of 110

Samuel, Sigmund 115–16
San Antonio Conservation Society 11
Santa Claus 166, 172
Sao Paulo Railway Company 79
Sarmiento, Domingo 81
Satyagraha 4, 6, 128–33, 137, 139, 141, 143
Satyagraha in South Africa 129
savings bank 43
Saxony 20, 59, 62, 89
Schäfer, Axel 29–30
Schletter, Heinrich Adolf 62
scholarship aid 111–12
school reform 2, 75–76, 78, 87, 94
school system
   American 21
   English 79–80, 82
Schurz, Carl 17
Schurz, Margarethe 17
Schweikert, Larry 10
Scotland 79–80
Second Annual Report of the State Board of Health of Massachusetts 40
Sedan Celebrations 92
Seidlitz, Woldemar von 6, 57, 68
self-help 36–37, 39, 43
Seminarum Philipinum 110
Seven Years War 116
Shaftesbury, Lord. *See* Ashley, Lord
Sharpeville Massacre 140
shiva 113
Shridharani, Krishnalal 142–43
sick care associations 113
Sistine Madonna 58, 62
Smithsonian Institution 66
Smuts, Jan Christiaan 131
social housing 29–31, 36, 38, 41, 43, 44
   associations 33, 37
   charity 18
   companies 5, 29–31, 35, 38, 41–44
   company 34, 36, 39
   concepts of 5, 38, 41
   experiments 38
   models 29–32, 38–39, 42, 44–46
   movement 36
   projects 31, 38, 42–44, 46, 114
   reform 2, 29, 44
   sector 36

social policies 13, 29–30
   European 30
social question 30–31
social reform 75, 87, 94, 162
social welfare policies 29–30
Society for Improving the Condition of the Labouring Classes 34, 36, 38
Sophie Charlotte, Duchess of Mecklenburg-Strelitz 158
South Africa 127–28, 130–31, 139–40, 149
South America 2, 76, 80, 88, 127, 147, 149
Southampton 79
Soviet Union 21
Soysal, Yasemin 11
Spain 59, 60, 113
Spar und Bauverein Hannover 36–37, 42–44
Spiess, Adolf 86
Sputnik Shock 21
St. Andrews School 79, 82
St. Francis of Assisi 145
St. Louis 17
St. Nicholas Day 166–67, 170–72
Stanley, Lord 31
Streit, Sigismund 111
Stride towards Freedom 143
Sturgis, R. Clipston 66
Stuttgart 68, 79, 84
Stuyvesant family 58
subculture 77, 93
   Conservative 77, 91–92
   Socialist 77, 91–92
suffragist movement 129
suffragists 129–30
Sweden 42
Switzerland 66, 79, 133

Taj Mahal 133
Taylor, J. Bayard 164, 166–68
Technical University at Berlin 135
terrorism 12
Texas 11
That Strange Little Brown Man Gandhi 133, 141
The Delineator 21
The Housing of the Working People 42
The Kingdom of God Is Within You 128
The Laws of Football as Played at Rugby School 88

The Life of Mahatma Gandhi 145
The Montessori Method 21
The Museum Commission in Europe 67
The New-York Mirror 166
The Rural and Domestic Life of Germany 167
The Rural Life of England 160
Third Annual Report of the Boston Co-operative Building Company 40, 43
Thomas, Ann Van Wynen 107
Thoreau, Henry David 128, 142, 145
Thurman, Howard 4, 140–41
Thurman, Sue 141
Tiananmen Square massacre 148
Ticknor, Anna 163
Ticknor, George 3, 4, 17–20, 58, 155–56, 162–69, 171
Tobias, Channing H. 140–41
Tolle, Marie 85
Tolstoy, Leo 127, 128
Tom Brown's Schooldays 80
Toronto 115–16
totalitarianism 137
transculturation 16
Transnational Nation 11
Transvaal 131
travel 4, 16–17, 32, 38, 41–42, 79–81, 84, 85
  accounts 42
  diaries 46
  journals 158
  logs 164–65, 169
  reports 30, 79, 81
trench warfare 127, 135
Trieste 60
tuition scholarships 110
Turgot, Anne Robert Jacques 112
Turgot, Robert Jacques 112
Turkey 60
Turnfest 92
tyrannicide 138–39
Tyrrell, Ian 11, 13

Über Museen des Ostens der Vereinigten Staaten von Nord-Amerika 65
Ungern-Sternberg, Wilhelm Hartwig August Freiherr von 20, 163
Union League Club 58–59, 63

United States 9–11, 16–18, 21–23, 29–30, 32, 38, 40, 57, 62–65, 67–68, 114, 127, 140–43, 155–56, 160–63, 165, 172
United States Supreme Court 142
universities 9, 108, 110
University College at Oxford 108
university library at Kiel 22
university model, German 15
University of Berlin 61, 64, 116
University of Chicago 142
University of Edinburgh 79
University of Freiburg 67
University of Göttingen 17, 58, 163–64
University of Heidelberg 116
University of Leipzig 79, 88
University of Marburg 110
University of Toronto 115–16
Unto This Last 128
urban hygiene discourse 89
urbanization 41, 89

Varrentrapp, Georg 35
Varrentrapp, Johann Georg 30, 35–36
Venice 111
Vienna 159
Vietnam 144
violent resistance 139
Voigt, J. A. 79
voluntary associations 101, 103, 112–13, 117

Wagner, Ernst 80
waqf 101, 102–3, 105–9, 117–18
waqf ahli 106–7
waqf khairi 106–7
War without Violence 143
Warren, Samuel D. 66–67
Washington 65, 141
Washington Crossing the Delaware 15
Washington, George 15
waste disposal 35
Waterlow, Sydney 39
Watertown 17
Watkins, John 159
Wecke, Margarethe 85
Weihnachten. See Christmas

Weihnachten ritual. See Christmas ritual
Werner, Michael 13, 15
Wesebeder, Johann 111
Wesleyan College 60
Western Hospital of Toronto 115
Western Travel 161
Wheelwright, Edmund M. 66
White, Alfred T. 29, 30, 41, 42
Wichern, Johann Hinrich 162–63, 168
Wiese, Ludwig 79–80
Windsor Palace 159
winter solstice 157
Winthrop family 58
Wisconsin 17
Woodroofe, Kathleen 31
World War I 30, 37, 41, 65, 91, 127, 132, 135
World War II 15, 37, 127, 146
Wright, Carroll Davidson 30

Young Men's Christian Association (YMCA) 140
Yugoslavia 148
Yule 157, 170
Yuma 144

zakat 101, 105
zedakah 101, 105
Zeitschrift für Turnen und Jugendspiel 85
Zimmermann, Bénédicte 15
zones of contact 103
zones of transition 103
Zürich 67
Zwingli, Huldrych 110

www.ingramcontent.com/pod-product-compliance
Lightning Source LLC
Chambersburg PA
CBHW021829300426
44114CB00009BA/381